Made in Heaven

Made in Heaven
The Marriages and Children of Hollywood Stars

Victoria Houseman

Bonus Books, Inc.

95 94 93 92 91   5 4 3 2 1

International Standard Book Number: 0-929387-24-4
Library of Congress 91-70343

Bonus Books, Inc.
160 East Illinois Street
Chicago, Illinois 60611

Printed in the United States of America

This book is dedicated
to the memory of
George C. Lyon

Contents

Acknowledgments   ix

Alphabetical Listing of Hollywood Stars and   1
    Personalities

Stars Who Never Married   329

Index   331

Acknowledgments

During the time that I was researching and writing this book, my family offered me invaluable support, encouragement, and advice. I would like to thank my father, Gerald Houseman, for his help in the pursuit of publication and in the search for photographs. I would also like to thank my mother, Penelope, and my brother, Kit, for their support, and my sister, Lisa, for her support and advice. All of my friends were very encouraging while I was working on this book—in particular Molli Crowder, Robin Lee, and Ericka Myers. I would also like to thank James Whitcraft for his invaluable assistance with the photographs that appear in this book, and my agent, Hy Cohen, for all of his hard work and consideration.

ABBOTT, Bud
(1895-1974)

Abbott wed vaudevillian *Betty Smith* on September 17, 1918, at the courthouse in Alexandria, Virginia. In 1944, they adopted a son, *Frank James Abbott, Jr.,* and in 1949 they adopted a daughter, *Rae Victoria.* The Abbots were married fifty-five years, until his death from cancer at age seventy-eight on April 24, 1974, in their Woodland Hills, California, home.

ABRAHAM, F. Murray
(1939-   )

The actor married *Kate Hannan* in California in 1962. Abraham will not reveal the names of their children, a daughter, born in 1970, and a son, born in 1972. They reside in New York City.

ADAMS, Edie
(1927-   )

The actress became a co-star on *The Ernie Kovacs Show* and married Kovacs in Mexico City on September 12, 1954. Their daughter, *Mia,* was born in 1959. The marriage ended suddenly when, in the early morning hours of January 14, 1962, Kovacs was killed in a car accident in Los Angeles at the age of forty-two. In 1964, Adams married music publisher *Martin (Marty) Mills,* Their son, *Joshua,* was born in 1968. The marriage ended in divorce on April 13, 1972. Later that same year, on June 4, 1972, Adams married jazz trumpeter *Pete Candoli,* who was divorced from *Betty HUTTON.* Adams and Candoli separated in 1979.

ADOREE, Renée
(1898-1933)

The French-born actress wed film star *Tom MOORE* on February 12, 1921. *Jack Pickford* and *Mabel Normand* were the attendants at their wedding. Adorée filed for divorce in Los Angeles on July 21, 1923, charging Moore with cruelty. The decree became final in October 1924. After broken engagements to composer *Rudolf Friml* and actor *Gaston Glass*, she wed businessman *William Sherman Gill* in Los Angeles on June 28, 1927. Gill received a divorce in Reno, Nevada, on February 2, 1929, testifying that Adorée had fits of temper.

AHERNE, Brian
(1902-1986)

The actor's first wife was *Joan FONTAINE*, whom he married on August 20, 1939, in Del Monte, California. Although Fontaine had once described Aherne as "the perfect husband," she received a divorce in Los Angeles on June 2, 1944, charging Aherne with extreme cruelty. Aherne was remarried on January 27, 1946, at Steven's Landing, New York, to *Eleanor de Liagre Labrot*, the sister of Broadway producer *Alfred de Liagre, Jr.* The Ahernes were married forty years, until his death on February 10, 1986, at age eighty-three in Venice, Florida. His widow commented that they had shared a "quiet, gracious life together."

ALBERGHETTI, Anna Maria
(1936-   )

On September 12, 1964, the Italian-born singer and actress married director *Claudio Guzman* at St. Victor's Roman Catholic Church in Los Angeles. The couple has a son, *Alexander*, born in 1965, and two daughters, *Pilar*, born October 11, 1966, and *Danielle*, born March 17, 1970.

ALBERT, Eddie
(1908-   )

Albert wed actress *MARGO* on December 5, 1945, at St. Patrick's Cathedral in New York City. The couple had a son, actor *Eddie Albert, Jr.*, born February 20, 1951, in Los Angeles. In

1954, they adopted a four-year-old Spanish orphan in Madrid, *Maria del Carmen*. Their nearly forty years of marriage ended with Margo's death, at age sixty-eight, on July 17, 1985, at their Pacific Palisades, California, home after a long illness.

ALDA, Alan
(1936-)

The actor-director, who is the son of *Robert ALDA*, married musician *Arlene Weiss* in Houston, Texas, in 1957. The Aldas have three daughters: *Eve*, born in 1958; *Elizabeth*, born in 1960; and *Beatrice*, born in 1961.

ALDA, Robert
(1914-1986)

On September 31, 1932, Alda married *Joan Brown*, a Miss New York beauty contest winner. Their son, actor-director *Alan ALDA*, was born on January 28, 1936, in New York City. The marriage ended in divorce in Las Vegas in 1955. That same year, on December 21, 1955, Alda wed Italian actress *Flora Marino*. A son, *Robert, Jr.*, was born in 1957. The thirty-year marriage ended with Alda's death at age seventy-two. He died on May 3, 1986, in their Los Angeles home from the aftereffects of a stroke.

ALEXANDER, Jane
(1939-)

The actress, born *Jane Quigley*, wed fellow drama student *Robert Alexander* on July 23, 1962. Their son, actor *Jason Edward Alexander*, was born in 1963. The Alexanders were divorced in 1969. Since March 29, 1975, the actress has been married to director *Edward Sherin*.

ALLEN, Fred
(1894-1956)

In 1928, Allen wed actress *Portland Hoffa*, who became his radio and vaudeville partner. The Allens were married twenty-eight years, until the comedian's death from a heart attack, at age sixty-one, outside their New York City home on March 17, 1956.

ALLEN, Gracie
(1902-1964)

On January 7, 1926, the comedienne married her vaudeville partner of three years, comedian *George BURNS*, in Cleveland. The couple adopted an infant daughter, *Sandra Jean*, in 1934. They adopted a son, *Ronald John*, in 1935. During their thirty-eight years of marriage, the couple was one of America's favorites, both on and off screen. Gracie Allen died of a heart attack on August 27, 1964, in Los Angeles at age sixty-two.

ALLEN, Woody
(1935-)

In 1955, Allen married schoolteacher *Harlene Rosson*. They were divorced in 1960. On February 2, 1966, Allen wed actress *Louise Lasser*, his co-star in several films. The marriage ended in divorce in 1971. Allen has two children with actress *Mia FARROW*: an adopted daughter, *Dylan*, and a son, *Satchel*, born on December 21, 1987.

ALLYSON, June
(1917-)

On August 19, 1945, Allyson married *Dick POWELL* in a ceremony held at the Los Angeles home of composer *Johnny Green*.

Louis B. Mayer gave the bride away. The Powells adopted a two-month-old daughter, *Pamela*, on August 10, 1948. Their son, *Richard Keith*, was born on December 24, 1950. Allyson was granted a divorce in Los Angeles on March 31, 1961. She was awarded a $2.5 million settlement and custody of their children. The interlocutory decree, granted on the grounds of cruelty, would have become final in one year, but the Powells were reunited. On January 3, 1963, Dick Powell died of cancer at their Los Angeles home. He was fifty-eight. On October 12, 1963, Allyson wed *Alfred Glenn Maxwell*, a former barber from Newport Beach, California. She divorced Maxwell on April 20, 1965, in Santa Ana, California, charging that Maxwell struck her, issued bad checks for gambling debts, and called her vile names in front of her children. Allyson and Maxwell were remarried on April 1, 1966, at the Sands Hotel in Las Vegas, but the couple was again divorced. Since October 30, 1976, she has been the wife of *Dr. David Prince Ashrow*. Among those attending the wedding ceremony in Palm Springs, California, were her old friends *Rita Hayworth, Gloria DeHaven*, and *Margaret O'Brien*.

AMECHE, Don
(1908-)

The actor wed dietician *Honore Prendergast* of Dubuque, Iowa, on November 26, 1932. The Ameches have six children: *Dominic Felix*, born in 1933; *Ronald John*, born in 1936; *Thomas Anthony*, born in 1940; *Lawrence Michael*, born in 1941; and two daughters, *Barbara* and *Cornelia*, adopted in the late forties. Their nicknames are Donnie, Ronnie, Tommie, Lonnie, Bonnie, and Connie. The couple has been separated since the mid-sixties.

AMES, Adrienne
(1907-1947)

At sixteen, she wed Texas oilman *Derward Truax*. A daughter, *Barbara*, was born the following year. At eighteen, Ames divorced Truax. In 1929, she married millionaire broker *Stephen Ames* of Beverly Hills. On October 30, 1933, the actress received a Reno divorce. The following day she married actor *Bruce Cabot* at the Carlsbad, New Mexico, home of his mother. Ames divorced Cabot in Los Angeles on April 6, 1937, after testifying that Cabot drank to excess. She never remarried.

AMES, Leon
(1903-)

The actor married starlet *Christine Gossett* on June 25, 1938. The couple has two children: a daughter, *Shelley,* born in 1941, and a son, *Leon, Jr.,* born in 1944.

ANDERSON, Dame Judith
(1898-)

On May 18, 1937, the Australian-born actress wed *Benjamin Harrison Lehman,* an English professor at the University of California at Berkeley, in Kingman, Arizona. Two years later, on August 23, 1939, the couple was divorced. She married theatrical producer and director *Luther Greene* on July 11, 1946. Divorced from Greene since June 26, 1951, Anderson has not remarried.

ANDRESS, Ursula
(1936-)

In 1957, the Swiss-born actress married actor-director *John Derek.* They separated in 1964 and were divorced in 1966. Andress has not remarried. She has a son, *Dimitri,* born in 1979, with actor *Harry Hamlin.*

ANDREWS, Dana
(1909-   )

On December 31, 1932, Andrews wed *Janet Murray*. Their son, *David Murray Andrews*, was born in 1933. Janet Andrews died in 1935. As a student at the Pasadena Playhouse, Andrews met *Mary Todd*, whom he married on November 17, 1939. The couple has three children: *Stephen*, born in 1944; *Catherine*, born in 1948; and *Susan*, born in 1949. Mary Todd Andrews filed for divorce in Los Angeles on May 28, 1968, alleging ''great mental and physical suffering.'' But she later withdrew her suit, and the couple remains married. His son David died in 1964.

ANDREWS, Julie
(1935-   )

The actress-singer married scenic designer *Tony Walton* on May 10, 1959, at St. Mary's Church of the Oatlands in Weybridge, England. A daughter, *Emma Kate*, was born in London on November 27, 1962. Andrews filed for divorce in California on the grounds of mental cruelty on November 14, 1967. The decree was granted the following year. Since November 13, 1969, Andrews has been married to director-producer *Blake Edwards*. The couple was married in Los Angeles. She has two step-daughters.

ANGELI, Pier
(1932-1971)

In November 1954, the Italian-born actress married singer-actor *Vic DAMONE*. Their son, *Perry* was born in 1955. Angeli filed for divorce in Santa Monica on November 10, 1958, on the grounds of mental cruelty. There was a brief reconciliation, but the divorce became final in 1959. On February 14, 1962, she married Italian bandleader *Armando Trovajoli* in London. Their son, *Howard Andrea*, was born on January 8, 1963. Angeli was separated from Trovajoli when she was found dead, a possible suicide, in her Los Angeles apartment on September 10, 1971.

ANN-MARGRET
(1941-   )

The actress-singer-dancer was born Ann-Margret Olsson in Stockholm, Sweden. She married her personal manager, *Roger Smith*, on May 8, 1967.

ARBUCKLE, Roscoe "Fatty"
(1887-1933)

In August 1908, the comedian married actress *Minta DUR-FEE*. Durfee testified in her divorce suit that she and Arbuckle had separated in 1917, even though she had stood by him during his rape trial in 1921, believing him innocent. Durfee received a divorce decree in Providence, Rhode Island, on December 31, 1923, charging Arbuckle with desertion and non-support. Arbuckle wed film actress *Doris Deane* on May 16, 1925, at her mother's home in San Marino, California. Deane filed for divorce in Los Angeles on September 17, 1929, charging Arbuckle with desertion and cruelty. On June 29, 1932, he wed *Addie Oakley Dukes McPhail*. Arbuckle died on their first wedding anniversary from a heart attack in their New York City home. He was forty-six.

ARDEN, Eve
(1912-1990)

Arden married *Edward Bergen*, a Hollywood literary agent, in Reno, Nevada, in June 1939. The couple adopted a daughter, *Liza*, in 1944. The Bergens were divorced in Reno on July 27, 1947. Later that same year, Arden adopted a second daughter, *Connie*. On August 25, 1951, Arden married actor and artist *Brooks West* at a New England farm. In the summer of 1952, the couple adopted a son, *Duncan Paris West*. A second son, *Douglas Brooks West*, was born in September 1953. West also adopted Arden's daughters. The couple was married for thirty-two years. On February 7, 1984, West died in California after a long illness.

ARKIN, Alan
(1934-)

Arkin married his first wife, identified simply as "a Bennington College girl," while studying there in 1955. The couple had two sons, *Adam*, born in 1956, and *Matthew*, born in 1960, before they were divorced. Since June 16, 1964, Arkin has been married to his one-time Broadway co-star, actress *Barbara Dana*. The couple has a son, *Anthony*, born in 1968. They reside in Connecticut.

ARLEN, Richard
(1899-1976)

In 1923, the actor was divorced from *Ruth Austin*, by whom he had a daughter, *Rosemarie*. On the set of the film *Wings* (1927), Arlen met actress *Jobyna Ralston*. They were married at the Mission Inn in Riverside, California, on January 28, 1927. Their son, *Richard Ralston Mattimore* (Arlen's legal surname), was born on May 18, 1933, in Los Angeles. Ralston divorced Arlen in Los Angeles on September 5, 1945. Arlen then married the widowed *Margaret Kinsella* in Mexico. The couple was married thirty years, until Arlen's death from emphysema at the age of seventy-five on March 28, 1976, in Riverside, California.

ARLISS, George
(1868-1946)

In 1899, the actor married actress *Florence Montgomery*. Their son, film director *Leslie Arliss*, was born in London in 1901. The couple was married forty-six years, until the actor's death from a bronchial ailment in London on February 5, 1946. He was seventy-seven.

ARNAZ, Desi
(1917 – 1986)

His marriage to *Lucille BALL* took place in Greenwich, Connecticut, on November 30, 1940. Their two children both became actors. *Lucie Desirée Arnaz* was born on July 17, 1951, and *Desi Arnaz, Jr.* (Desiderio Alberto IV) was born on January 19, 1953. The announcement that they would divorce did not surprise their friends. Arnaz stated: "Our divorce will be completely amicable, and there will be no contest." Ball received a divorce in Santa Monica on May 4, 1960, testifying that their marriage had been a "nightmare." Their company, Desilu Productions, was divided in half. On March 2, 1963, Arnaz married *Edith Mack Hirsch*. He was widowed in 1985, after twenty-two years of marriage.

ARQUETTE, Rosanna
(1960 –)

The actress married film composer *James Newton Howard* in Big Sur, California, in September 1986. The couple separated in May 1988.

ARTHUR, Jean
(1905 –)

The actress was married for one day in 1928 to photographer *Julian Anker*. The marriage was annulled after Arthur stated that she had not known that her studio contract did not permit her to marry. On June 11, 1932, she wed singer *Frank Ross, Jr.*, who later became a film producer. Arthur divorced Ross on March 14, 1949, after sixteen years of marriage. Ross later married actress *Joan CAULFIELD*. Arthur has not remarried.

ASHCROFT, Dame Peggy
(1907-   )

Ashcroft wed publisher *Rupert Charles Hart-Davis* on December 23, 1929. They were divorced in June 1931. In November of 1934, she married theatre actor, director, and producer *Theodore Komisarjevsky*. Ashcroft received a divorce from Komisarjevsky in London on June 15, 1937, on the grounds of adultery. On September 14, 1940, the actress married barrister (now Lord) *Jeremy Nicholas Hutchinson*. Their daughter, *Eliza*, was born in 1941, and their son, stage director *Nicholas Hutchinson*, was born in 1945. In December 1965, Ashcroft divorced Hutchinson in London on the grounds of adultery after twenty-five years of marriage. She has not remarried.

ASHLEY, Elizabeth
(1939-   )

Ashley married actor *James Farentino* in September of 1962. The marriage ended in divorce in 1965. On April 17, 1966, she married actor *George PEPPARD* at the Bel-Air Hotel. Their son, *Christian Moore Peppard*, was born on March 12, 1968. Ashley received a divorce, and custody of Christian, in Los Angeles on April 30, 1972, on the grounds of irreconcilable differences. In May 1976, Ashley announced that she had married British actor *James McCarthy* in 1975.

ASTAIRE, Fred
(1899-1987)

On July 12, 1933, Astaire wed socialite *Phyllis Livingstone Potter* in Brooklyn, New York. At the time of their marriage, Potter had a three-year-old son, Peter, from a former marriage. *Fred Astaire, Jr.* was born in Los Angeles on January 21, 1936. Their daughter, *Ava*, was born on March 28, 1942, in Los Angeles. Their twenty-one years of marriage ended in Phyllis Astaire's death. She died of cancer at the age of forty-six on September 13, 1954, at their Beverly Hills home. Astaire did not remarry until June 1980, when he wed *Robyn Smith*, one of the first women jockeys, in California. The marriage ended in Astaire's death from pneumonia on June 22, 1987, in Los Angeles. He was eighty-eight.

ASTOR, Mary
(1906-1987)

On February 24, 1928, Astor married director *Kenneth Hawks* (brother of *Howard Hawks* and *William Hawks*, who married *Bessie LOVE*) at her home in Los Angeles. Three years later, on January 2, 1930, Hawks and nine others were killed when two planes collided during the filming of a parachute drop. Astor was remarried on June 29, 1931, in Yuma, Arizona, to *Dr. Franklyn Thorpe*. Their daughter, *Marylyn Haouli* (Hawaiian for "triumphant joy"), was born in Honolulu on June 15, 1932. Her marriage to Thorpe ended in divorce on April 12, 1935, in Los Angeles when Thorpe was granted an interlocutory divorce decree. "She repeatedly told me she no longer cared for me. She said she had no interest in my work and that we had nothing in common. She criticized my earning power as compared to hers," Thorpe testified. Astor eloped to Yuma, Arizona, with actor-writer *Manuel Del Campo* on February 18, 1937. Their son, *Anthony Paul Del Campo*, was born in Los Angeles on June 5, 1939. On December 14, 1942, Astor divorced Del Campo in Los Angeles and was given custody of their son. Her fourth and last marriage, to *Sergeant Thomas Gordon Wheelock*, took place on December 24, 1945. The couple was divorced in 1953.

ATTENBOROUGH, Sir Richard
(1923-   )

Attenborough married actress *Sheila Sim*, whom he had met at the Royal Academy of Dramatic Arts in London, on January 22, 1945. The couple has a son, film director *Michael Attenborough*, born in 1950; and two daughters: *Jane*, born in 1955; and *Charlotte*, born June 29, 1959. Michael Attenborough married actress *Jane Seymour* in 1971. The couple was later divorced.

AUTRY, Gene
(1907-)

Autry met *Ina Mae Spivey* when she was a student at Teacher's College in St. Louis. They were married on April 1, 1932. The couple was married forty-eight years until, on May 20, 1980, Spivey died in their home in Palm Springs, California. The following year, on July 19, 1981, Autry wed *Jacqueline Ellam*, a bank vice-president, at the First United Methodist Church in Burbank, California.

AVALON, Frankie
(1939-)

On January 19, 1963, the singer-actor married dental technician *Kathryn (Kay) Deibel* at St. Charles Catholic Church in North Hollywood. The Avalons have eight children: *Frankie, Jr.*, born September 29, 1963; *Anthony*, born in November 1964; *Dina Mary*, born April 15, 1966; *Laura*, born in 1968; *Joseph*, born August 28, 1969; *Nicholas*, born in 1971; *Kathryn*, born July 24, 1972; and *Carla*, born in 1974.

AYKROYD, Dan
(1952-)

The actor-writer married *Maureen Lewis* on May 10, 1974. The couple had three sons, *Mark, Lloyd*, and *Oscar*, but were divorced after less than five years of marriage. Since April 29, 1983, Aykroyd has been married to actress *Donna Dixon*.

AYRES, Agnes
(1896-1940)

Ayres married *Capt. Frank P. Schuker* during World War I. Schuker was granted a divorce in 1921. In October 1924, the actress announced that she had married Mexican diplomat *S. Manuel Reachi* on July 13, 1924. Their daughter, *Maria Eugenia*, was born in Los Angeles on March 25, 1926. Ayres divorced Reachi in Los Angeles on June 10, 1927, on the grounds of failure to provide and desertion. She never remarried.

AYRES, Lew
(1908-)

Ayres married actress *Lola Lane* in Las Vegas on September 15, 1931. The couple separated in 1932, and Lane received a divorce in Los Angeles on February 3, 1933. She testified that Ayres once told her to go out and get a divorce if she did not like what he did. On November 14, 1934, he married *Ginger ROGERS* in the Little Church of the Flowers in Glendale, California. *Janet Gaynor* and *Mary Brian* were bridesmaids. The couple separated in 1936. They were divorced in 1941. Ayres did not remarry until February 7, 1964, when he married English-born *Diana Hall*. Their son, *Justin Bret Ayres* was born on December 27, 1968.

BACALL, Lauren
(1924-)

The marriage of *Humphrey BOGART* and Lauren Bacall took place on May 21, 1945, at Malabar Farm, the home of novelist *Louis Bromfield*, near Mansfield, Ohio. Their son, *Stephen Humphrey Bogart* (named for the character Bogart played in *To Have and Have Not*, the film in which they met), was born in Los Angeles on January 7, 1949. A daughter, *Leslie Howard Bogart* (named for the actor), was born on August 23, 1952. Bogart died of cancer at the age of fifty-seven on January 14, 1957, at their home in Holmby Hills, California. Unable to obtain a marriage license in Vienna or Nevada, Bacall and actor *Jason ROBARDS, Jr.*, were married in Ensenada, Mexico, on July 4, 1961. Their son, *Sam*, who became an actor, was born in New York City on December 16, 1961. The couple was divorced in Juarez, Mexico, on September 10, 1969, on the grounds of incompatibility. Bacall has not remarried.

BAKER, Carroll
(1931-)

In January 1953, the actress married hotelier *Louie Ritter* in Montreal, Canada. Eight months later, in August 1953, the couple was divorced in New York City. On April 3, 1955, Baker married director *Jack Garfein* in the New York City apartment of *Lee* and *Paula Strasberg*. Their daughter, *Blanche Joy*, was born on December 20, 1956, and their son, *Herschel David*, was born on January 17, 1958. Both of their children were born in New York City. Garfein filed for divorce in Los Angeles on August 14, 1968, charging cruelty. The decree was granted in 1969. Since 1978, Baker has been the wife of British actor and author *Donald Burton*. The couple lives in London.

BALL, Lucille
(1911-1989)

Her marriage to actor and musician *Desi ARNAZ* took place in Greenwich, Connecticut, on November 30, 1940. The couple became one of America's favorites, both on and off screen. Their daughter, actress *Lucie Desirée Arnaz*, was born on July

17, 1951. Their son, Desiderio Alberto IV, actor *Desi Arnaz, Jr.*, was born on January 19, 1953. After announcing their separation, Desi Arnaz commented: "Our divorce will be completely amicable. And there will be no contest." Ball received a divorce in Santa Monica on May 4, 1960, after testifying that their marriage was a "nightmare." Their profitable Desilu Productions was divided in half. She married comedian *Gary Morton* on November 20, 1961, at Marble Collegiate Church in New York City. Their twenty-seven years of marriage ended with Ball's death from a heart attack in Los Angeles on April 26, 1989. She was seventy-seven.

BANCROFT, Anne
(1931-)

On July 4, 1954, the actress married *Martin A. May*. The couple was divorced on February 13, 1958. Since August 1964, she has been married to *Mel BROOKS*. Their son, *Maximilian*, was born on May 22, 1972.

BANKHEAD, Tallulah
(1903-1968)

She eloped to Jasper, Alabama, her childhood home, on August 31, 1937, with actor *John Emery*. "He's mad as a hatter. But then, so am I," the actress said. Less than four years later, on June 13, 1941, she received a Reno divorce on the grounds of mental cruelty. She never remarried.

BANKY, Vilma
(1898-)

Producer *Samuel Goldwyn* brought Banky to the United States from Hungary in 1925 and two years later, on June 26, 1927, gave her away at her wedding to film star *Rod LAROCQUE* at the Church of the Good Shepherd in Beverly Hills. Nearly one hundred policemen were needed to keep the crowds outside under control. The LaRocques were married forty-two years until LaRocque's death after a short illness on October 16, 1969, at their Beverly Hills home. Banky has not remarried.

BARA, Theda
(1890 - 1955)

In June 1921, Bara wed film director *Charles J. Brabin* in Connecticut. The couple lived in Beverly Hills during their thirty-three years of marriage, which ended in Bara's death from cancer in Los Angeles on April 7, 1955. Brabin died in 1957.

BARDOT, Brigitte
(1934-   )

Bardot married film director *Roger Vadim* in her native France on December 20, 1952. The marriage ended in divorce in Paris on December 6, 1957, on mutual charges of incompatibility. Vadim later married *Jane FONDA*. Bardot wed actor *Jacques Charriers* on June 18, 1959, at the city hall in Louveciennes, France, a suburb of Paris. Their son, *Nicolas Jacques Charriers*, was born in Paris on January 11, 1960. Bardot divorced Charriers in Paris on January 30, 1963. On July 14, 1966, she married German industrialist and sportsman *Gunther Sachs* in Las Vegas. She received a divorce in Filisur, Switzerland, on September 2, 1969. Bardot has not remarried.

BARI, Lynn
(1913 - 1989)

In 1939, she married her agent, *Walter Kane*. Four years later, on November 26, 1943, she received a final divorce decree from Kane in Los Angeles. Two days later, on November 28, 1943, she married *Sid Luft*, a test pilot who became a film producer. The wedding was held at the Los Angeles home of producer *William Perlberg*. Their son, *John Michael*, was born in 1948. Bari was granted a divorce from Luft in Los Angeles on December 26, 1950, on the grounds of cruelty. Luft later married *Judy*

GARLAND. Bari wed psychiatrist *Dr. Nathan Rickles* in 1955. The marriage ended in divorce on July 26, 1972.

BARKER, Lex
(1919-1973)

The actor was married five times. On January 27, 1942, Barker, who was from a socially prominent New York family, married socialite *Constance Thurlow* in New York City. The couple had a daughter, *Lynn*, born in 1944, and a son, *Alexander C. Barker III* (nicknamed "Zan"), born in 1948. Thurlow received a final decree of divorce in Los Angeles on November 16, 1950, on the grounds of cruelty. She was given custody of their children. Five months later, on April 6, 1951, Barker wed film star *Arlene DAHL* in the chapel of the Central Presbyterian Church in New York City. Dahl received a divorce in Santa Monica less than two years later, on October 15, 1952, after testifying that Barker had called her a "hick from Minnesota." The decree became final on November 13, 1953. Meanwhile, on September 7, 1953, Barker had married *Lana TURNER* in Turin, Italy. Turner filed for divorce in Santa Monica on June 28, 1957, charging Barker with "cruel and inhuman conduct." Barker married Swiss drama student *Irene Labhart* in Lucerne, Switzerland, on March 14, 1959. Their son, *Christopher*, was born in 1960. Two years later, on October 23, 1962, Irene Barker, who was thirty-two, died suddenly of a heart attack in Rome. On March 6, 1965, the actor married *Maria del Carmen Cervera*, Miss Spain of 1961, in Geneva, Switzerland. The marriage ended in Barker's death at the age of fifty-three in New York City on May 11, 1973.

BARKIN, Ellen
(1955-)

Barkin married her co-star from *Sea of Love*, Irish actor *Gabriel Byrne*, in 1988. Their son, *Jack*, was born in New York City on October 16, 1989.

BARRIE, Wendy
(1912-1978)

Her only marriage was to textile manufacturer *David L. Meyers* whom she wed on June 5, 1945. They separated in 1949, and Barrie received a divorce in Reno on April 24, 1950.

BARRYMORE, Diana
(1921-1960)

The actress was born Diana Strange Blythe (the legal surname of all the Barrymores) and was the daughter of *John BARRYMORE* and his second wife, poet *Michael Strange*. On July 30, 1942, Diana married actor *Bramwell Fletcher*, who was divorced from *Helen CHANDLER*, in an elegant wedding held at the Los Angeles home of *Basil* and *Ouida Rathbone*. The marriage ended in divorce in Las Vegas on June 27, 1946, on the grounds of mental cruelty. Barrymore wed professional tennis player *John R. Howard* in Boston on January 17, 1947. Six months later, the couple was divorced. She then married actor *Robert Wilcox* in Newark, New Jersey, on October 17, 1950. She was widowed on June 11, 1955, when Wilcox died of a heart attack aboard a train bound for Rochester, New York, at the age of forty-four.

BARRYMORE, Ethel
(1879-1959)

The second child born to actors *Maurice Barrymore* and *Georgianna Drew*, she was the sister of *Lionel BARRYMORE* and *John BARRYMORE*. She wed New York stockbroker *Russell Griswold Colt* on March 14, 1909. The ceremony took place in the rectory of the Roman Catholic Church of the Most Precious Blood in Hyde Park, Massachusetts. The Colts had three children: *Samuel Peabody*, born November 29, 1909; *Ethel Barrymore*, born April 30, 1912; and *John Drew* (named for her famous uncle), born September 9, 1913. Charging Colt with non-support, abuse, and neglect, Barrymore divorced her husband in Providence, Rhode Island, on July 5, 1923. She never remarried.

BARRYMORE, John
(1882-1942)

The actor was the youngest child of actors *Maurice Barrymore* and *Georgianna Drew* and the brother of actors *Lionel BARRYMORE* and *Ethel BARRYMORE*. He married socialite *Katharine Corri Harris* on September 1, 1910 in St. Xavier's Church in New York City. Harris obtained a divorce in California in December of 1917 charging desertion. On August 5, 1920, he wed Blanche Oelrichs Thomas, better known as poet *Michael Strange*, at the Ritz-Carlton Hotel in New York City. Their daughter, Diana Strange Blythe, actress *Diana BARRYMORE*, was born in New York City on March 3, 1921. The marriage ended in divorce in Kingston, New York, on November 19, 1928. Six days later, on November 24, 1928, he married actress *Dolores COSTELLO*, the daughter of actor *Maurice COSTELLO*, at her parents' Beverly Hills home. A daughter, *Dolores Ethel Mae* (nicknamed "Dede"), was born in Los Angeles on April 8, 1930. A son, *John Blythe BARRYMORE, Jr.*, an actor, was born in Los Angeles on June 4, 1932. Costello divorced Barrymore in Los Angeles on the grounds of desertion on August 24, 1934. She was given custody of their children. The actor eloped to Yuma, Arizona, on November 9, 1936, with actress *Elaine Jacobs*, his protégé. Jacobs divorced him in Los Angeles on November 26, 1940, charging cruelty and testifying that he had caused her "a great deal of anguish, sleeplessness, and loss of weight." Barrymore never remarried.

BARRYMORE, John, Jr.
(1932-)

The actor was born John Blythe Barrymore, Jr., the son of *John BARRYMORE* and his third wife, *Dolores COSTELLO*. He is the half-brother of *Diana BARRYMORE*. On December 23, 1952, he eloped to Las Vegas with actress *Cara Williams*. Their son, *John Blythe Barrymore III*, was born on May 15, 1954. The marriage ended in divorce in 1959. He married Italian starlet *Gabriella "Gaby" Palazzoli* on October 28, 1960, at the Church of Saint Sebastiano in Rome. A daughter, *Blythe*, was born in Rome in 1962. Divorced from Palazzoli in 1964, Barrymore has not remarried.

BARRYMORE, Lionel
(1878-1954)

The actor was the oldest child of actors *Maurice Barrymore* and *Georgianna Drew* and the brother of *Ethel BARRYMORE* and *John BARRYMORE*. In 1904, he wed actress *Doris Rankin*. A daughter, *Ethel Barrymore II*, was born in 1909, but died the following year. Their second daughter, *Mary*, was born in 1916 but also died at the age of one. Rankin received a divorce in New York City on December 21, 1922. A year later, on July 16, 1923, Barrymore married actress *Irene Fenwick* in Rome. Their marriage ended in Fenwick's death, at the age of forty-nine, following a lengthy illness. She died on December 24, 1936, at their Beverly Hills home. Barrymore never remarried.

BARTHELMESS, Richard
(1895-1963)

On June 18, 1920, the actor wed Ziegfeld star *Mary Hay* at the Church of the Heavenly Rest in New York City. Their daughter, *Mary Hay Barthelmess*, was born in 1923. The couple separated in May 1925, and Hay received a Parisian divorce on December 29, 1926. He married *Jessica Stewart Sargent* on May 20, 1928. Sargent had a son, *Stewart*, from a former marriage. Their thirty-five years of marriage ended with the actor's death from cancer at the age of sixty-eight on August 17, 1963, at their Long Island, New York, home.

BASINGER, Kim
(1953-)

In 1980, the actress married make-up man and painter *Ron Britton*. Britton filed for divorce in December of 1988.

BAXTER, Anne
(1923-1985)

Baxter married actor *John HODIAK* at the Burlingame, California, home of her parents, *Stuart* and *Catherine Baxter*, on July 7, 1946. Their daughter, *Katrina*, was born on July 9, 1951. Baxter received a divorce in Los Angeles on January 27, 1953, after testifying that Hodiak had poor manners. She was given custody of Katrina. She married land developer *Randolph Galt* in Honolulu on February 18, 1960. The couple settled on his cattle station in Australia. Two daughters were born: *Melissa*, on October 5, 1961, and *Maginal*, on March 11, 1963. The couple separated in 1967, and she received a divorce in Santa Monica on the grounds of irreconcilable differences on January 29, 1970. On January 30, 1977, she wed banker *David Klee*. Ten months later, on October 15, 1977, Klee died from an illness at the age of seventy in New York City. Baxter never remarried.

BAXTER, Warner
(1891-1951)

The actor married *Viola Caldwell* in 1911. He was widowed seven months later. In January 1918, Baxter married actress *Winifred Bryson*. The Baxters were married thirty-three years, until his death from pneumonia at age fifty-nine at their Beverly Hills home on May 7, 1951.

BAYNE, Beverly
(1894-1982)

On July 29, 1918, the actress married her leading man, *Francis X. BUSHMAN*, at Bronx City Hall in New York City. Their son,

Richard, was born on June 9, 1919. Bayne divorced her husband, charging desertion, in Los Angeles on June 2, 1925. She married Chicago businessman *Charles T. Hvass* in 1937 and settled in Scottsdale, Arizona. The marriage ended in divorce in 1944. She never remarried. Her son died in 1969.

BEERY, Noah
(1884-1946)

The actor was the older brother of *Wallace BEERY*. He married *Marguerite (Rita) Lindsey* in Boston in July 1910. Their son, actor *Noah Beery, Jr.*, was born in New York City on August 10, 1915. Marguerite Beery filed for divorce in Los Angeles on December 5, 1928, but a decree was never granted. The couple remained separated until the actor's death from a heart attack at the age of sixty-two in Los Angeles on April 1, 1946. Noah Beery, Jr. married *Maxine Jones*, the daughter of cowboy star *Buck Jones*.

BEERY, Wallace
(1885-1949)

The actor was the younger brother of *Noah BEERY*. He eloped to Pasadena, California, with *Gloria SWANSON* on her seventeenth birthday, March 27, 1916. Two years later, on December 13, 1918, Beery obtained a divorce on the grounds of desertion. Beery did not remarry until 1930, when he wed *Rita Gilman*. In 1933, he adopted fifteen-year-old *Carol Ann*, the daughter of his aunt. She became an actress. The marriage ended in Beery's death on April 5, 1949 in Beverly Hills. He died from a heart ailment at the age of sixty-four.

BEGLEY, Ed, Jr.
(1949-)

The son of actor *Ed Begley*, he married *Ingrid Margaret Taylor* in 1976. Their daughter, *Amanda*, was born in 1977, and their son, *Nicholas*, was born in 1979. The couple was divorced in October of 1989.

BELAFONTE, Harry
(1927-)

On June 18, 1948, the singer-actor married *Marguerite Byrd*, a child psychology teacher at New York University. Two daughters were born: *Adrienne* in 1949, and actress-model *Shari Belafonte* in 1954. On February 28, 1957, Marguerite Belafonte received a divorce in Las Vegas. She charged Belafonte with extreme cruelty and was given custody of their daughters. Belafonte married dancer *Julie Robinson* in Tecate, Mexico, on March 8, 1957. The marriage was not disclosed until a month later, on April 9, 1957. The couple has a son, *David Michael*, born September 24, 1957, and a daughter, *Gina*, an actress, born September 8, 1961. Both children were born in New York City.

BEL GEDDES, Barbara
(1922-)

On January 24, 1944, the actress, who is the daughter of stage designer *Norman Bel Geddes*, wed *Carl Schreur*. Their daughter, *Susan*, was born on January 25, 1945. The marriage ended in divorce in 1951. That same year, on April 15, 1951, Bel Geddes married Broadway director *Windsor Lewis* in Wooddale, Delaware. Their daughter, *Betsy*, was born in 1953. The couple was married twenty-one years until his death after a long illness on May 15, 1972 in New York City. Bel Geddes has not remarried.

BELL, Rex
(1905-1962)

The cowboy-actor eloped to Las Vegas with *Clara BOW* on December 3, 1931. Their oldest son, *Rex Anthony (Tony) Bell*, was born on December 16, 1934, followed by *George Robert Bell*, born on June 14, 1938. The couple was separated during much of their marriage. Bell died from a coronary occlusion in Las Vegas on July 4, 1962.

BELLAMY, Ralph
(1904-)

The actor married *Alice Delbridge* on December 28, 1927. The couple had one daughter, *Lynn*, before their divorce in Detroit in June of 1931. Bellamy married actress *Catherine Willard* in Reno on July 6, 1931. The couple adopted an infant son, *Willard*, in the late thirties. Catherine Bellamy received a divorce in Reno on August 6, 1945, on the grounds of mental cruelty. Later that same month, he married swing organist *Ethel M. Smith* in Westchester County, New York. Bellamy received a divorce from Smith in Gooding, Idaho, on November 24, 1947, charging Smith with desertion. Since November 27, 1949, Bellamy has been married to *Alice Murphy*. The couple was married in New York City.

BELUSHI, Jim
(1954-)

Belushi married an actress in 1980, the same year their son, *Robert*, was born. The marriage ended in divorce in the late eighties. On September 22, 1990, Belushi wed actress *Marjorie Bransfield* at St. Nicholas's Albanian Orthodox Church in Chicago. He is the younger brother of the late *John BELUSHI*.

BELUSHI, John
(1949-1982)

In 1976, Belushi married his high school sweetheart, *Judith Jacklin*, who became a children's book designer and illustrator. The marriage ended in Belushi's death at the age of thirty-three in Hollywood on March 5, 1982. His younger brother is actor *Jim BELUSHI*.

BENJAMIN, Richard
(1938-)

Benjamin married actress *Paula PRENTISS* in 1961. The couple has one son, *Ross Alexander*, born on March 26, 1974.

BENNETT, Constance
(1904-1965)

Bennett was born in New York City, the daughter of matinee idol *Richard Bennett*, and the sister of actresses *Barbara* (1906–1958) and *Joan BENNETT*. She eloped to Greenwich, Connecticut, on June 6, 1921, with *Chester Hirst Moorhead*, a college student. The union was annulled in 1923. On November 23, 1925, she again eloped to Greenwich, this time with *Philip Morgan Plant*, heir to a steamship and railroad fortune. They were married by the same justice of the peace who had married her to Moorhead. Her second marriage ended in divorce in Paris in December 1929. She wed *Henri, Marquis de la Falaise de la Coudraye*, who was divorced from *Gloria SWANSON*, on November 22, 1931, at the Beverly Hills home of director *George Fitzmaurice*. Bennett received a divorce in Reno on November 14, 1940, on the grounds of desertion. About this time, Bennett began being seen with a son, *Peter*. At first she claimed that she and Plant had adopted him not long before their divorce. But it was soon learned that he was the illegitimate son of Bennett's cousin and had been born in England on January 21, 1939. Bennett adopted him. Actor *Gilbert ROLAND* became her fourth husband in Yuma, Arizona, on April 20, 1941. They quickly adopted a daughter, *Lorinda*. Later that same year, on December 11, 1941, a second daughter, *Gyl Christina*, was born. The couple separated in September 1944, and was divorced on June 13, 1945. Bennett was given custody of their daughters. She married *Col. John Theron Coulter* on June 22, 1946, in the St. Francis Chapel of the Mission Inn in Riverside, California. Her fifth marriage lasted nineteen years. On July 24, 1965, at the age of fifty-nine, Bennett died from a cerebral hemorrhage in Fort Dix, New Jersey.

BENNETT, Enid
(1895-1969)

In 1918, the Australian-born film actress married director *Fred Niblo*. Their thirty years of marriage ended in Niblo's death from pneumonia, at the age of seventy-four, in New Orleans on November 11, 1948. On June 20, 1963, Bennett wed producer *Sidney Franklin*. Franklin's former wife, *Ann Denitz*, had married *Nelson EDDY*. Bennett and Franklin were married five years, until she died from a heart attack at their Malibu home on May 14, 1969. Franklin died in 1972.

BENNETT, Joan
(1910-1990)

The youngest of matinee idol *Richard Bennett*'s three daughters, she is the sister of actresses *Barbara* and *Constance BENNETT*. On September 15, 1926, she married stage producer *John Marion Fox* at St. Luke's Church in Chelsea, London. The couple had a daughter, *Diane*, born in Los Angeles on February 20, 1928. Bennett divorced Fox in August of 1928. She married screenwriter *Gene Markey*, in a Los Angeles hotel on March 16, 1932. Constance was matron-of-honor. Their daughter, *Melinda Markey*, was born in Los Angeles on Joan's twenty-fourth birthday, February 27, 1934. Bennett divorced Markey in Los Angeles on June 3, 1937, testifying that Markey often left the house in "spasms of temper." Markey later married *Hedy LAMARR* and *Myrna LOY*. Bennett married producer *Walter Wanger* at the courthouse in Phoenix, Arizona, on January 13, 1940. Two daughters were born: *Stephanie*, on June 26, 1943, and *Shelley*, on July 4, 1948. After twenty-five years of marriage, Bennett divorced Wanger in Juarez, Mexico, in 1965 on the grounds of incompatibility. On Valentine's Day of 1978, she married author and publisher *David Wilde*. The couple was married by a state supreme court justice in White Plains, New York. On December 7, 1990, Bennett died from cardiac arrest at their Scarsdale, New York, home. She was eighty.

BENNY, Jack
(1894-1974)

The comedian married Sadye Marks, actress *Mary Livingstone*, on January 25, 1927. In June of 1934, the couple adopted a daughter, *Joan Naomi*. Their forty-seven years of marriage ended in Benny's death from cancer in Los Angeles on December 26, 1974. He was eighty years old. Mary Livingstone Benny died in 1983.

BERGEN, Candice
(1946-)

The actress and photojournalist is the daughter of *Edgar BERGEN*. She married French film director *Louis Malle* at his French château on September 27, 1980. She has two stepchildren. Their daughter, *Chloe*, was born in October 1985.

BERGEN, Edgar
(1903-1978)

The ventriloquist and actor married model and actress *Frances Westcott* in Mexico on June 28, 1945. Their daughter, actress *Candice BERGEN*, was born the following year on May 8, 1946, in Beverly Hills. Their son, *Kris Edgar*, was born on October 12, 1961. The Bergens were married thirty-three years, until his death in Las Vegas on October 1, 1978, at the age of seventy-five.

BERGEN, Polly
(1930-)

In 1950, the actress wed actor *Jerome Courtland* in Las Vegas. The marriage ended in divorce in Los Angeles on February 18,

1955. On February 13, 1956, Bergen married her agent, *Frederic (Freddie) Fields*. Fields had a daughter, *Kathy*, from a former marriage. A daughter, *Pamela Kerry* (nicknamed "P.K."), was born in 1957, followed by a son, *Peter*, born in 1959. The marriage ended in divorce in 1976. On June 25, 1982, Bergen wed lawyer and businessman *Jeffrey Endervelt*. She filed for divorce from Endervelt in April 1990.

BERGMAN, Ingrid
(1915-1982)

Bergman married *Dr. Petter Aron Lindstrom* a dentist, in a church in Stöde, Sweden, on July 10, 1937. Their daughter, *Friedel Pia*, was born in Sweden on September 20, 1938. The couple then moved to the United States. In 1949, she left her husband and daughter for Italian film director *Roberto Rossellini*. A son, *Robertino*, was born to the couple in Rome on February 2, 1950. Lindstrom divorced her in Los Angeles on November 1, 1950. Joint custody was given to Bergman and Lindstrom. Bergman and Rossellini were married by proxy in Juarez, Mexico, on May 24, 1950. Twin daughters, *Isotta* and model-actress *Isabella Rossellini*, were born in Rome on June 18, 1952. Her marriage to Rossellini was annulled in Rome on July 10, 1958, on the grounds that, by Swedish law, Bergman was still married to Lindstrom. She wed her third husband, Swedish producer *Lars Schmidt*, at the Caxton Hall registry office in London on December 21, 1958. The marriage ended in divorce in 1975.

BERLE, Milton
(1908-   )

In 1941, the comedian married dancer-actress *Joyce Matthews*. The couple adopted a daughter, *Victoria Melanie*. They were divorced in Reno in October of 1947. On June 16, 1949, Berle and Matthews were remarried in New York City. They were divorced for the second time in 1950. Berle married press agent *Ruth Cosgrove* in New York City on December 9, 1953. The couple adopted a son, *William*, in 1962. Their thirty-five years of marriage ended in Cosgrove's death in April of 1989.

BLACK, Karen
(1942-)

She was Karen Ziegler when she dropped out of high school to marry *Charles Black* in 1960. After divorcing Black, she wed actor *Robert "Skip" Burton* on April 18, 1973. The couple was divorced fourteen months later, in October 1974. On July 4, 1975, Black married writer-actor *L. Minor (Kit) Carson*. Their son, *Hunter*, was born on December 26, 1975. After divorcing Carson, she married film editor *Steven Eckelbery* in 1987. Their daughter, *Celine*, was born in 1987.

BLAINE, Vivian
(1921-)

Blaine married her agent, *Manuel (Manny) Frank*, on January 10, 1945. The marriage ended in divorce in Arkansas on December 10, 1956. She wed *Milton R. Rackmil*, President of Universal Pictures and Decca Records, on May 9, 1959. Two years later, on July 25, 1961, she received a divorce. Since December 14, 1973, she has been married to real estate executive *Stuart Clark*.

BLAIR, Janet
(1921-)

As a vocalist for *Hal Kemp's* Orchestra, she met pianist and arranger *Louis (Lou) Busch*. They were married at the Lake Arrowhead, California, home of friends on July 12, 1943. Blair and Busch were divorced in 1950. She wed *Nick Mayo* on October 5, 1953. The couple had a daughter, *Amanda*, born on February

22, 1959, and a son, *Andrew*, born in 1961. The marriage ended in divorce in 1972.

BLONDELL, Joan
(1909-1979)

On January 4, 1933, Blondell and cameraman *George S. Barnes* were married in Phoenix, Arizona. A son, *Norman Scott Barnes*, was born in Los Angeles on November 2, 1934. Their marriage ended in divorce on September 4, 1935, in Los Angeles. Blondell charged mental cruelty and was given custody of their son. She wed film star *Dick POWELL* on September 19, 1936, aboard the ocean liner *Santa Paula* before the ship sailed from Los Angeles to New York City. Their daughter, *Ellen Powell*, was born on July 1, 1938. In February of 1938, Powell had adopted Blondell's son Norman, whose surname became Powell. It took four minutes for Blondell to receive a divorce from Powell in Los Angeles on July 14, 1944. She charged him with numerous acts of cruelty. On July 4, 1947, she married producer *Mike Todd* at the El Rancho Vegas Hotel in Las Vegas. On June 8, 1950, Blondell divorced him in Las Vegas on the grounds of cruelty. Todd later married *Elizabeth TAYLOR*. Blondell never remarried.

BLOOM, Claire
(1940-)

On September 19, 1959, Bloom married actor *Rod STEIGER* in Los Angeles. Their daughter, *Anna Justine*, now an opera singer, was born on February 13, 1960. The couple was divorced in 1969. Later that same year, on August 14, 1969, the actress wed stage producer *Hilliard Elkins*. She later divorced Elkins. After a fifteen-year courtship, she married author *Philip Roth* in New York City on May 2, 1990.

BLYTH, Ann
(1928-)

On June 27, 1953, she wed obstetrician *Dr. James McNulty* at St. Charles Roman Catholic Church in North Hollywood. Bridesmaids were actresses *Joan Leslie, Jane Withers*, and *Betty Lynn*. Singer *Dennis Day*, the brother of the groom, was best man. The couple has five children: *Timothy Patrick* born in 1954; *Maureen Ann*, born in 1955; *Katheen Mary*, born in 1957; *Terrence Grady*, born in 1960; and *Eileen Alana*, born in 1963. They reside in Los Angeles.

BOARDMAN, Eleanor
(1898-)

The actress married film director *King Vidor* (divorced from *Florence VIDOR*) on September 8, 1926, at the Beverly Hills home of *Marion Davies*. The couple had two daughters: *Antonia*, born in 1927, and *Belinda*, born in 1930. Boardman divorced Vidor in Los Angeles on April 11, 1933, charging him with cruelty and association with another woman. In 1940, she wed film director *Harry d'Abbadie D'Arrast*. Divorced in the late forties, she has never remarried.

BOGART, Humphrey
(1899-1957)

Bogart married his Broadway co-star, *Helen Menken*, at her New York City home on May 20, 1926. Her sister, actress *Grace Menken*, married *Bert Lytell*. Helen Menken received a divorce in Chicago on November 18, 1927, after eighteen months of marriage. She charged cruelty and testified that Bogart had struck her on two occasions. In the fall of 1928, he married actress *Mary Phillips*. She divorced him in Los Angeles in 1937, and the decree became final in 1938. Bogart married actress *Mayo Methot* on August 20, 1938, but the couple soon became known as the "Battling Bogarts." Separated from Methot, he met actress *Lauren BACALL* when they co-starred for the first time in *To Have and Have Not* (1945). Methot was granted a divorce in a private hearing in Las Vegas on May 10, 1945. Eleven days later, on May 21, 1945, Bogart and Bacall were married at Malabar Farm, the home of novelist *Louis Bromfield*, near Mansfield, Ohio. Their son, *Stephen Humphrey Bogart* (named for the character Bogart played in *To Have and Have Not*), was born in Los Angeles on January 7, 1949. Their daughter, *Leslie Howard Bogart* (named for the actor), was born on August 23, 1952. The marriage ended in Bogart's death from cancer on January 14, 1957, at their home in Holmby Hills, California. He was fifty-seven.

BOLGER, Ray
(1904-1987)

The dancer-actor married his vaudeville partner, *Gwendolyn Rickard* on July 9, 1929. The couple resided in Beverly Hills during their fifty-three years of marriage which ended in Bolger's death from cancer on January 15, 1987, in Los Angeles. Bolger was eighty-three.

BOND, Ward
(1903-1960)

The actor married *Doris Sellers Childs* in 1936. The marriage ended in divorce in 1944. In 1954, Bond married talent agent *Mary Louise May*. The marriage ended with his death from a heart attack at the age of fifty-seven in Dallas, Texas on November 5, 1960.

BOONE, Pat
(1934-)

Boone eloped with *Shirley Foley*, the daughter of radio and television singer *Red Foley*, on November 7, 1953. The couple has four daughters: *Cheryl Lynn*, born in 1954; *Linda Lee*, born in 1955; Deborah Ann, singer *Debby Boone*, born in 1956; and

Laura Gene, born in 1958. Debby Boone married *Gabriel Ferrer*, the son of *José FERRER*, in 1979.

BOOTH, Shirley
(1907-)

The actress married radio comedian *Edward F. Gardiner* on November 23, 1929. The marriage ended in divorce in 1942. The following year, on September 24, 1943, Booth married *William H. Baker, Jr.*, in New York City. Baker was an investment counselor who later became a farmer and painter. The couple had been married seven years when Baker died from a heart ailment at the age of forty-three in New York City on March 4, 1951. Booth has not remarried.

BORGNINE, Ernest
(1917-)

While serving in the Navy, he met *Rhoda Kemins* a pharmacist's mate, whom he married on September 3, 1949. A daughter, *Nancy Alison* was born in 1952. Their marriage ended in divorce in Santa Monica on August 26, 1958. Kemins testified that Borgnine's temper tantrums had wrecked their marriage. He wed Mexican-born actress *Katy Jurado* in her Cuernavaca, Mexico, home on December 31, 1959. Their divorce became final in June 1964. He married actress *Ethel MERMAN* in his Beverly Hills home on June 27, 1964. The couple separated thirty-eight days later, and Merman received a divorce in Santa Monica on November 18, 1964, charging Borgnine with extreme cruelty. On June 30, 1965, he married *Donna Granoucci Rancourt* in Juarez, Mexico. The couple had a daughter, *Sharon Lynn*, born on August 5, 1965, and a son, *Christopher*, born on August 9, 1966. Donna Borgnine received a divorce in Los Angeles on July 17, 1972. Since February 24, 1973, Borgnine has been married to *Tove Traesnaes*.

BOW, Clara
(1905-1965)

Bow eloped to Las Vegas with cowboy actor *Rex BELL* on December 3, 1931. The couple had two sons: *Rex Anthony (Tony)*, born on December 16, 1934, and *George Robert*, born on June 14, 1938. The couple was separated during much of their marriage, which ended in Bell's death from a coronary occlusion in Las Vegas on July 4, 1962.

BOYD, William
(1898-1972)

In 1921, the cowboy actor married actress *Ruth Miller*. They were divorced in 1924. On January 13, 1926, he wed actress *Elinor Fair* in Santa Ana, California. Fair received a divorce in 1929, which became final in 1930. Later that same year, Boyd married actress *Dorothy Sebastian*. Sebastian was granted a divorce in Los Angeles on May 29, 1936, charging Boyd with cruelty. On June 5, 1937, Boyd married actress *Grace Bradley*. The couple was married thirty-five years until the actor's death on September 12, 1972, in Laguna Beach, California. Boyd was seventy-four.

BOYER, Charles
(1897-1978)

The actor eloped to Yuma, Arizona, on Valentine's Day, February 14, 1934, with British actress *Pat Paterson*. Their son, *Michael*, was born in Los Angeles on December 10, 1943. He committed suicide in 1965. The couple had been married forty-four years when, on August 24, 1978, Pat Boyer died of cancer at the age of sixty-seven in Phoenix, Arizona. Two days later, on August 26, 1978, Charles Boyer died from an overdose of sleeping pills.

BRACKEN, Eddie
(1920-)

On September 25, 1939, the comedian married model *Connie Nickerson*. The Brackens have five children: *Judith Ann*, born in 1942; *Carolyn*, born November 22, 1944; *Michael Edward*, born November 19, 1945; *Susan Kathleen*, born September 9, 1948; and *David Vincent*, born November 18, 1950. All of their children were born in Santa Monica.

BRADY, Alice
(1892-1939)

On May 20, 1919, Brady wed actor *James L. Crane* in New York City. Two years later, on January 13, 1922, the actress received a divorce in New York City on the grounds of adultery. Their son, *Donald*, was born two months later, in March 1922. Brady never remarried.

BRANAGH, Kenneth
(1960-)

The Irish-born actor and director married British actress *Emma Thompson* at the estate Cliveden, near Taplow, Berkshire, England, in August 1989.

BRANDO, Marlon
(1924-)

Brando married film actress *Anna Kashfi* on October 11, 1957, at the Eagle Rock, California, home of his aunt. Their son, *Christian Devi*, was born in Los Angeles on May 11, 1958. Kashfi received a divorce (and a half-million dollar property settlement) on April 22, 1959, in Santa Monica. In June 1960, Brando married Mexican actress *Movita*. The marriage was not announced until June 29, 1961, when it also became public knowledge that the Brandos had a son, *Miko*, born earlier that year. In 1962, the actor had a son, *Tehotu*, with Polynesian actress *Tarita Tariipaia*. On January 23, 1967, a daughter, *Rebecca*, was born to Brando and Movita. Their marriage was annulled later that year on the grounds that Movita had not been legally divorced from her former husband when she married Brando. A daughter, *Tarita Cheyenne*, was born to Brando and Tarita Teriipaia in 1970.

BRAZZI, Rossano
(1916-)

Brazzi married *Countess Lydia Bertolini*, an actress, in his native Italy on January 25, 1940. The couple resides in Rome.

BRENT, George
(1904-1979)

The actor was married five times. In 1922, he wed *Helen Campbell*. The marriage ended in divorce in 1929. On August 13, 1932, Brent and actress *Ruth CHATTERTON* were married by a justice of the peace in Harrison, New York. Two years later, on October 4, 1934, Chatterton received a divorce in Los Angeles, telling the judge that Brent was "sulky, unreasonable, and domineering." Brent wed Australian-born film actress *Constance Worth* in Ensenada, Mexico, on May 10, 1937. The couple separated thirty-five days later, and Brent tried to get the marriage annulled but failed. Worth received a divorce in Los Angeles on December 7, 1937. Brent was wed for the fourth time, to film star *Ann SHERIDAN*, on January 5, 1942. The wedding was held at the Palm Beach, Florida, home of his sister, *Mrs. Sam H. Harris*, the widow of the producer. Sheridan was granted a divorce exactly one year later, on January 5, 1943, in Mexico City. Brent married model *Janet Michaels* in Yuma, Arizona, on December 17, 1947. The couple had two children: *Suzanne*, born on August 3, 1950, and *Barry*, born on December 14, 1954.

Both of their children were born in Santa Monica. Their twenty-seven years of marriage ended in 1974 with the death of Michaels after a long illness.

BRIAN, Mary
(1908-)

The actress married magazine illustrator *Jon Whitcomb* on May 4, 1941, at the First Baptist Church in Los Angeles. Four months later, on August 8, 1941, Brian divorced Whitcomb in Carson City, Nevada, on the grounds of mental cruelty. In 1947, she wed film editor *George Tomasini*. Their twenty years of marriage ended in Tomasini's death in 1967. Brian has not remarried.

BRIDGES, Jeff
(1949-)

The actor, who is the son of *Lloyd BRIDGES*, married photographer *Susan Geston* on June 5, 1977. The couple has two daughters: *Isabelle*, born in 1981, and *Jessica*, born in 1982.

BRIDGES, Lloyd
(1913-)

Bridges married actress *Dorothy Simpson* in 1938. Their oldest son, Lloyd Vernet Bridges III, born December 9, 1941, became actor *Beau Bridges*. Their second son, actor *Jeff BRIDGES*, was born on December 4, 1949. Their daughter, *Lucinda*, was born in 1953.

BRONSON, Betty
(1906-1971)

On March 16, 1932, the actress married wealthy North Carolinian *Ludwig Lauerhass* at the courthouse in Santa Barbara, California. The couple had one son, *Ludwig, Jr.*, born in 1935. Their thirty-eight years of marriage ended in Bronson's death, following a brief illness, in Pasadena, California, on October 19, 1971. She was sixty-four.

BRONSON, Charles
(1921-)

Bronson married actress *Harriet Tendler* on September 30, 1949. The couple had one daughter, *Suzanne*, born February 27, 1955, and a son, *Tony*, born in February 1961. The Bronsons separated late in 1964 and were divorced in 1965. In October 1969, Bronson married British-born actress *Jill Ireland*. Ireland had three children from a former marriage to actor *David McCallum* which had ended in divorce. The Bronsons's sixth child, a daughter *Zuleika*, was born in 1971. Their twenty years of marriage ended in Ireland's death from cancer at the age of fifty-four on May 18, 1990, at their Malibu home.

BROOKS, Geraldine
(1925-1977)

Brooks married television writer *Herbert Sargent* on March 8, 1958. They were divorced in 1961. In June 1964, she married screenwriter and novelist *Budd Schulberg*. Their thirteen years of marriage ended in her death from cancer on June 19, 1977, in Riverhead, New York. Brooks was fifty-two.

BROOKS, Louise
(1906-1985)

The actress married film director *Edward Sutherland* on July 21, 1926, at the municipal building in New York City. Sutherland, who had been an assistant director for *Charlie Chaplin*, was divorced from *Marjorie DAW*. Less than two years later, on June 20, 1928, Brooks received a divorce in Los Angeles on the grounds of extreme cruelty. She married farm-equipment manufacturer *Deering Davis* in Chicago on October 10, 1933. The couple separated six months later, and Brooks received a divorce in Wichita, Kansas, on February 10, 1938, charging Davis with neglect. She never remarried.

BROOKS, Mel
(1926-   )

In the summer of 1952, the comedian and director married actress-dancer *Florence Baum*. By 1955, the couple had two children: *Stefanie* and *Nicky*. A second son, *Eddie*, was born by 1958. The marriage ended in divorce in 1959. In August of 1964, Brooks married actress *Anne BANCROFT*. They have a son, *Maximilian*, born on May 22, 1972.

BRUCE, Virginia
(1910-1982)

Bruce married film star *John GILBERT* on August 10, 1932, at a Los Angeles film studio. *Irving Thalberg* was best man and *Mrs. Donald Ogden Stewart* was matron-of-honor. Their daughter, *Susan Ann*, was born on August 2, 1933, in Los Angeles. The marriage quickly ended in divorce in Los Angeles on May 25, 1934. Married for one year and eight months, Bruce testified that Gilbert was often intoxicated and had been abusive. In December 1937, Bruce married MGM producer and director *J. Walter Ruben*. Their son, *Christopher*, was born in 1941. Ruben died, at the age of forty-three, from an illness on September 4, 1942, at their Los Angeles home. On August 27, 1946, she married Turkish writer and film producer *Ali M. Ipar* at the Los Angeles home of friends. The couple settled in Istanbul. The Ipars were forced to divorce on July 28, 1951, in Istanbul when Ipar received a commission in the Turkish military. Turkish law for-

bade the giving of commissions to any man married to a for-
eigner. On November 13, 1952, the couple was remarried in a
civil ceremony in their Istanbul home. They were divorced in the
United States in 1964 on the grounds of incompatibility. She
never remarried.

BRYNNER, Yul
(1920-1985)

On September 6, 1944, Brynner married actress *Virginia
Gilmore*. Their son, *Yul Brynner III* (called "Rock"), was born
in December 1946. Gilmore received a divorce in Juarez, Mexico, on March 26, 1960. Five days later, on March 31, 1960,
Brynner wed *Doris Kleiner* of Santiago, Chile, in Mexico City.
Their daughter, *Victoria*, was born in Lausanne, Switzerland, on
November 6, 1962. The marriage ended in divorce in 1971. Later
that same year, on September 23, 1971, Brynner wed French-
born widow *Jacqueline DeCroisset* in Normandy, France. In February 1974, the couple adopted a daughter, *Mia*, in San
Francisco. A second daughter, *Melody*, was adopted in San Francisco on April 10, 1975. Both of their daughters were Vietnamese orphans. The marriage ended in divorce in 1983. That same
year, the actor wed *Kathy Lee*, a dancer in his final tour of *The
King and I*. The marriage ended in his death from cancer at the
age of sixty-five in New York City on October 9, 1985.

BUJOLD, Genevieve
(1942-)

In 1965, the Canadian actress married film director *Paul Al-
mond*. Their son, *Matthew*, was born in 1968. The couple was
divorced in 1973.

BURKE, Billie
(1885-1970)

As a Broadway star, Burke married showman *Florenz Ziegfeld,
Jr.*, on April 11, 1914, in the back room of a Hoboken, New Jersey,
parsonage. Their daughter, *Patricia Burke Ziegfeld*, was born in

New York City on October 23, 1916. The Ziegfelds had been married eighteen years when Florenz Ziegfeld died from pleurisy and pneumonia at the age of sixty-three in Los Angeles on July 22, 1932. Burke never remarried.

BURNS, George
(1896-)

The comedian married his vaudeville partner of three years, *Gracie ALLEN*, on January 7, 1926, in Cleveland. They adopted an infant daughter, *Sandra Jean*, in 1934, and a son, *Ronald John*, in 1935. The couple remained a popular comic duo during their thirty-eight years of marriage. Gracie Allen died from a heart attack in Los Angeles on August 27, 1964. She was sixty-two. Burns has not remarried.

BURSTYN, Ellen
(1932-)

In 1950, the actress (then known as Edna Rae) married poet *William Alexander*. After divorcing Alexander, she married film director *Paul Roberts* in 1957. The marriage ended in divorce. In 1961, she married actor *Neil Burstyn*. Their son, *Jefferson,* was born in 1962. Divorced since 1970, the actress has not remarried.

BURTON, Richard
(1925-1984)

The actor married *Sybil Williams* in his native Wales on February 5, 1949. The couple had two daughters: actress *Kate Burton*, born September 11, 1957, and *Jessica*, born in 1959. Both of their daughters were born in Geneva, Switzerland. While in Italy filming *Cleopatra* (1963), Burton fell in love with his co-star, *Elizabeth TAYLOR*. Sybil Williams Burton received a divorce in

Puerto Vallarta, Mexico, in February of 1963. She charged Burton with "abandonment of the home and cruel and inhumane treatment." She did not mention Elizabeth Taylor (who had divorced her husband, *Eddie FISHER*) by name. Burton and Taylor were married in Montreal, Canada, on March 15, 1964. Their separations and reconciliations received much notice in the press until, on June 26, 1974, Taylor received a divorce on the grounds of incompatibility in Gstaad, Switzerland. Then, on October 10, 1975, the couple was remarried in a mudhut village on a Botswana game preserve. The union lasted less than a year; Burton received a Haitian divorce on July 30, 1976. Three weeks later, on August 21, 1976, Burton married British model *Susan Hunt* in Arlington, Virginia. The marriage ended in divorce in 1983. That same year, on July 3, he married *Sally Anne Hay* in the presidential suite of a Las Vegas hotel. She had worked as a continuity supervisor on one of his films. A year later, on August 5, 1984, Burton died suddenly from a hemorrhage in Geneva, Switzerland. He was fifty-eight.

BUSCH, Mae
(1897 - 1946)

In 1915, Busch married actor *J. Francis MacDonald*. The marriage ended in divorce in 1920. The actress wed *John E. Cassell* in 1925. They were divorced less than a year later. On February 9, 1936, Busch married civil engineer *Thomas C. Tate* in Los Angeles. They were married until her death, at the age of forty-nine, after a long illness on April 19, 1946, in Woodland Hills, California.

BUSHMAN, Francis X.
(1883 - 1966)

Bushman married clothing designer *Josephine Fladume* in Baltimore in 1902. By 1909, the couple had five children: *Josephine, Ralph* (actor *Francis X. Bushman, Jr.*, born in 1903), *Virginia* (who married film director *Jack Conway*), *Lenore* (who had a brief film career), and *Bruce*. Bushman's popularity plummeted in 1918 when his fans discovered that he, a married man with five children, was divorcing his wife to marry his leading lady, *Beverly BAYNE*. Josephine Bushman received a divorce (and custody of their children) in Baltimore on July 26, 1918. Three days later, on July 29, 1918, Bushman and Bayne were married at Bronx City Hall in New York City. Their son, *Richard*, was born on June 9, 1919. Richard died in 1969. Bayne received a divorce in Los Angeles on June 2, 1925, charging desertion. In 1932, Bushman married *Norma Emily Atkins*, owner of a chain of beauty salons in Los Angeles. Their twenty-four years of marriage ended with her death, at the age of fifty-two, in Woodland Hills, California, on February 4, 1956. Later that same year, on August 15, 1956, he married *Iva Millicent Richardson*, a former agent, in Las Vegas. The couple had been married ten years when, on August 23, 1966, Bushman died from a heart attack due to a fall in their Pacific Palisades, California, home. He was eighty-three. Iva Bushman died at the age of ninety-five on April 14, 1988.

BUTTONS, Red
(1919-)

The comedian and entertainer married burlesque performer *Roxanne* in 1947. They were divorced in 1951. That same year, Buttons married *Helayne McNorton*. They were divorced in 1963. Since 1964, he has been married to *Alicia Pratt*. The couple has one daughter, *Amy*, born in Los Angeles on February 11, 1966.

CAAN, James
(1939-)

Caan eloped to North Carolina on July 8, 1961, with dancer *Dee Jay Mattis*. Their daughter, *Tara*, was born in 1964. The marriage ended in divorce in 1966. He wed model *Sheila Ryan* on January 13, 1976, at the Las Vegas home of friends. Their son, *Scott Andrew*, was born later that same year. The couple was divorced by 1979. Caan has an adopted son, *Shane Hayes*, the same age as his son Scott. On September 9, 1990, Caan wed *Ingrid Hajek* aboard a yacht in Marina Del Ray, California.

CAESAR, Sid
(1922-)

The comedian married *Florence Levy* on July 17, 1943. The couple has three children: *Michele*, born in 1947; *Richard,* born in 1951; and *Karen*, born July 13, 1956.

CAGNEY, James
(1899-1986)

In 1922, Cagney married *Frances Willard (Bill) Vernon* after the Broadway show in which they met, *Pitter Patter*, closed. In 1941, the couple adopted a son, *James, Jr.*, and a daughter, *Cathleen*, nicknamed "Casey." Their sixty-four years of marriage ended in Cagney's death, at the age of eighty-six, on Easter Day, March 30, 1986, at their farm in upstate New York. James Cagney, Jr. died in 1984.

CAINE, Michael
(1933-)

Caine married actress *Patricia Haines* in his native England in 1955. Their daughter, *Dominique*, was born in 1957. Haines divorced him later that same year on the grounds of desertion. On

January 13, 1973, Caine married actress *Shakira Baksh* (Miss Guyana of 1967) in Las Vegas. Their daughter, *Natasha Halima*, was born in London on July 15, 1973.

CALHERN, Louis
(1895-1956)

Calhern married actress-writer *Ilka CHASE* in New England in June 1926. Seven months later, in February 1927, Chase divorced him in New York City on the grounds of adultery. He wed society actress *Julia Hoyt* at Noroton Presbyterian Church in Darien, Connecticut, on September 17, 1927. Hoyt received a Reno divorce on August 6, 1932. The following year, on April 20, 1933, Calhern married actress *Natalie Schaefer* in Los Angeles. After divorcing Schaefer, he married actress *Marianne Stewart* in Plainfield, New Jersey, on November 25, 1946. Stewart divorced him in Juarez, Mexico, on July 19, 1955.

CALHOUN, Alice
(1904-1966)

The silent screen star married attorney *Mendel Silberberg* in May of 1926. Two months later, in July of 1926, Silberberg filed for divorce stating that Calhoun had been engaged to another man at the time of their marriage. Calhoun married *Max Chotiner*, head of a Los Angeles chain of theatres, in Ventura, California, on January 1, 1927. Their thirty-nine years of marriage ended in her death from cancer in Los Angeles on June 3, 1966.

CALHOUN, Rory
(1922-)

Calhoun married singer-actress *Lita Baron* on August 29, 1948. The couple had three daughters: *Cindy Frances*, born in 1957;

Tami Elizabeth, born in 1960; and *Lorri Marie*, born in 1961. In July 1970, Lita Calhoun received a divorce in Santa Monica after twenty-one years of marriage. On April 20, 1971, Calhoun married Australian journalist *Sue Rhodes Boswell*. Their daughter, *Rorye*, was born later that same year.

CALVET, Corinne
(1925-   )

The French-born actress married actor *John Bromfield* in Boulder City, Nevada, in 1948. She received a divorce in Los Angeles on March 16, 1954. On April 12, 1955, she wed actor *Jeff Stone* in Morocco. A son, *Robin*, was born in 1956. The couple also adopted a son, *Michael*. On March 29, 1960, Calvet received a divorce in Santa Monica, after testifying that Stone's conduct had damaged her health. She married producer *Al Gannoway* on September 16, 1966. The marriage ended in divorce in 1968. That same year, on July 1, 1968, she wed producer *Robert Wirt* from whom she is now divorced. She has not remarried.

CANNON, Dyan
(1939-   )

The actress became the fourth wife of *Cary GRANT* in a secret wedding in Nevada on July 22, 1965. A daughter, *Jennifer* (Grant's only child), was born in Burbank, California, on February 26, 1966. Cannon received a divorce in Los Angeles on March 21, 1968. In her divorce suit, Cannon testified that Grant was a habitual LSD user and asked for custody of Jennifer, allowing Grant only daytime visits with a nurse present. The court gave her custody but concluded that Grant was no longer an LSD user and gave him visitation rights. Cannon married attorney *Stanley Finberg* in April 1985. She filed for divorce in Los Angeles on the grounds of irreconcilable differences in October of 1990.

CANTOR, Eddie
(1892-1964)

The comedian married *Ida Tobias* in his native New York City on June 9, 1914. Cantor often joked about having five daughters but no sons. His daughters were: *Marjorie*, born March 31, 1915; *Natalie*, born April 27, 1916; *Edna*, born June 10, 1919; *Marilyn*, born September 16, 1921; and *Janet*, born October 8, 1927. The Cantors had been married forty-eight years when Ida Cantor died from a heart attack at the age of seventy at their Beverly Hills home on August 8, 1962. His oldest daughter, Marjorie, had died of cancer at the age of forty-four on May 17, 1959.

CARLISLE, Kitty
(1914-   )

On August 10, 1946, the actress-singer married playwright and screenwriter *Moss Hart* in New Hope, Pennsylvania. The couple had a son, *Christopher*, born in 1947, and a daughter, *Cathy*, born in 1950. Their fifteen-year marriage ended in Hart's death from a heart attack at the age of fifty-seven on December 20, 1961, in Palm Springs, California. Carlisle, who uses the name Kitty Carlisle Hart, has not remarried.

CAROL, Sue
(1907-1982)

In the mid-twenties, Carol wed *Allen H. Keefer*, a lawyer for a Chicago stockyard firm. They separated soon after their marriage and were divorced in 1929. That same year, on July 29, 1929, she wed actor *Nick Stuart* in Ventura, California. A daughter, *Carol Lee* (named for the professional last names of herself and a close friend, singer *Dixie Lee*, who married *Bing CROSBY*), was born in 1932. Separated from Stuart in 1933, Carol filed for divorce in Los Angeles on August 24, 1934, charging that Stuart berated, abused, and criticized her. She married writer *Howard Wilson* in 1936, but the marriage ended in divorce. She became a Hollywood talent agent and met a young actor named *Alan LADD*, who became her client. They were married in Mexico on March 15, 1942. The couple had a daughter, child actress *Alana Ladd*, born April 21, 1943, and a son, actor *David Ladd*, born February 5, 1947. Both of their children were born in Los Angeles. The marriage ended in Ladd's death from a heart attack at the age of fifty in their Palm Springs home on January 29, 1964. Carol never remarried.

CARON, Leslie
(1931-)

On September 23, 1951, Caron married meat packing heir *George A. Hormel II* in Las Vegas. Hormel obtained a divorce in Los Angeles on March 31, 1954, saying his wife preferred the "intense artistic life to life with him." The actress-dancer wed British stage director *Peter Hall* on August 6, 1956, in the Marylebone Town Hall in London. The couple had a son, *Christopher*, born in 1957, and a daughter, *Jennifer*, born September 21, 1958. Peter Hall received a divorce in London on February 5, 1965, charging his wife with adultery. *Warren Beatty*, named as co-respondant, was ordered to pay the costs of the divorce case. On January 1, 1969, Caron married American film producer *Michael Laughlin* in Frenchman's Cove, Jamaica. The marriage ended in divorce in 1977.

CARRADINE, John
(1906-1989)

The actor married *Ardanelle McCool Cosner* in 1935. The couple had two sons: *Bruce*, born in 1935, and John Arthur, who became actor, singer, and songwriter *David Carradine*, born on December 8, 1936. The marriage ended in divorce in 1941. Carradine wed actress *Sonia Sorel* in 1945. Three sons were born: *Christopher*, in 1947; actor *Keith Carradine*, on August 8, 1951; and actor *Robert Carradine*, in 1954. The couple was divorced in

1956. In 1957, Carradine wed *Doris Rich*. The couple had been married fourteen years when Rich was killed in a fire on May 18, 1971. In 1974, the actor married *Emily Cisneros*, from whom he was later divorced. His son David has a son, *Tom*, with actress *Barbara HERSHEY*. His son Keith is the father of actress *Martha Plimpton*.

CARROLL, Madeleine
(1906-1987)

On October 2, 1931, Carroll wed *Capt. Philip Ashley*, a London real estate broker, in her native England. After a lengthy separation, Carroll divorced Ashley in London on December 12, 1939, charging Ashley with misconduct. On June 30, 1942, Carroll announced that she had been married to actor *Sterling HAYDEN* for three months. The wedding had taken place in Peterboro, New Hampshire, on Valentine's Day, February 14, 1942. Four years later, on May 8, 1946, Carroll received a divorce in Reno on the grounds of cruelty. She married French film producer *Henri Lavorel* in Paris two months later, on July 13, 1946. Divorced in 1949, Carroll married magazine publisher *Andrew Heiskell* on September 1, 1950. Their daughter, *Anne-Madeleine*, was born in 1952. She died in 1983. Heiskell received a divorce in Litchfield, Connecticut, on January 22, 1965, on the grounds of desertion. Carroll never remarried.

CARROLL, Nancy
(1905-1965)

As a young Broadway chorine, she married playwright *Jack Kirkland* in New York City in June 1924. A daughter, *Patricia*, was born in New York City on July 18, 1925. Carroll received a divorce in Nogales, Mexico, in June 1931. Shortly after, on July 3, 1931, she wed magazine editor *Francis Bolton Mallory* in Newton, Connecticut. She divorced Mallory in Carson City, Nevada, in September 1935. She did not remarry until 1953 when she wed Dutch industrialist *C.H.J. Groen*. When Carroll arrived in New York City in the summer of 1965, there were rumors that she and her husband were estranged. That same summer, on August 6, 1965, Carroll died of natural causes in New York City. She was fifty-nine.

CARSON, Jack
(1910-1963)

During the thirties, Carson married and divorced his vaudeville partner, *Betty Ann Linde*. In 1940, the actor wed radio singer *Kay St. Germain*. The couple had a son, *Jack, Jr.*, born in 1941, and a daughter, *Germain*, born in 1945. Kay Carson obtained a divorce in Los Angeles on April 3, 1950, charging her husband with desertion. On August 1, 1952, Carson married actress *Lola Albright* at the Little Brown Church in the Valley, near Los Angeles. Albright received a divorce in Los Angeles on November 10, 1958, stating that their careers clashed. The actor married *Sandra June Tucker* on January 26, 1961. Less than two years later, on January 2, 1963, Carson died from cancer in Los Angeles.

CASSAVETES, John
(1929-1989)

On March 19, 1958, Cassavetes wed actress *Gena ROWLANDS*. The couple had three children: *Nicholas*, born in 1959; *Alexander*, born in 1965; and *Zoe*, born in 1970. Their thirty years of marriage ended in his death after a long illness on February 3, 1989, in Los Angeles. He was fifty-nine.

CATES, Phoebe
(1963-)

The actress and model married *Kevin KLINE* in New York City on March 5, 1989.

CAULFIELD, Joan
(1922-   )

On April 29, 1950, the actress wed producer *Frank Ross* (divorced from *Jean ARTHUR*). The union ended in divorce in Santa Monica on April 9, 1959. Caulfield testified that Ross "did not want to be bothered with children." *Kevin Caulfield Ross* was born late in 1959. He was born after the divorce which became final in 1960. Caulfield married dentist *Dr. Robert H. Peterson* on November 24, 1960, at her Beverly Hills home. Their son, *John*, was born in Los Angeles on March 22, 1962. Caulfield divorced Peterson in Santa Monica on May 19, 1966. She has not remarried.

CHADWICK, Helene
(1897-1940)

In 1918, the silent film star wed director *William A. Wellman* at the Mission Inn in Riverside, California. Chadwick divorced Wellman in Los Angeles on September 6, 1933, on the grounds of non-support. She never remarried.

CHAMPION, Gower
(1921-1980)

On October 5, 1947, the dancer-choreographer wed dancer *Marjorie Belcher* in Los Angeles. Belcher began to use the professional name of *Marge CHAMPION* when the couple became a popular duo in films. The couple had two sons: *Blake Gower*, born in 1956, and *Gregg*, born February 14, 1962. The Champions separated in 1972, and Marge received a divorce in Santa Monica on December 21, 1973, after twenty-six years of marriage. In July 1976, Champion wed *Carla Russell* at his Malibu home. Gregg Champion was best man. The marriage ended in Champion's death from cancer at the age of fifty-nine in New York City on August 25, 1980. One of his sons, actor-dancer

Blake Champion, was killed in a car accident in Lee, Massachusetts, on May 21, 1987.

CHAMPION, Marge
(1921-)

In the early forties, the actress-dancer, then known as *Marjorie Belcher*, married commercial artist *Art Babbitt* in Los Angeles. The marriage ended in divorce two years later. She married dancer and choreographer *Gower CHAMPION* in Los Angeles on October 5, 1947. The couple had two sons: *Blake Gower*, born in 1956, and *Gregg*, born February 14, 1962. The Champions separated in 1972, and Marge received a divorce in Santa Monica on December 21, 1973, after twenty-six years of marriage. She married film director *Boris Sagal* on January 1, 1977. Four years later, on May 22, 1981, Sagal was killed in a filming accident in Portland, Oregon. One of her sons, actor-dancer Blake Champion, was killed in a car accident in Lee, Massachusetts on May 21, 1987.

CHANDLER, Helen
(1906-1965)

On February 3, 1930, the actress married writer *Cyril Hume*. The marriage ended in divorce in 1934. She wed actor *Bramwell Fletcher* on Valentine's Day, 1935, at Riverside Church in New York City. After their divorce in 1940, Fletcher married *Diana BARRYMORE*. Chandler never remarried.

CHANDLER, Jeff
(1918-1961)

Chandler wed actress *Marjorie Hoshelle* in Los Angeles on October 13, 1946. The couple had two daughters: *Jamie*, born in May 1947, and *Dana*, born in 1949. Hoshelle received a divorce in

Los Angeles on April 15, 1954. The decree was to become final in one year, but the couple reconciled so the decree was never finalized. She received a second divorce in Los Angeles on the grounds of extreme mental cruelty on June 29, 1959. The divorce became final in 1960.

CHANEY, Lon
(1883-1930)

In the spring of 1905, the actor married singer *Cleva Creighton*. Their son, Creighton Chaney, who became actor *Lon Chaney, Jr.*, was born in Oklahoma City on February 10, 1906. Divorced in 1914, Chaney married *Hazel Hastings Bennett* that same year. The couple was married sixteen years until Chaney's death from cancer at the age of forty-seven, on August 26, 1930, in Los Angeles.

CHAPLIN, Charlie
(1889-1977)

Chaplin wed sixteen-year-old screen actress *Mildred HARRIS* in Los Angeles on October 23, 1918. A son, *Norman Spencer Chaplin*, was born in Los Angeles on July 7, 1919, but died three days later. The marriage ended in divorce in Los Angeles on November 12, 1920, on the grounds of cruelty. Chaplin wed his sixteen-year-old protégé, *Lita Grey*, in Guayamas, Mexico, on November 26, 1924. Grey was originally to be his leading lady in *The Gold Rush* (1925) but was replaced by *Georgia Hale*. Their oldest son, *Charles Spencer Chaplin, Jr.*, was born in Los Angeles in May 1925. He became an actor, but died in 1968. Their second son, *Sydney Earle Chaplin* (named for Chaplin's half-brother), was born in Los Angeles on March 30, 1926. After a year-long court battle, Lita Grey Chaplin was granted a divorce in Los Angeles on August 22, 1927. Charging Chaplin with cruelty and neglect, she was given custody of their sons and a $625,000 settlement, as well as $200,000 in a trust for the children. Chaplin married screen actress *Paulette GODDARD* in

Canton, China, in June 1936. The couple separated in 1940, and Goddard received a divorce in Juarez, Mexico, on June 4, 1942, on the grounds of incompatibility of characters. On June 16, 1943, Chaplin married *Oona O'Neill*, the actress-daughter of playwright *Eugene O'Neill*. The couple was married at the Santa Barbara home of Justice of the Peace *Linton P. Moore*. The couple had eight children. Actress *Geraldine CHAPLIN* was born on July 31, 1944, followed by actor *Michael John Chaplin*, born on March 7, 1946. *Josephine Hannah* (Hannah was the name of Chaplin's mother) was born on March 28, 1949. *Victoria* was born on May 19, 1951; *Eugene Anthony* on August 23, 1953; *Jane Cecil* on May 23, 1957; and *Annette Emily* on December 3, 1959. Their youngest child, *Christopher James*, was born on July 8, 1962. The Chaplins were married thirty-four years. Chaplin died in his sleep in Corsier, Switzerland, on Christmas Day, 1977. He was eighty-eight.

CHAPLIN, Geraldine
(1944-)

The actress was born in Santa Monica, California, the oldest of the eight children of *Charlie CHAPLIN* and *Oona O'Neill*. She has a son, *Shane Saura Chaplin O'Neill*, born on December 31, 1974, in Madrid, Spain, with Spanish film director *Carlos Saura*.

CHARISSE, Cyd
(1921-)

She was *Tula Finklea* when she married her ballet teacher, the famous Los Angeles dance instructor *Nico Charisse*, in France on August 12, 1939. Their son, *Nicky*, was born on May 7, 1942, in Los Angeles. The marriage ended in divorce in 1947. On May 9, 1948, she married singer-actor *Tony MARTIN*. Their son, *Tony*, was born on August 28, 1950. Martin also adopted her son Nicky.

CHASE, Chevy
(1943-   )

Chase's first marriage, to a model, ended in divorce after a short time. On December 4, 1976, he married actress *Jacqueline Carlin*. The couple was divorced in May 1980. Since 1982, Chase has been married to film production assistant *Jayni Luke*. The couple has three daughters: *Cydney Cathalene* (Cathalene was the name of Chase's mother), born on January 4, 1983; *Caley Leigh*, born in 1985; and *Emily*, born in 1988.

CHASE, Ilka
(1903-1978)

In June 1926, the actress-writer married actor *Louis CALHERN* in New England. Seven months later, in February 1927, Chase received a divorce in New York City on the grounds of adultery. On July 13, 1935, she wed New York theatrical agency executive *William B. Murray* in Greenwich, Connecticut. She was granted a divorce from Murray in Las Vegas on December 4, 1946, after eleven years of marriage. Three days later, on December 7, 1946, she wed New York doctor *Norton Sager Brown* in Las Vegas. Their thirty-one years of marriage ended in Chase's death at the age of seventy-two on February 15, 1978, in Mexico City, Mexico.

CHATTERTON, Ruth
(1893-1961)

On December 20, 1924, Chatterton married her Broadway co-star, actor *Ralph FORBES*, at the Church of the Beloved Disciple in New York City. The union ended in divorce in Minden, Nevada, on August 12, 1932. They remained friends. The next day, August 13, 1932, Chatterton and actor *George BRENT* were married in Harrison, New York. Two years later, on October 4, 1934, Chatterton divorced Brent in Los Angeles, testifying that Brent was "sulky, unreasonable, and domineering." In 1942, she married actor *Barry Thomson*. She was widowed in 1960.

CHER
(1946-   )

The singer-actress married *Sonny Bono* secretly in 1969 before the birth of their daughter, *Chastity*, later that same year. The couple always stated that they were married in Tijuana, Mexico, on October 27, 1964. Cher received a divorce from Bono on June 27, 1975, in Santa Monica. Three days later, on June 30, 1975, she wed singer *Gregg Allman* at Caesar's Palace in Las Vegas. The couple separated five days later and on July 9, 1975, Cher filed for divorce in Santa Monica. Allman is the father of her son, *Elijah Blue*, born on September 20, 1976.

CHEVALIER, Maurice
(1888-1972)

The entertainer's only marriage was to dancer *Yvonne Vallée*, whom he married on October 10, 1926. The couple was divorced in 1935.

CLAIRE, Ina
(1892-1985)

Claire married Chicago music critic *James Whittaker* on July 9, 1919, in Wheaton, Illinois. They kept their marriage a secret until the following February. Her marriage to Whittaker ended in divorce in Chicago on October 19, 1925. Charging Whittaker with cruelty and desertion, she testified that he had thrown her out of their New York apartment. On May 9, 1929, she eloped to Las Vegas with film star *John GILBERT*. They were married by a Justice of the Peace. The marriage was shortlived. Claire received a divorce in Los Angeles on August 4, 1931, testifying that it was "impossible to live with him anymore." In 1939, she married lawyer and financier *William R. Wallace, Jr.* The couple settled into a home on Nob Hill in San Francisco. She was widowed in 1975.

CLARK, Marguerite
(1883-1940)

One of the biggest stars of the 1910s, Clark married aviator *Harry Palmerson Williams* on August 15, 1918, at the First Methodist Church in Greenwich, Connecticut. Their seventeen years of marriage ended suddenly when, on May 19, 1936, Williams was killed in a plane crash outside of Baton Rouge, Louisiana. Their home in New Orleans is now the *Milton H. Latter* Memorial branch of the New Orleans public library.

CLARK, Petula
(1932-)

In 1961, the singer-actress married French recording executive *Claude Wolff*, who became her manager. The couple has two daughters: *Barbara Michele*, born in 1962; and *Catherine Natalie*, born in 1963; and a son, *Patrick Philippe*, born September 7, 1972.

CLARKE, Mae
(1907-)

The actress has been married and divorced three times. She wed actor *Lew Brice*, the brother of *Fanny Brice*, in 1926; *Capt. Stevens Bancroft* in 1937; and *Capt. Herbert Langdon* in 1946.

CLAYBURGH, Jill
(1944-)

Clayburgh married playwright *David Rabe* in March 1979. Their daughter, *Lily*, was born in 1982.

CLOSE, Glenn
(1947-)

Close married rock guitarist *Cabot Wade* in 1969. The marriage ended in divorce two and a half years later. On September 1, 1984, she wed New York businessman *James Marlas* on Nantucket Island, Massachusetts. They were divorced a year later. The actress has a daughter, *Annie Maude*, born April 26, 1988, with producer *John Starke*.

CODY, Lew
(1884-1934)

During the years 1910 to 1913, Cody married, divorced and remarried actress *Dorothy DALTON*. They were divorced for the second time in Los Angeles in 1914. On September 17, 1926, he wed *Mabel NORMAND* in Ventura, California. Less than four years later, on February 23, 1930, Normand died of tuberculosis in a Monrovia, California, sanitarium.

COLBERT, Claudette
(1905-)

The French-born actress wed actor-director *Norman Foster* in London in 1928. Colbert received a Mexican divorce on August 30, 1935. On Christmas Eve of 1935, she married *Dr. Joel Pressman* in Yuma, Arizona. Their thirty-nine years of marriage ended in Pressman's death from cancer at the age of sixty-seven on February 26, 1968, in Los Angeles. Colbert has not remarried.

COLLINS, Joan
(1933-   )

On May 24, 1952, Collins married actor *Maxwell Reed* in her native England. After a long separation, she received a divorce in Los Angeles in 1956. She wed *Anthony Newly*, the British-born actor, composer, and singer on May 27, 1963. The couple had a daughter, *Tara Cynara*, born October 12, 1963, and a son, *Alexander Anthony*, called Sacha, born on September 8, 1965. The couple was divorced in 1970. *Ronald S. Kass*, a record company executive and film producer, became her third husband in March of 1972. Their daughter, *Katyana (Katy)*, was born in June of 1972. Divorced from Kass in 1983, Collins wed Swedish pop singer-turned-businessman *Peter Holm* in October 1985. After lengthy divorce proceedings, Collins divorced Holm in Los Angeles on August 25, 1987.

COLLYER, June
(1907-1968)

On July 21, 1931, Collyer wed actor *Stuart ERWIN* in Yuma, Arizona. The couple had two children: *Stuart, Jr.*, born September 15, 1932, and *Judy*, born in July 1935. The couple was married thirty-six years until Erwin's death from a heart attack at the age of sixty-five in Los Angeles on December 21, 1967. Collyer died just three months later on March 16, 1968.

COLMAN, Ronald
(1891-1958)

The British-born star married actress *Thelma Victoria Raye* on September 18, 1920, in the Hanover Square registry office in London. The marriage ended in divorce in London in 1935 after a lengthy separation. Colman wed actress *Benita HUME* on September 30, 1938, at San Ysidro Ranch, his home near Santa Barbara. *Col. Tim McCoy* was best man. Their daughter, *Juliet Benita Colman*, was born in Los Angeles in July 1944. She published a biography of her father in 1975. Their nineteen-year marriage was considered one of Hollywood's happiest. The marriage ended when Colman died from a lung infection on May 19, 1958, at their ranch. He was sixty-seven.

COMPSON, Betty
(1897-1974)

The film star married director *James Cruze* on October 14, 1924, at her home in Flint Ridge, near Los Angeles. In 1929, the couple separated, reconciled and separated again for the last time. Compson was granted a divorce in Los Angeles on May 20, 1930, on the grounds of mental cruelty. She wed her manager, *Irving Weinberg*, on December 13, 1933. The ceremony took place in Albuquerque, New Mexico, aboard a train bound for California. Less than four years later, on March 25, 1937, Compson divorced Weinberg in Los Angeles. She testified that he left her home at night to be with another woman. In the early forties, she met and married *Jack Silvius Gall*, a former professional boxer who became a navy athletic specialist. She was widowed in 1962.

CONNERY, Sean
(1930-)

Connery wed actress *Diane Cilento* in Gibralter on November 30, 1962. Cilento had a daughter, *Giovanna*, from a former marriage, and the couple had a son, actor *Jason Connery*, born in Rome on January 12, 1963. After a two-year separation, Connery obtained a divorce in London in October of 1973 on the grounds of irretrievable breakdown. He married French-born divorcée *Micheline Rocquebrun* in Gibralter on May 6, 1975.

CONTI, Tom
(1941-)

Conti married British actress *Kara Wilson* on July 2, 1967. The couple has a daughter, *Nina*, born in 1974.

COOGAN, Jackie
(1914-1984)

The former child actor married *Betty GRABLE* at St. Brendan's Catholic Church in Los Angeles on November 20, 1937. Financial difficulties led to their divorce less than two years later, on October 11, 1939, in Los Angeles. He married nightclub entertainer *Flower Parry* on August 10, 1941, in Gardnerville, Nevada. A son, *Anthony*, was born in Los Angeles on March 4, 1942. Parry was granted a divorce on June 29, 1943, in Los Angeles on the grounds of mental cruelty. She was given custody of their son. On December 26, 1946, Coogan married singer *Ann Mc-Cormack* at the Los Angeles home of *Judge Edward Brand*. A daughter, *Joan*, was born in Los Angeles on April 2, 1948. Mc-Cormack received a divorce in Los Angeles on September 14, 1950. The decree became final on September 20, 1951. McCormack was given custody of Joan. In April 1952, Coogan married dancer *Dorothy (Dodie) Lamphere* in Mexico City. The marriage was kept a secret until July 1953. Their daughter, *Leslie*, was born in 1953, and their son, *Christopher*, was born fourteen years later, on July 9, 1967. The Coogans were married nearly thirty-two years until the actor's death from a heart attack on March 1, 1984, in Santa Monica. He was sixty-nine.

COOPER, Gary
(1901-1961)

Cooper married socialite *Veronica Balfe* in her mother's New York City home on December 15, 1933. Balfe, who was called "Rocky," had had a brief screen career using the professional name *Sandra Shaw*. Their daughter, *Maria*, was born on September 15, 1937, in Los Angeles. The marriage ended in Cooper's death from cancer at the age of sixty on May 13, 1961, in Los Angeles.

COOPER, Dame Gladys
(1888-1971)

On December 12, 1908, the actress wed *Capt. Herbert Buckminster* in London. The couple had two children: *Joan*, born in 1910, and *John*, born July 18, 1915. The marriage ended in divorce in December 1922. On June 15, 1928, Cooper married *Sir Neville Pearson*. Their daughter, *Sally*, was born in January 1930. Pearson received a divorce in Carlisle, England, on October 16, 1936, naming actor *Philip Merivale* as co-respondant. Cooper and Merivale were married in Chicago on April 30, 1937. Eight years later, on March 13, 1946, Merivale died from a heart ailment in Los Angeles at the age of fifty-nine. The actress never remarried.

COOPER, Jackie
(1921-)

On December 11, 1944, the former child star married *June Horne*, the daughter of film director *James W. Horne*, in the wedding chapel of Wilshire Methodist Church in Los Angeles. Their son, *John Anthony*, was born in 1946. Late in 1948, Cooper divorced Horne in Little Rock, Arkansas, and married actress *Hildy Parks* in New York City. Horne received her own decree in Los Angeles on November 4, 1949, charging Cooper with cruelty. She was given custody of their son. Cooper's marriage to Parks ended in divorce in Jacksonville, Florida, in April 1954. Later that month, on April 29, 1954, he married *Barbara Kraus* in Washington, D.C. The couple has three children: *Russell*, born in 1956; *Julie*, born in 1958; and *Cristina*, born in 1959.

COOPER, Miriam
(1891-1976)

In February 1916, Cooper married actor-director *Raoul WALSH* at a Hopi Indian reservation near Albuquerque, New Mexico. The couple adopted two sons from the New York Foundling Hospital: *Jackie*, in 1918, and *Bobby*, in 1922. Cooper divorced her husband in Los Angeles in 1926 on the grounds of incompatibility. The decree became final in 1927. She never remarried.

CORTEZ, Ricardo
(1899-1977)

On January 30, 1926, the film star married actress *Alma RUBENS* in Riverside, California. Rubens died from pneumonia in Los Angeles on January 21, 1931. Cortez married New York socialite *Christine Coniff Lee* in Phoenix, Arizona, on January 8, 1934. Testifying that Cortez was unaffectionate, Lee received a divorce in Los Angeles on June 14, 1940, on the grounds of cruelty. A decade later, in 1950, he wed *Margarette Bell* of Chicago. The union lasted until his death at the age of seventy-seven on April 28, 1977, in New York City.

COSTELLO, Dolores
(1905-1979)

The younger daughter of actor *Maurice COSTELLO*, she became the third wife of *John BARRYMORE* on November 24, 1928, in a ceremony held at her parents' Beverly Hills home. A daughter, *Dolores Ethel Mae* (nicknamed "Dede") was born in Los Angeles on April 8, 1930. A son, actor *John Blythe BARRYMORE, Jr.*, was born in Los Angeles on June 4, 1932. The marriage ended in divorce in Los Angeles on August 24, 1934. Costello charged desertion and was given custody of the children. On November 29, 1939, she wed *Dr. John Vruwink*, a Beverly Hills physician, in Prescott, Arizona. The union ended in divorce on July 12, 1951, in Los Angeles. Costello testified that "He seldom talked to her, and when he did, he only criticized." She never remarried and was known throughout the rest of her life as Dolores Costello Barrymore. Her older sister, actress *Helene Costello* (1903-1957), was married and divorced five times and had one daughter, *Deirdre*.

COSTELLO, Lou
(1906-1959)

On January 30, 1934, the comedian married Scottish-born dancer *Ann Battler* in a Boston church. Their first daughter, *Patricia Ann*, was born on September 28, 1936, in Providence, Rhode Island. A second daughter, *Carole Lou*, was born on December 23, 1939, also in Providence. Their son, *Lou Costello, Jr.* (nicknamed "Butch"), was born on November 6, 1942. Two days before his first birthday, on November 4, 1943, Butch accidentally fell into the family swimming pool and was drowned. Costello felt the tragedy deeply, but a third daughter, *Christine,* was born in Los Angeles on August 15, 1947. Their twenty-five years of marriage ended in the comedian's death from a heart attack at the age of fifty-three on March 3, 1959, in Beverly Hills. Ann Costello died later that same year. Christine Costello published a biography of her father in 1981.

COSTELLO, Maurice
(1877-1950)

In 1902, Costello, who was to become a Broadway matinee idol and an early screen star, married *Mae Altschuh* in Brooklyn, New York. The couple had two daughters: *Helene*, born June 21, 1903, in New York City, and *Dolores COSTELLO*, born September 17, 1905, in Pittsburgh, Pennsylvania. Both of their daughters became film actresses which their father blamed for the failure of his marriage. He claimed that his efforts to give his daughters helpful advice about their careers were frustrated by his wife. He divorced her in Los Angeles in September 1927. On

August 29, 1939, Costello married actress *Ruth Reeves* in Tijuana, Mexico. Reeves divorced him in Los Angeles on October 29, 1941, on charges of extreme cruelty. Costello never remarried.

COSTNER, Kevin
(1955-   )

Costner married *Cindy Silva*, whom he had met in college, in 1978. The couple has two daughters, *Annie*, born in 1984; and *Lily*, born in 1986; and a son, *Joe*, born in 1988.

COTTEN, Joseph
(1905-   )

In October 1931, the actor married magazine writer and editor *Lenore Kip* in Miami, Florida. Their twenty-nine years of marriage ended in her death at the age of fifty-five from cancer in Rome on January 7, 1960. Cotten married actress *Patricia Medina* later that same year, on October 20, 1960, at the Bel-Air home of *David O. Selznick* and *Jennifer Jones*.

COURTENAY, Tom
(1937-   )

On January 11, 1973, the actor married his stage co-star, British actress *Cheryl Kennedy*. The couple is now divorced.

CRAIN, Jeanne
(1925-   )

On December 31, 1946, Crain married business executive *Paul Frederick Brinkman* at the Church of the Blessed Sacrament in

Los Angeles. Four children were born: *Paul, Jr.*, born April 6, 1947; *Michael*, born January 21, 1949; *Timothy*, born August 2, 1950; and *Jeanine*, born March 5, 1952. Crain obtained an interlocutory divorce decree (to become final in one year) in Los Angeles on August 6, 1956. The couple was reconciled in December of 1956, and the decree never became final. Three more children were born: *Lisabette*, on November 21, 1958; *Maria*, on January 10, 1961; and their seventh, *Christopher*, on May 25, 1965.

CRAWFORD, Broderick
(1911-1986)

The actor was the son of vaudevillian *Lester Crawford* and actress *Helen Broderick*. On November 21, 1940, he married actress *Kay Griffith*. The couple had two sons: *Christopher*, born in 1947, and *Kelly*, born in 1951. They separated in 1951 and were divorced in 1953. He wed actress *Joan Tabor* in the Baptist Little Church of the West in Las Vegas on January 4, 1962. He adopted her seven-year-old daughter, *Lauren*. Five years later, on April 26, 1967, Tabor received a divorce in Los Angeles. Crawford wed *Mary Alice Michael* in St. Louis, Missouri, on August 8, 1973. The couple was married for twelve years until his death at the age of seventy-four from the aftereffects of a stroke on April 26, 1986, in Rancho Mirage, near Palm Springs, California.

CRAWFORD, Joan
(1906-1977)

During the twenties, Crawford was married to musician *James Barratt Welton*, with whom she moved to Los Angeles. The marriage ended in divorce soon after she began her film career in 1925. When she married actor *Douglas FAIRBANKS, Jr.*, on June 3, 1929, at St. Malachy's Catholic Church in New York City, it was publicized as her first marriage. But troubling rumors stated that Crawford had married Fairbanks only to further

her own career and that her in-laws, *Douglas FAIRBANKS* and *Mary PICKFORD*, did not approve of the match. Crawford divorced Fairbanks in Los Angeles on May 12, 1933, testifying that he was "jealous and suspicious" of her. She wed her leading man *Franchot TONE* in Englewood Cliffs, New Jersey, on October 11, 1935. Crawford received a divorce in Los Angeles on April 11, 1939, on the grounds of mental cruelty. They remained friends. That same year, Crawford adopted a daughter, actress-writer *Christina Crawford*. Six weeks after they first met, Crawford married actor *Phillip Terry* at the Ventura, California, ranch of a friend, lawyer *Neil McCarthy*, on July 21, 1942. On April 4, 1943, they adopted an eight-year-old orphan, *Phillip, Jr.* His name was changed to *Christopher* after their divorce in Los Angeles on April 25, 1946. Terry, according to Crawford, interfered with her movie work, criticized her selection of parts, and found fault with her personally. In between marriages, she adopted "twin" daughters (born one month apart), *Cynthia* and *Cathy*. On May 10, 1955, Crawford married *Alfred N. Steele*, president of Pepsi-Cola Company, at a Las Vegas hotel. Crawford hoped to spend the rest of her life with Steele and became a Pepsi-Cola board member. But on April 19, 1959, at the age of fifty-seven, Steele died in his sleep, apparently from a heart attack, in New York City. Crawford never remarried.

CRISP, Donald
(1880-1974)

On August 15, 1932, the actor-director married screenwriter *Jane Murfin* in California. Widowed in 1957, Crisp never remarried.

CRONYN, Hume
(1911-)

Cronyn married actress *Jessica TANDY* on September 27, 1942. Tandy has a daughter, *Susan*, from a former marriage to actor

Jack HAWKINS. The couple also has a son, *Christopher*, born in 1946, and a daughter, *Tandy*, born in 1947.

CROSBY, Bing
(1903-1977)

Crosby married singer *Dixie Lee* on September 29, 1930. The couple had four sons: *Gary* (named for their friend *Gary COOPER*), born on June 25, 1933; twins, *Dennis* and *Eddie*, born on July 13, 1934; and *Lindsay*, born on January 5, 1938. Lee died of cancer in Los Angeles on November 1, 1952. Crosby eloped to Las Vegas on October 24, 1957, with starlet *Kathryn (Kathy) Grant*. The couple had three children: *Harry, Jr.* (Bing Crosby was born Harry Lillis Crosby), born on August 8, 1958; a daughter, *Mary Frances*, born on September 14, 1959; and a second son, *Nathaniel*, born on October 29, 1961. The couple resided in Hillsborough, California. Their nearly twenty years of marriage ended in Crosby's death from a heart attack at the age of seventy-four in Madrid, Spain, on October 14, 1977. His son Lindsay committed suicide at the age of fifty-one in Las Virgenes, California, on December 11, 1989.

CRUISE, Tom
(1962-)

The actor married actress *Mimi Rogers* on May 9, 1987, in New York City. The couple filed for divorce in February 1990, and the decree was granted later that same year. On Christmas Eve, 1990, Cruise wed Australian actress *Nicole Kidman* in Telluride, Colorado.

CRYSTAL, Billy
(1947-)

The comedian married *Janice Goldfinger* in 1970. The couple has two daughters: *Jennifer*, born in 1973, and *Lindsay*, born October 21, 1977.

CURTIS, Jamie Lee
(1958-   )

The actress is the daughter of *Tony CURTIS* and *Janet LEIGH*. She married actor *Christopher Guest* in December of 1984 at the Beverly Hills home of director *Rob Reiner*. The couple has an adopted daughter, *Annie*, born in the spring of 1987.

CURTIS, Tony
(1925-   )

On June 4, 1951, Curtis and film star *Janet LEIGH* were married in Greenwich, Connecticut. The couple had two daughters: *Kelly Lee*, born June 17, 1956, and actress *Jamie Lee CURTIS*, born November 21, 1958. Curtis and Leigh were considered Hollywood's ideal couple, but on July 11, 1962, Leigh was granted a divorce in Santa Monica on the grounds of extreme cruelty. Curtis married actress *Christine Kaufmann* at the Riviera Hotel in Las Vegas on February 8, 1963. Two daughters were born: *Alexandra*, born on July 19, 1964, followed by *Allegra*, born on July 12, 1966. Kaufmann divorced Curtis in Juarez, Mexico, on April 16, 1968. She was given custody of their daughters. Four days later, on April 20, 1968, Curtis wed model *Leslie Allen* at the Sahara Hotel in Las Vegas. The couple had two sons: *Nicholas*, born December 3, 1971, and *Benjamin*, born May 2, 1973. Curtis and Allen were divorced in 1981.

DAFOE, Willem
(1955-   )

The actor has a son, *Jack*, born in 1982, with stage actress and director *Elizabeth LeCompte*.

DAHL, Arlene
(1924-   )

On April 16, 1951, Dahl married actor *Lex BARKER* in Central Presbyterian Church in New York City. Less than two years later, on October 15, 1952, Dahl received a divorce in Santa Monica, after testifying that Barker had called her a "hick from Minnesota." The decree became final on November 13, 1953. In 1954, the actress married *Fernando LAMAS*. Their son, actor *Lorenzo Lamas*, was born on January 20, 1958. She received a divorce in Santa Monica in August 1960 on the grounds of mental cruelty. She married *Christian R. Holmes*, heir to the Fleischman Yeast fortune, in Pueblo, Mexico, on October 15, 1960. A daughter, *Christina*, was born on August 3, 1961. Dahl obtained a divorce in Santa Monica on October 13, 1964, charging mental cruelty. She wed importer and wine expert *Alexis Lichine* on December 23, 1964, in Bridgetown, Barbados. Divorced in 1969, she wed business executive *Rounsevelle W. Schaum*, her fifth husband, later that year. The couple was married at Marble Collegiate Church in New York City on December 7, 1969. A son, *Rounsevelle Andreas*, was born on December 8, 1970, in New York City. The marriage ended in divorce in 1976. In the summer of 1984, Dahl married perfume executive *Marc Rosen* aboard a cruise ship in the Mediterranean.

DAILEY, Dan
(1914-1978)

Dailey was first married to *Esther Rodier*. The brief marriage ended in divorce in 1941. In 1942, he wed *Elizabeth Hofert*. A son, *Dan Dailey III*, was born in 1947. The couple was divorced in 1951. On February 5, 1955, Dailey wed *Gwendolyn Carter*

O'Connor (the divorced wife of *Donald O'CONNOR*) in Las Vegas. Seven years later, on August 24, 1962, Gwen Dailey was granted a divorce in Los Angeles on the grounds of extreme cruelty. Dailey married *Nora Warner* on December 14, 1968. She filed for divorce in Santa Monica on September 8, 1972, on the grounds of irreconcilable differences. The actor never remarried. His son committed suicide in 1975.

DALTON, Dorothy
(1894-1972)

During the years 1910 to 1913, Dalton married, divorced, and remarried actor *Lew CODY*. The couple was divorced for the second time in Los Angeles in 1914. On April 22, 1924, she wed theatrical producer *Arthur Hammerstein* (the father of *Elaine HAMMERSTEIN*) in Chicago. A daughter, *Carol*, was born in the early thirties. The Hammersteins were married thirty-three years until his death, at age eighty-two, on October 12, 1955, in Palm Beach, Florida. Dalton never remarried.

DAMITA, Lili
(1901-)

The French-born actress eloped to Yuma, Arizona, on June 19, 1935, with *Errol FLYNN*. Their son, *Sean Flynn*, was born on May 31, 1941, in Los Angeles. Sean Flynn became an actor but disappeared in Vietnam while serving as a war correspondent. Damita received a divorce from Flynn in Los Angeles on March 31, 1942, testifying that her husband paid more attention to his yachts than to her. In 1962, she wed *Allen R. Loomis*. They reside in Beverly Hills.

DAMONE, Vic
(1928-)

The singer-actor married Italian actress *Pier ANGELI* in November 1954. Their son, *Perry*, was born in 1955. Angeli filed for divorce in Santa Monica on November 20, 1958, on the grounds of mental cruelty. There was a brief reconciliation, but the divorce became final in 1959. In 1963, Damone married actress *Judy Rawlins*. The couple had three daughters: *Victoria Catherine*, born in 1965; *Andrea*, born in 1966; and *Daniella*, born in 1968. The marriage ended in divorce in 1971. On April 12, 1974, Damone married socialite *Becky Ann Jones*. Later divorced, he married actress-singer *Diahann Carroll* in Atlantic City, New Jersey, in January 1987.

DANA, Viola
(1897-1987)

In 1915, the actress wed film director *John Hancock Collins* in New Jersey. Collins died on October 23, 1918, a victim of the flu epidemic. He was twenty-eight. Dana was remarried on June 20, 1925, in Los Angeles, to former college athlete-turned-Western film star *Maurice B. "Lefty" Flynn*. The couple separated in December 1928. Dana divorced her husband in Los Angeles on February 14, 1929. She testified that Flynn was "intoxicated for two and a half years in our three years of married life." On October 15, 1930, she wed professional golfer *Jimmy W. Thomson* in Colorado Springs, Colorado. The marriage ended in divorce in Los Angeles on March 30, 1945. She charged that Thomson paid too much attention to other women—and wanted her to pay more attention to other men. She never remarried. Her sister, silent film star *Shirley Mason* (1901–1979), married film director *Bernard J. Durning*. Widowed, Mason married film director *Sidney Lanfield*. The couple had two daughters and was married until Lanfield's death in 1972.

DANDRIDGE, Dorothy
(1923-1965)

At seventeen, in 1940, Dandridge married *Harold Nicholas* of the Nicholas Brothers dancing team. Their daughter, *Marolyn*, was born the following year. The couple was divorced after five years of marriage. On June 22, 1959, Dandridge wed Beverly Hills restaurateur *Jack Denison* in the Greek Orthodox Cathedral of St. Sophia in Beverly Hills. The marriage ended in divorce in 1962.

DANIELS, Bebe
(1901 - 1971)

On June 14, 1930, Daniels and *Ben LYON*, two of the most popular film stars of the silent era, were married in a Hollywood hotel. *Louella Parsons* was matron-of-honor and the bridesmaids were *Lila LEE, Constance TALMADGE, Betty COMPSON,* and *Adela Rogers Hyland*. The couple settled in London where their daughter, *Barbara*, was born on September 9, 1931. The couple adopted a son, *Richard*, a child actor, who was born in 1937. The couple was married forty years until her death from a cerebral hemorrhage, at age seventy, in London on March 16, 1971.

DANIELS, Jeff
(1955-)

The actor married *Kathleen Treado*, whom he had met in his childhood home of Chelsea, Michigan, on July 13, 1979. Their son, *Ben*, was born in November 1984.

DARIN, Bobby
(1936 - 1973)

The actor-singer married *Sandra DEE* in the Elizabeth, New Jersey, home of a friend, *Donald Kirschner*, on December 1, 1960. Their son, *Dodd Mitchell*, was born on December 16, 1961. Dee received a divorce in Los Angeles on March 7, 1967, after testifying that Darin "woke up one morning and didn't want to be married anymore." He then left their home. Darin wed *Andrea Joy Yeager*, a legal secretary from Beverly Hills, on

June 27, 1973, in Walnut Grove, California. Less than six months later, on December 20, 1973, Darin died following heart surgery.

DARNELL, Linda
(1921-1965)

The actress eloped to Las Vegas with cameraman *J. Peverell Marley* on April 18, 1943. In 1948, the couple adopted a five-week-old baby, *Charlotte Mildred*, nicknamed "Lola." The couple was divorced in 1951. On February 25, 1954, she wed *Philip Liebmann*, of a New York City brewery family, in Bernalillo, New Mexico. They were divorced in Mexico in December 1955. On March 3, 1957, she married pilot *Merle Roy Robertson*. Her third and last marriage ended in divorce on November 23, 1963 in Los Angeles.

DAVENPORT, Dorothy
(1895-1977)

The daughter of actors *Harry* and *Alice Davenport*, she came from a theatrical family. On October 13, 1913, she married *Wallace REID* at Christ Episcopal Church in Los Angeles. In 1917, their son, *William Wallace Reid, Jr.*, was born. The Reids also adopted a daughter, *Betty Ann*. Reid was being treated for injuries received in a train crash when he became addicted to the drug morphine, which was used as a painkiller. On January 18, 1923, Reid, age thirty-two, died in a California sanitarium. Using the names of Mrs. Wallace Reid or Dorothy Reid, she became a screenwriter, producer, and director. In 1923, the same year as her husband's death, she produced *Human Wreckage*, an anti-drug film. She never remarried.

DAVIES, Marion
(1897-1961)

Two months after the death of long time companion, *William Randolph Hearst*, Davies surprised friends by marrying Merchant Marine *Capt. Horace Gates Brown*. The couple was married on October 31, 1951, in the wedding chapel of the El Rancho

Vegas Hotel in Las Vegas. Although Davies claimed that Brown was a cousin of Hearst, many denied it, including the Brown family. Davies filed for divorce in 1952 and again in 1954, but both times she withdrew her suit. The marriage ended in her death from cancer on September 22, 1961, in Los Angeles.

DAVIS, Bette
(1908-1989)

The actress married orchestra leader *Oscar Harmon Nelson, Jr.*, in Yuma, Arizona, on August 18, 1932. They had met as students at the Cushingham Academy in Ashburnham, Massachusetts. Testifying that Davis "thought her work was more important than her marriage," Nelson divorced her in Los Angeles on December 6, 1938. Davis wed *Arthur Farnsworth*, manager of a New Hampshire hotel, on December 31, 1941, at the Rockrim, Arizona, home of friends, *Mr. and Mrs. Justin Dart*. Eighteen months later, in August 1943, Farnsworth collapsed from the aftereffects of a fall the year before. The next day, August 25, 1943, he died from a bloodclot. Davis was remarried on November 30, 1945, to artist *William Grant Sherry*. The couple was married in the St. Francis Chapel of the Mission Inn in Riverside, California. Their daughter, *Barbara Davis Sherry*, was born in Santa Ana, California, on May 1, 1947. On July 3, 1950, Davis divorced Sherry in Juarez, Mexico, on the grounds of incompatibility. She was given custody of Barbara. Twenty-five days later, on July 28, 1950, she wed her leading man, actor *Gary Merrill*, in Juarez. In 1951, the couple adopted a daughter, *Margot*, and, in 1952, they adopted a son, *Michael*. Davis received a divorce in Portland, Maine, on July 6, 1960, charging Merrill with cruel and abusive treatment. She never remarried.

DAVIS, Geena
(1957-   )

The actress married *Richard Emmolo* in 1981. The marriage ended in divorce after eighteen months. On November 1, 1987, Davis wed actor *Jeff GOLDBLUM* in Las Vegas. She filed for divorce in Los Angeles on the grounds of irreconcilable differences in October 1990.

DAVIS, Mildred
(1900-1969)

The actress was *Harold LLOYD*'s leading lady in several films before she married the comedian on February 10, 1923, at St. John's Protestant Episcopal Church in Los Angeles. Their first daughter, *Mildred Gloria*, was born in May 1924. In the fall of 1930, the couple adopted four-year-old *Gloria Freeman* from a foundling home in Pasadena, California. She was renamed *Marjorie Elizabeth* and called "Peggy." A son, actor-singer *Harold Clayton Lloyd, Jr.*, was born on January 25, 1931. He died in 1974. Davis died from a heart attack at the age of sixty-nine in Santa Monica on August 18, 1969, after forty-six years of marriage.

DAVIS, Ossie
(1917-   )

Davis married actress *Ruby DEE* on December 9, 1948. Their first daughter, *Nora*, was born in 1950; their son, *Guy*, in 1952; and their second daughter, *LaVerne* in 1956. The couple often works together in films and for civil rights and humanitarian causes.

DAVIS, Sammy, Jr.
(1925-1990)

Davis married singer *Loray White* on January 10, 1958. Fifteen months later, on April 23, 1959, White received a divorce in Las Vegas on the grounds of mental cruelty. On November 13, 1960, the entertainer wed Swedish-born actress *May Britt* at his Los Angeles home. *Frank SINATRA* was best man. Their daughter, *Tracey*, was born on July 5, 1961. The couple also adopted two sons, *Mark* and *Jeff*. They separated on November 1, 1967. Britt was granted a divorce on December 19, 1968, in Santa Monica. She testified that during their marriage "there was no family life to speak of," and was given custody of their children. On May 11, 1970, Davis married dancer *Altovise Gore* in Philadelphia. A few months before his death, the couple adopted a thirteen-year-old son, *Manny*. Their twenty years of marriage ended in Davis's death from cancer at their Beverly Hills home on May 16, 1990. He was sixty-four.

DAW, Marjorie
(1902-)

The silent film star married director *Edward Sutherland* at Pickfair, the home of *Douglas FAIRBANKS* and *Mary PICKFORD*, in Beverly Hills on April 21, 1923. Mary Pickford was matron-of-honor and *Charlie CHAPLIN* was best man. Early in 1925, Daw announced that she was seeking a divorce from Sutherland, saying that "we simply could not get along." The divorce was granted in July 1925. Sutherland later married *Louise BROOKS*. On January 23, 1929, Daw married producer and agent *Myron Selznick*, the brother of *David O. Selznick*, at the Municipal Chapel in New York City. Their daughter, *Jean*, was born in 1936. Daw received a divorce, charging cruelty, on April 3, 1942, in Los Angeles. Selznick died in 1944. Daw has not remarried.

DAY, Doris
(1924-)

In March 1941, at the age of seventeen, the actress-singer married trombonist *Al Jordon* at New York City hall. A son, *Terrence (Terry)*, was born in New York City on February 8, 1942. Day divorced Jordon in 1943. She married songwriter *George Weidler*, the brother of child actress *Virginia Weidler*, in Mount Vernon, New York, on March 30, 1946. Three years later, on May 31, 1949, Day divorced him in Los Angeles. On her twenty-seventh birthday, April 3, 1951, she wed producer-manager *Martin*

(Marty) Melcher at the Burbank city hall. Melcher, who was divorced from *Patti Andrews* of the Andrews Sisters, adopted her son Terrence. The couple was married seventeen years until his death from a stroke, at age fifty-two, on April 20, 1968, in Los Angeles. After his death, Day discovered that he had mismanaged and embezzled her life savings and had signed a contract for her to appear on a television series. She married businessman *Barry Comden* in Carmel, California, on April 14, 1976. On January 5, 1981, Day filed for divorce in Los Angeles. The decree was granted later that year.

DAY, Laraine
(1917-   )

On May 16, 1942, the actress married singer *Ray Hendricks* in the gardens of her Los Angeles home. Day divorced Hendricks in Los Angeles on January 20, 1947, charging him with cruelty. The next day, she received a second divorce decree in Juarez, Mexico, and married *Leo Durocher*, then manager of the Brooklyn Dodgers, in El Paso, Texas. But her Mexican divorce was declared void in the state of California. Day and Durocher were remarried a year later, on February 15, 1948, at her Santa Monica home. Soon after their marriage, the couple adopted two young children, *Melinda Michele* and *Christopher*. Day obtained a divorce from Durocher in Juarez, Mexico, on June 14, 1960, on the grounds of incompatibility. She was given custody of their children. On March 8, 1961, the actress married television executive *Mike Grilikhes*. The three-hour ceremony took place at the Mormon Temple in Los Angeles. The couple has two daughters: *Dana Laraine*, born in 1962, and *Gigi*, born in 1965.

DECAMP, Rosemary
(1914-   )

The actress wed *Judge John Shidler* in 1941. The couple has four daughters: *Margaret*, born in 1946; *Martha*, born in 1947; *Valerie*, born in 1952; and *Nita*, born in 1954.

DE CARLO, Yvonne
(1922-)

On November 21, 1955, the actress married stuntman and actor *Robert Morgan*. The Morgans had two sons: *Bruce*, born July 8, 1956, and *Michael*, born November 14, 1957. Divorced in 1976, the actress has not remarried.

DEE, Frances
(1907-)

Dee wed film star *Joel McCREA* on October 20, 1933, at White Methodist Church in Rye, New York. The couple had three sons: *Joel*, born September 7, 1934; *David*, born November 15, 1936; and *Peter*, born in 1955. McCrea died on their fifty-seventh wedding anniversary, October 20, 1990, from lung trouble in Woodland Hills, California.

DEE, Ruby
(1924-)

Dee married actor *Ossie DAVIS* on December 9, 1948. Their first daughter, *Nora*, was born in 1950; their son, *Guy*, in 1952; and their second daughter, *LaVerne*, in 1956. The couple often works together in films and for civil rights and humanitarian causes.

DEE, Sandra
(1942-)

On December 1, 1960, the actress married actor-singer *Bobby DARIN* at the Elizabeth, New Jersey, home of a friend, *Donald Kirschner*. Their son, *Dodd Mitchell*, was born on December 16, 1961. Dee received a divorce in Los Angeles on March 7, 1967, after testifying that Darin "woke up one morning and didn't want to be married anymore." She has not remarried.

DE HAVEN, Gloria
(1924-)

The actress is the daughter of silent film and vaudeville stars *Carter De Haven* and *Flora Parker* and is the sister of producer *Carter De Haven, Jr.* She married actor *John PAYNE* in Beverly Hills on December 28, 1944. The couple had two children: *Kathie*, born in 1945, and *Thomas,* born in 1948. De Haven was granted a divorce in Los Angeles on February 9, 1950, after testifying that their careers clashed. She was given custody of their children. She wed *Martin S. Kimmel*, a New York real estate agent, in Pittsburgh on June 21, 1953. Fourteen months later, on August 25, 1954, the actress was granted a divorce in Las Vegas on the grounds of irreconcilable differences. In 1956, she wed *Richard W. Fincher*, a Miami, Florida, auto dealer. He later became a congressman. The couple had two children: *Harry*, born in 1958, and *Faith*, born August 31, 1962. De Haven obtained a divorce in Miami on September 27, 1963, charging extreme cruelty. But on January 20, 1965, she remarried Fincher. Divorced for the second time in 1968, she has not remarried.

DE HAVILLAND, Olivia
(1916-)

De Havilland, the older sister of actress *Joan FONTAINE*, wed screenwriter and author *Marcus Goodrich* on August 26, 1946. The wedding took place at Langerlane Farm, near Canondale, Connecticut, the home of friends, *Mr. and Mrs. Lawrence Langner*, directors of the New York Theatre Guild. A son, *Benjamin Briggs Goodrich*, was born in Los Angeles in September 1951. De Havilland received a divorce in Los Angeles on August 28, 1952. The interlocutory decree became final a year later. On April 2, 1955, the actress married *Pierre Galante*, who later became editor of *Paris Match* magazine, in the village schoolhouse of Yvoy-Le-Marron, France. Their daughter, *Gisele*, was born in Neuilly, France, on July 18, 1956. The couple was divorced in 1979.

DEL RIO, Dolores
(1905-1983)

In 1920, at the age of fifteen, the actress married *Jaime Martinez Del Rio*, an attorney, in her childhood home, Mexico City. The couple separated when she went to Hollywood to pursue a career in films. In 1928, she sued for divorce, but her husband died of blood poisoning in a German sanitarium later that year. On August 6, 1930, she wed art director *Cedric Gibbons* at the old Spanish mission in Santa Barbara, California. The marriage ended in divorce on January 17, 1941, in Los Angeles. Del Rio testified that his cold and indifferent attitude made her nervous and ill. On November 24, 1959, she became the wife of American stage producer *Lewis Riley*, who produced his shows in South America. The couple had houses in Coyocan, a fashionable suburb of Mexico City, and in Newport Beach, California. Their twenty-three years of marriage ended in Del Rio's death after a long illness at their Newport Beach home on April 11, 1983. She was seventy-seven.

DE MILLE, Katherine
(1911-)

On October 3, 1937, the actress, the daughter of *Cecil B. DeMille*, married actor *Anthony QUINN* at All Saints Church in Los Angeles. The couple had five children: *Christopher*, born in 1939; *Christina*, born in 1941; *Kathleen*, born in 1942; *Duncan*, born in 1945; and *Valentina*, born in 1952. Their son Christopher drowned in 1941. On January 21, 1965, after twenty-seven years of marriage, De Mille received a divorce in Juarez, Mexico, on the grounds of incompatibility. Quinn said that he felt a sense of duty towards his two sons in Italy—his children with Italian actress *Iolanda Addolori*, whom he later married. De Mille herself has never remarried.

DEMPSTER, Carol
(1902-)

On August 15, 1929, the actress married *Edwin S. Larsen*, a New York investment banker, on the lawn of her country home, a mile outside of Ludingtonville, New York. The couple divides their time between LaJolla, California, and Palm Springs.

DENEUVE, Catherine
(1943-)

The French actress married British photographer *David Bailey* on August 18, 1965. The marriage ended in divorce in 1970. Her son, *Christian*, born in 1963, is the son of French film director *Roger Vadim*. She has a daughter, *Chiara-Charlotte*, born in 1972, with Italian actor *Marcello MASTROIANNI*.

DE NIRO, Robert
(1943-)

In the spring of 1976, De Niro wed actress *Diahnne Abbott* in an Ethical Culture meeting house in New York City. Abbott had a daughter, *Drina*, from a former marriage. Their son, *Raphael*, was born in 1976. The marriage ended in divorce in 1978. De Niro has a daughter, *Nina Nadeja*, born in 1982, with singer and songwriter *Helena Springs*.

DENNIS, Sandy
(1937-   )

The actress married jazz musician and composer *Gerry Mulligan* in June 1965, after a three-week courtship. They separated in 1976.

DEVINE, Andy
(1905-1977)

On October 28, 1933, the actor married *Dorothy Irene House*, whom he had met on the set of one of his movies, in Las Vegas. The couple had two sons: *Timothy*, born in November 1934, and *Dennis*, born in January 1939. Their forty-three years of marriage ended in the actor's death from leukemia on February 18, 1977, in Orange, California. He was seventy-one.

DE VITO, Danny
(1944-   )

De Vito began living with actress *Rhea Perlman* in 1970 and married her on January 8, 1982. The couple has two daughters, *Lucy Chet*, born in March 1983; and *Gracie Fan*, born in March 1985; and a son, *Jake Daniel*, born in November 1987.

DEWHURST, Colleen
(1926-   )

Dewhurst married actor *James Vickery* in 1947. They were divorced in 1959. In 1960, she wed *George C. SCOTT*. Two sons were born: *Alexander* in 1961, and *Campbell*, an actor, in 1962. The couple was divorced in Juarez, Mexico, in July of 1965. Then, on July 4, 1967, Dewhurst and Scott were remarried at his South Salem, New York, farm. Divorced from Scott for the second time in Santo Domingo on February 3, 1972, Dewhurst has not remarried.

DEXTER, Elliott
(1870-1941)

The actor married film star *Marie DORO* in New York City in November 1915. The marriage ended in divorce. On November 27, 1922, Dexter wed *Nina Chisolm Untermeyer* at the Los Angeles home of *Cecil B. DeMille*. Nina Dexter was granted a divorce in Los Angeles on October 20, 1927, charging Dexter with desertion and non-support. Dexter never remarried.

DICKINSON, Angie
(1931-)

In 1952, the actress, then known as *Angeline Brown*, married college football player *Gene Dickinson* They were divorced in 1959. In 1965, she married composer *Burt Bacharach* in Paris. Their daughter, *Lea Nikki*, was born in Los Angeles on July 12, 1966. The Bacharachs separated in 1976, and she filed for divorce in November 1980. Their divorce became final in 1981.

DIETRICH, Marlene
(1901-)

On May 13, 1924, she wed Czechoslovakian production assistant *Rudolf Siebe* in her native Germany. Their daughter, *Maria* (actress *Maria Riva*), was born in 1925. The couple separated when Dietrich came to the United States in 1930. Siebe and their daughter remained in Germany. The marriage ended in his death in 1975.

DIX, Richard
(1894-1949)

On October 20, 1931, the film star wed San Francisco socialite *Winifred Coe* in Yuma, Arizona. Their daughter, *Martha Mary Ellen*, was born in January 1933. Winifred Dix received a divorce in Juarez, Mexico, on June 29, 1933, after less than two years of marriage. Dix married his secretary, *Virginia Webster* on June 29, 1934, in Jersey City, New Jersey. Twin sons, *Richard* and *Robert*, were born in Los Angeles on May 8, 1935. The couple also adopted a daughter, *Sara Sue*. Their fifteen years of marriage ended in his death from a heart attack at the age of fifty-four on September 20, 1949, in Los Angeles.

DONAHUE, Troy
(1936-)

The actor married *Suzanne PLESHETTE* on January 4, 1964. Nine months later, on September 8, 1964, Pleshette received a divorce in Santa Monica after testifying that their marital problems had begun seventeen days after their wedding. In 1966, Donahue married *Valerie Allen*. They were divorced in 1968. On November 15, 1969, he married secretary *Alma Sharpe*.

DONAT, Robert
(1905-1958)

In 1928, Donat married actress-dancer *Ella Annesley Voysey* in Wilmslow Chester, England. The Donats had a daughter, *Joanna*, born May 19, 1931; and two sons, *John*, born September 12, 1933, and *Brian*, born August 3, 1936. The couple was divorced in 1946 after a lengthy separation. On May 4, 1953, Donat wed actress *Renée Asherson* near London. The couple separated in 1956. The actor died two years later from an asthma attack on June 9, 1958, in London. He was fifty-three.

DONLEVY, Brian
(1899-1972)

On October 5, 1928, Donlevy wed Ziegfeld girl *Yvonne Grey*. The marriage ended in divorce in February 1936. Donlevy married actress and singer *Marjorie Lane* on December 22, 1936, in Tijuana, Mexico. They were remarried on December 31, 1936, at Wilshire Methodist Church in Los Angeles. Their daughter, *Judith Ann*, was born on February 20, 1943. The marriage ended in divorce in 1947. On February 25, 1966, he married *Lillian Arch Lugosi*, the divorced wife of actor *Bela LUGOSI*. The marriage ended in his death from cancer in Los Angeles on April 5, 1972.

DORO, Marie
(1882-1956)

Doro married film star *Elliott DEXTER* in New York City in November 1915. She divorced Dexter and never remarried.

DORS, Diana
(1931-1984)

In 1951, Dors married *Denis Hamilton* in her native England. She filed for divorce in London on December 4, 1957, and the decree was granted early in 1958. On April 12, 1959, she wed British comedian *Dickie Dawson* at the New York City apartment of singer *Fran Warren*. The couple had two sons: *Mark*, born in 1960, and *Gary*, born in 1962. The marriage ended in divorce in 1967. On November 23, 1968, she married actor *Alan Lake*. Their son, *Jason,* was born in 1969. The couple was married fifteen years until her death from cancer at the age of fifty-two in London on May 4, 1984.

DOUGLAS, Kirk
(1916-)

The actor married *Diana Dill*, whom he had met at the American Academy of Dramatic Arts, in California on November 2, 1943. Their oldest son, actor-producer *Michael DOUGLAS*, was born on September 25, 1944, in New Brunswick, New Jersey. Their second son, *Joel*, was born in New York City on January 23, 1947. The marriage ended in divorce in 1951. Douglas married Belgian-born *Anne Buydens* in Las Vegas on May 29, 1954. The couple has two sons: *Peter*, born November 25, 1955, and *Eric*, born June 21, 1958.

DOUGLAS, Melvyn
(1901-1981)

In the mid-twenties, the actor was briefly married to actress *Rosalind Hitower*. The couple had one son, *Gregory*, before their divorce. Douglas married actress *Helen Gahagan* on April 5, 1931, at the Brooklyn, New York, home of her mother. The couple had two children: *Peter*, born October 8, 1933, and *Mary Helen*, born August 14, 1938. Both of their children were born in Los Angeles. Their forty-nine years of marriage ended in Gahagan's death from cancer at the age of seventy-nine on June 28, 1980, in New York City.

DOUGLAS, Michael
(1944-)

The actor-producer is the oldest son of *Kirk DOUGLAS*. On March 20, 1977, he married *Diandra Luker*, the daughter of a Spanish diplomat. They have one son, *Cameron*, born in 1979.

DOVE, Billie
(1900-)

The film star married director-producer *Irvin Willat* in Santa Monica on October 27, 1923. Dove's romance with *Howard*

Hughes ended her marriage to Willat. The couple was divorced in Los Angeles on July 1, 1930. On May 4, 1932, she wed millionaire rancher *Robert Kenaston* in Yuma, Arizona. Their son, *Robert Allen Kenaston, Jr.*, was born in Santa Monica on April 18, 1934. They adopted a daughter, *Gail*, in 1937. The couple was divorced in 1971, after thirty-nine years of marriage. In the mid-seventies, Dove married architect *John Miller*. Their brief marriage ended in divorce after only a few months. She now lives in Palm Springs.

DRESSLER, Marie
(1869 - 1934)

The actress never made public her marital life. She married *George E. Huppert* about 1894, a marriage which ended in 1896.

DREW, Ellen
(1915 -   )

Drew married Hollywood make-up man *Fred Wallace* in 1935. Their son, *David*, was born later that same year. Wallace received a divorce in Reno on October 19, 1940, on the grounds of incompatibility. She wed screenwriter *Sydney S. Bartlett* at Cal Neva Lodge on the shores of Lake Tahoe on August 16, 1941. She received an interlocutory divorce decree from Bartlett in Los Angeles on July 19, 1946. The divorce was to become final in one year, but the couple reconciled and the decree never became final. On June 17, 1949, she again filed for divorce from Bartlett, and the decree was granted on July 19, 1949. Drew married socialite and business executive *William T. Walker* on May 30, 1951, at his ranch near Indio, California. The couple was divorced in Los Angeles in 1968. Since December 29, 1970, the actress has been married to retired business executive *James Edward Herbert*. The couple was married in Palm Desert, California.

DREYFUSS, Richard
(1947-)

On March 20, 1983, Dreyfuss married television writer and producer *Jeramie Rain*, after a two-month courtship. The couple has a daughter, *Emily*, born November 19, 1983; and two sons: *Benjamin*, born June 14, 1986, and *Harry Spencer*, born August 9, 1990.

DUKE, Patty
(1946-)

On November 26, 1965, the actress married television director and producer *Harry G. Falk, Jr.*, in Studio City, California. Separated in 1968, Duke was granted a divorce in Los Angeles on March 24, 1970. Two months later, on May 11, 1970, she wed rock promoter *Michael Tell*. The couple separated three weeks later. A son, *Sean*, was born to the actress on February 25, 1971. Duke was granted an annulment from Tell in Santa Monica on June 4, 1971, after stating that her son was not his child. It later became known that the child's father was actor *John Astin*. On August 5, 1972, Astin and Duke were married. A second son, *MacKenzie*, was born on May 12, 1973. The couple was divorced in 1985. Duke married *Sgt. Michael Pearce* in Stateline, Nevada, on March 15, 1986.

DUNAWAY, Faye
(1941-)

Dunaway married rock singer *Peter Wolf*, of the J. Geils Band, on August 7, 1974. She met photographer *Terrence O'Neill* in 1977 and was divorced from Wolf soon after. Her son with O'Neill, *Liam*, was born in 1980. In 1983, she announced that she had married O'Neill in a secret ceremony. The couple is now divorced.

DUNNE, Irene
(1898-1990)

On July 16, 1928, the actress married dentist *Dr. Francis J. Griffin*. They adopted a four-year-old daughter, *Anna Mary Bush*, from the New York Foundling Hospital on March 17, 1936. The Griffins were married thirty-seven years until his death from a heart ailment at age seventy-nine on October 15, 1965. Dunne never remarried.

DURANTE, Jimmy
(1893-1980)

In 1921, Durante wed singer *Jeanne Olson*. After twenty-two years of marriage, Olson died of a heart ailment at their Los Angeles home on February 14, 1953. After a sixteen-year courtship, Durante married *Marjorie Little*. The wedding took place on December 14, 1960, in the Actor's Chapel of St. Malachy's Roman Catholic Church in New York City. The comedian's only child, *Alicia Cecilia*, was adopted as an infant on Christmas Day, 1961. Their nineteen years of marriage ended in Durante's death from pneumonia on January 29, 1980, in Santa Monica, California. He was eighty-six.

DURBIN, Deanna
(1921-   )

On April 18, 1941, two thousand fans gathered outside a Hollywood church as Durbin married assistant director and producer *Vaughn Paul* in the presence of nine hundred guests. The marriage ended in divorce two years later on December 14, 1943, in Los Angeles. Durbin told the judge that her husband criticized her film work. She wed producer *Felix Jackson* in the Little Church of the West in Las Vegas on June 13, 1945. A daughter, *Jessica Louise*, was born to the couple in Los Angeles on February 7, 1946. Durbin divorced Jackson in Los Angeles on October

27, 1949, charging mental cruelty. Since December 21, 1950, she has been the wife of French film director *Charles Henri David*. The couple was married in Surremougne, France. Their son, *Peter Henri*, was born in 1951.

DURFEE, Minta
(1897-1975)

In August 1908, the actress married comedian *Roscoe "Fatty" ARBUCKLE*. In her divorce suit, Durfee charged that Arbuckle had deserted her in 1917, although she stood by him during his rape trial in 1921, believing him innocent. She received a divorce in Providence, Rhode Island, on December 31, 1923, on the grounds of desertion and non-support. She never remarried.

DURYEA, Dan
(1907-1968)

The actor married *Helen Bryan* on April 15, 1932. The couple had two sons: *Peter*, born July 14, 1939, and *Richard*, born July 14, 1942. The Duryeas were married thirty-five years before Bryan died from a heart ailment on January 21, 1967.

DUVALL, Robert
(1931-)

On December 31, 1964, Duvall married actress *Barbara Benjamin*. The marriage ended in divorce in 1975. In August 1982, Duvall wed actress *Gail Youngs* on an island off the coast of Maine. The couple was divorced in 1989.

DVORAK, Ann
(1912-1979)

The actress eloped to Yuma, Arizona, on March 17, 1932, with actor-director *Leslie Fenton*. The marriage ended in divorce fourteen years later on August 2, 1946. Dvorak wed Russian dancer *Igor Dega* on August 7, 1947. Exactly four years later, on August 7, 1951, she divorced Dega on the grounds of extreme mental cruelty. In the mid-fifties, she married architect *Nicholas Wade* and moved to Honolulu. She was widowed in the late seventies.

EAGELS, Jeanne
(1894-1929)

At fifteen, Eagels married actor *Morris Dubrinsky*, owner of a traveling tent show. A son was born to the couple, whom she gave to friends to raise. Her son never learned who his mother was. Her marriage to Dubrinsky was later annulled. On August 27, 1925, she married *Edward Harris (Ted) Coy*, a former Yale football star, in Stanford, Connecticut. Eagels was granted a divorce in Chicago on the grounds of cruelty on July 14, 1928.

EASTWOOD, Clint
(1930-)

Eastwood married swimsuit designer and model *Maggie Johnson* on December 19, 1953. The couple had a son, *Kyle Clinton*, born in 1968, and a daughter, *Allison*, born May 22, 1972. The couple separated in 1979 and divorced in 1983.

EDDY, Nelson
(1901-1967)

In January 1939, the singer-actor married *Ann Denitz Franklin*, the divorced wife of producer *Sidney Franklin*, who later married *Enid BENNETT*. The Eddys remained one of Hollywood's happiest married couples until on March 6, 1967 Eddy died after being stricken with a heart attack during a concert tour in Miami Beach, Florida. He was sixty-five.

EGGAR, Samantha
(1939-)

In 1964, the actress married actor and producer *Tom Stern*. The couple had a son, *Nicholas*, born in 1965, and a daughter, *Jenna Louise*, born in 1967. Divorced from Stern in 1971, Eggar has not remarried.

EILERS, Sally
(1908-1978)

The actress married cowboy film star *Hoot GIBSON* at his Saugus, California, ranch on June 27, 1930. The marriage ended in divorce in Chihuahua, Mexico, on September 24, 1933. Four days later, on September 28, 1933, she wed producer *Harry Joe Brown*. Their son, *Harry, Jr.*, was born in 1934. Brown and Eilers obtained a mutual-consent divorce in Juarez, Mexico, on August 26, 1943. Two days later, Eilers and *Lieut. Howard Barney* of the U.S. Navy were married in Santa Fe Methodist Church in Santa Fe, New Mexico. The union ended in divorce in 1949. In the early fifties, Eilers married film director *John Hollingsworth Morse*. Divorced from Morse in 1958, Eilers never remarried.

EKBERG, Anita
(1931-   )

The Swedish-born actress married actor *Anthony Steele* in Florence, Italy, on May 22, 1956. The couple separated in January 1959, and Ekberg received a divorce in Santa Monica on May 14, 1959. Charging extreme mental cruelty, she testified that Steele was "insanely jealous." On April 9, 1963, she wed actor *Rick Van Nutter* in a civil ceremony at the town hall in Viganello (near Lugano), Switzerland.

ELDRIDGE, Florence
(1901-1988)

She wed actor *Fredric MARCH* in Mexico on May 30, 1927. The couple adopted a daughter, *Penelope*, in 1932, and a son, *Anthony*, in 1935. Their forty-seven years of marriage ended in March's death from cancer at age seventy-seven on April 14, 1975, in Los Angeles. Eldridge never remarried.

ELLIOTT, Denholm
(1922-)

On March 1, 1954, Elliott married actress *Virginia MacKenna*. They were divorced in 1957. Since June 15, 1962, the actor has been married to *Susan Robinson*.

EMERSON, Faye
(1917-1983)

Emerson wed *William Wallace Crawford, Jr.*, a San Diego auto dealer, on October 29, 1938. Their son, *William Wallace Crawford III*, was born in 1939. The union ended in divorce in 1942. On December 3, 1944, the actress married *Col. Elliott Roosevelt*, the son of *Franklin D. Roosevelt*, at the Yavapai observation station overlooking the Grand Canyon. Five years later, on January 17, 1950, Emerson received a divorce on the grounds of mental cruelty in Cuernavaca, Mexico. Later that year, on December 12, 1950, she returned to Cuernavaca where she married bandleader *Lyle C. "Skitch" Henderson*. The ceremony, held at the home of friends, was performed by the mayor of the city. Her third and last marriage ended in divorce on January 7, 1958, in Mexico City.

ERWIN, Stuart
(1902-1967)

On July 21, 1931, Erwin married actress *June COLLYER* in Yuma, Arizona. The Erwins had two children: *Stuart, Jr.*, born September 15, 1932, and *Judy Dorothea*, born in July 1935. The couple was married thirty-six years, until Erwin's death from a heart attack at age sixty-five on December 21, 1967. Collyer died three months later on March 16, 1968.

ETTING, Ruth
(1896-1978)

On July 12, 1922, the singer-actress eloped to Crown Point, Indiana, with mobster *Martin Snyder*. Etting divorced Snyder in Chicago on November 30, 1937, on the grounds of desertion and cruelty. On October 15, 1938, Snyder shot pianist *Harry Myrl Alderman*, with whom Etting had fallen in love. During Snyder's trial (he was eventually convicted of attempted murder), Alderman and Etting flew to Las Vegas where, on December 14, 1938, they were married in the chambers of *Judge William Orr*. Their twenty-seven years of marriage ended in Alderman's death from a liver ailment on November 16, 1966, in Colorado Springs, Colorado.

EVANS, Dale
(1912-   )

In January 1927, she eloped to Blitheville, Arkansas, with a classmate, *Thomas Fox*. A son, *Thomas, Jr.*, was born on November 28, 1927. In 1929, at the age of seventeen, she was divorced from Fox. In the late thirties, she wed pianist *Robert Dale Butts*, and together they went to California. The union ended in divorce in 1945. Cowboy actor *Roy ROGERS* was a widower with three children when Dale Evans married him on December 31, 1947, at the Flying L Ranch near Davis, Oklahoma. On August 26, 1950, a daughter, *Robin Elizabeth*, was born. The baby was born with Downs Syndrome (mental retardation and physical malformation) and a heart condition. She died two days before her second birthday, on August 24, 1952, from mumps. A grieving Dale Evans Rogers published a book, *Angel Unaware* (1953), which told her daughter's story. In October 1952, the couple adopted a three-fourths Choctaw Indian baby, *Mary Little Doe* (nicknamed "Dodie"), from Hope Cottage in Dallas, Texas. Also that year, they adopted a six-year-old son, *Harry*, from a foster home in Covington, Kentucky. He was renamed *John David* and nicknamed "Sandy." In 1954, an eleven-year-old British girl, *Marion*, was adopted. They adopted *Debbie*, a Korean orphan, in 1955. On August 17, 1964, Debbie was killed in a bus crash near San Clemente, California. Sandy was serving in the army in Germany when he choked to death on October 31, 1965. In honor of her two children, she published *Dear Debbie* and *Salute to Sandy* in 1965. All the proceeds from her books are donated to charity.

EVANS, Dame Edith
(1888-1976)

The actress married *Guy Booth*, a manager of British oil fields in South America, on September 9, 1925, at St. Saviour's Church in London. Booth died in England on January 9, 1935, after a long illness. Evans never remarried.

EVANS, Madge
(1909-1981)

Evans married playwright *Sidney Kinglsey*, whom she had met while playing at the summer theatre in Ogunquit, Maine, in July 1939. Evans often helped her husband with the researching and writing of his plays. Their forty years of marriage ended in her death from cancer on April 26, 1981, at their Oakland, New Jersey, home. She was seventy-one.

FABRAY, Nanette
(1920-   )

The actress-singer wed press agent *David Tebet* on October 26, 1947. The marriage ended in divorce in July 1951. In 1957, Fabray married playwright *Ranald MacDougall*. Their son, *Jamie*, was born on September 29, 1958. MacDougall died at the age of fifty-eight in Los Angeles on December 12, 1973. Fabray has not remarried.

FAIRBANKS, Douglas
(1883-1939)

While playing on Broadway in 1907, Fairbanks married *Anna Beth Sully*, the socialite daughter of a soap manufacturer. Their son, actor *Douglas FAIRBANKS, Jr.*, was born in New York City on December 9, 1909. During a WW I liberty bond tour, Fairbanks met *Mary PICKFORD*. They fell in love, although their friends did not become aware of it until 1917. Sully sued for divorce and received a decree (and custody of their son) on March 5, 1919, in New Rochelle, New York. Pickford was divorced from her husband, actor *Owen MOORE*, and, on March 30, 1920, Fairbanks and Pickford were married in Los Angeles. *Marjorie Daw* was bridesmaid and *Robert Fairbanks*, brother of the groom, was best man. The era of Pickfair, their Beverly Hills home, as the social center of Los Angeles had begun. Doug and Mary were considered to be truly a match made in heaven and were the world's most popular couple. The era came to an end on January 13, 1936, when Pickford received her final divorce decree in Los Angeles. Doug's preference of Europe, Mary's of Hollywood, combined with their faltering careers, were blamed for the divorce. Two months after the divorce, on March 7, 1936, Fairbanks wed *Lady Sylvia Ashley* in Paris. Ashley had recently been divorced by Lord Ashley in a suit which had named Fairbanks as co-respondant. The Fairbankses had been married three years when, on December 12, 1939, the actor died from a heart attack at the age of fifty-six in their home in Santa Monica. Sylvia Fairbanks later married *Clark GABLE*.

FAIRBANKS, Douglas, Jr.
(1909-)

The actor is the son of *Douglas FAIRBANKS* and his first wife, *Anna Beth Sully*. On June 3, 1929, he married *Joan CRAW-FORD* at St. Malachy's Catholic Church in New York City. But rumors flew that Crawford had married Fairbanks only to further her own career and that the older Fairbanks and his second wife, *Mary PICKFORD*, did not approve of the marriage. Crawford received a divorce in Los Angeles on May 12, 1933, after testifying that Fairbanks was "jealous and suspicious" of her. On April 22, 1939, Fairbanks wed divorced socialite *Mary Lee Eppling Hartford* at the Methodist Episcopal Church in the Westwood area of Los Angeles. The couple had three daughters: *Daphne*, born in April 1940; *Victoria*, born in 1943; and *Melissa*, born in 1947. The Fairbankses were married forty-nine years until on September 14, 1988, Mary Lee Fairbanks died of cancer at the age of seventy-five in West Palm Beach, Florida.

FARMER, Frances
(1913-1970)

She eloped to Yuma, Arizona, on February 8, 1936, with actor *Leif Erickson*. Erickson received a Reno divorce on June 12, 1942. Farmer married Seattle engineer *Alfred Lobley* on July 27, 1953. They were divorced on March 7, 1958. Later that month, on March 20, 1958, she wed *Leland (Lee) Mikesell* in Las Vegas. The marriage ended in divorce in 1963.

FARNUM, Dustin
(1874-1929)

The silent film star (and brother of *William FARNUM*) wed actress *Agnes Muir Johnson* in 1898. The marriage ended in divorce in November of 1908. On March 23, 1909, he married actress *Mary Bessie Conwell* in Chicago. Farnum received a

Reno divorce on the grounds of desertion on August 19, 1924. He then hurried back to Los Angeles where, on August 24, 1924, he married one of his leading ladies, *Winifred Kingston*, at the Wilshire Presbyterian Church parsonage. Their daughter, *Estelle*, was born in 1925. Farnum died from a kidney ailment on July 3, 1929, in New York City. He was fifty-five.

FARNUM, William
(1876-1953)

Farnum, one of the biggest stars of the early silent screen (and brother of *Dustin FARNUM*), married *Mabel Eaton* in 1901. The marriage ended in divorce. He married actress *Olive Ann White* on December 2, 1906, in Sag Harbor, on Long Island. White received a divorce in San Francisco on May 5, 1931, after testifying that Farnum had deserted her in 1928. She was given their Sag Harbor home in the property settlement. On June 8, 1932, Farnum married screenwriter *Isabelle Lunds Major* at a Santa Barbara hotel. The groom was attended by *Douglas FAIRBANKS*. Their twenty-one years of marriage ended in Farnum's death from cancer at age seventy-six in Los Angeles on June 5, 1953.

FARRAR, Geraldine
(1882-1967)

The opera singer and actress married actor *Lou TELLEGEN* at her New York City home on February 8, 1916. The union ended in divorce on January 23, 1923, in New York City. Farrar charged Tellegen with misconduct and alleged that he had committed adultery on several occasions. She never remarried.

FARRELL, Charles
(1901-1990)

Farrell married film star *Virginia Valli* on Valentine's Day, 1931, in Yonkers, New York. After a honeymoon in Europe, the couple settled in Palm Springs where they founded the Palm Springs Racquetball Club. Their thirty-seven years of marriage ended in

Valli's death at the age of seventy-three on September 25, 1968, from the aftereffects of a stroke that had occurred in 1966. Farrell never remarried.

FARRELL, Glenda
(1904-1971)

During the twenties, Farrell married WW I veteran *Thomas Richards* in Los Angeles. They had an unsuccessful vaudeville act together and a son, *Thomas, Jr.* The marriage ended in divorce, and her son's last name was later changed to Farrell. She did not remarry until January 19, 1941, when she wed *Dr. Henry Ross* in the Passaic, New Jersey, home of *Dr. Irving Saxe*, a friend of the groom's. *Mary BRIAN* was maid-of-honor. Their thirty years of marriage ended in Farrell's death after a long illness on May 1, 1971, at their New York City home. She was sixty-six.

FARROW, Mia
(1945-)

The actress is the daughter of film director *John Farrow* and actress *Maureen O'SULLIVAN*. She married *Frank SINATRA*, at the age of nineteen, on July 19, 1966, at the Las Vegas home of *Jack Entratter*, owner of the Sands Hotel. They separated in November 1967, and Farrow received a divorce in Juarez, Mexico, on August 16, 1968. On February 26, 1970, twin sons, *Matthew Phineas* and *Sacha Villiers*, were born in London to Farrow and composer-conductor *André Previn*. After Previn's divorce from his wife, songwriter *Dorothy Langdon*, became final, Farrow and Previn were married on September 11, 1970, at the Rosslyn Hill Unitarian Church in London. They adopted a daughter, *Lark Song*, a Vietnamese orphan, and, on March 14, 1974, a son, *Fletcher Farrow Previn*, was born in London. The Previns adopted three more Vietnamese orphans, *Summer Song*, *Gigi Soon Mi*, and *Misha*, in the years that followed. The marriage ended in divorce on January 31, 1979, in Santo Domingo. Farrow has two children with *Woody ALLEN*: an adopted daughter, *Dy-*

lan, and a son, *Satchel*, born December 21, 1987. Her sisters, *Tisa Farrow* and *Stephanie Farrow*, are also actresses.

FAWCETT, Farrah
(1946-   )

On July 28, 1973, the actress-model wed actor *Lee Majors*. She used the professional name *Farrah Fawcett-Majors* until their divorce in Los Angeles on February 12, 1982. On June 18, 1988, she married actor *Ryan O'NEAL* in Paris. At the time of their marriage, the couple had a son, *Redmond James O'Neal*, born on January 30, 1985, in Los Angeles.

FAYE, Alice
(1912-   )

On September 4, 1937, she eloped to Yuma, Arizona, with singer-actor *Tony MARTIN*. The couple separated early in 1940, and Faye received a divorce on the grounds of mental cruelty in Los Angeles later that year, on March 22, 1940. Faye surprised her friends (and her studio) when she eloped with bandleader and actor *Phil HARRIS* to Ensenada, Mexico, on May 12, 1941. The couple has two daughters: *Alice*, born May 19, 1942, and *Phyllis*, born April 26, 1944.

FAZENDA, Louise
(1895-1962)

In 1917, the comedienne wed film director *Noel M. Francis*. The marriage ended in divorce in 1926. In November 1927, Fazenda married producer *Hal B. Wallis*. Their son, *Hal Brent Wallis, Jr.*, was born in Los Angeles on April 10, 1933. Their forty-four years of marriage ended in Fazenda's death from a cerebral hemorrhage at the age of sixty-seven at their home in Holmby Hills,

California, on April 17, 1962. Wallis later married actress *Martha HYER*.

FERRER, José
(1912-   )

On December 8, 1938, Ferrer married actress *Uta Hagen*. Their daughter, *Leticia Thyra*, was born in 1940. In 1948, the couple, who had achieved success on the Broadway stage, was divorced. Later that year, on June 19, 1948, Ferrer married actress *Phyllis Hill* in Greenwich, Connecticut. Hill was granted a mutual-consent divorce in Juarez, Mexico, on July 7, 1953, on the grounds of incompatibility. Six days later, on July 13, 1953, the actor-director married singer and actress *Rosemary Clooney* in Durant, Oklahoma. The couple had five children: *Miguel*, born February 7, 1955; *Maria*, born in August 1956; *Gabriel*, born in 1957; *Monsita*, born in 1958; and *Rafael* born March 23, 1960. Clooney was granted a divorce in Santa Monica on May 9, 1962. The interlocutory decree was to become final in one year, but the couple was reconciled, and the decree never became final. The Ferrers were divorced in Santa Monica late in 1967 on the grounds of extreme cruelty. Since the late sixties, the actor has been married to British-born *Stella Daphne Magee*. Concerning the exact date of their marriage he says: "The date of our marriage is known only to three people my wife, myself, and the man who married us. Even my children don't know." His son Gabriel married singer *Debby Boone*, the daughter of *Pat BOONE*, in 1979.

FERRER, Mel
(1917-   )

The actor, director, and producer married sculptress *Frances Pilchard* on October 23, 1937. Divorced, he married *Barbara C. Tripp* in 1940. A daughter, *Mela*, was born later that same year, and a son, *Christopher*, was born the following year. Divorced from Tripp, Ferrer and Pilchard were remarried in 1942. Their daughter, *Pepa*, was born in 1942, and their son, *Mark*, was born in 1944. Ferrer and Pilchard were divorced for the second time in 1953. On September 25, 1954, Ferrer married *Audrey HEP-BURN* in Burgenstock, Switzerland. Their son, *Sean*, was born in Lucerne, Switzerland, on January 17, 1960. The couple was divorced in France in 1968, after fourteen years of marriage. Ferrer married Belgian-born book editor *Elizabeth Soukotine* on February 18, 1971.

FIELD, Betty
(1918-1973)

On January 12, 1942, the actress married playwright *Elmer Rice*. Three children were born: *John Alden*, born in December 1942; *Judith*, born in 1944; and *Paul*, born in 1949. The couple separated in 1956 and was divorced later that same year. In 1957, Field married lawyer and criminologist *Edwin J. Lukas* (a cousin of actor *Paul LUKAS*). Divorced, she married artist *Raymond L. Olivere* in Detroit on March 22, 1968. The couple was married until her death from a cerebral hemorrhage at the age of fifty-five on September 13, 1973, in Hyannis, Massachusetts.

FIELD, Sally
(1946-)

On September 16, 1968, the actress married *Steve Craig*, her high school sweetheart, in Las Vegas. The couple had two sons: *Peter*, born in 1969, and *Elijah*, born May 22, 1972. The marriage ended in divorce in 1973. In December 1984, she wed producer *Alan Greisman* in her Tarzana, California, home. Their son, *Samuel*, was born in Los Angeles on December 2, 1987.

FIELDS, Dame Gracie
(1898-1979)

In 1923, the actress-singer married comedian and manager *Archie Pitt*. Fields was granted a provisional divorce decree in London on July 21, 1939, on the grounds of misconduct. The decree became final on January 29, 1940. Two months later, on March

18, 1940, Fields wed *Monty Banks*, a British-born silent film comedian turned film producer. He also directed Fields in some of her films. The couple was married at the Los Angeles home of her parents. Their ten years of marriage ended in Banks's death from a heart attack at age fifty-two on January 7, 1950, in Arona, Italy. Rumanian-born *Boris Alperovici* visited Fields's villa on Capri to fix a broken radio and married her on February 18, 1952, at St. Stephen's Catholic Cathedral on the island. Their twenty-seven years of marriage ended in Fields's death from pneumonia at the age of eighty-one on September 27, 1979, at her Capri home.

FIELDS, W.C.
(1879-1946)

In 1900, while touring in vaudeville, he married a fellow performer, *Harriet Hughes*. Their son, *William Claude, Jr.*, was born in 1904. The couple was separated during most of their marriage, which ended in the comedian's death from cirrhosis of the liver in Los Angeles on Christmas Day, 1946. He was sixty-six.

FINCH, Peter
(1916-1977)

On April 21, 1943, the actor married ballet dancer *Tamara Tchinarova* in Sydney, Australia. A daughter, *Anita*, was born in 1950. The couple was divorced in 1959, after sixteen years of marriage. Later that year, on July 4, 1959, Finch wed South African-born actress *Yolande Turner*. The couple had two children: *Samantha*, born April 27, 1960, and *Charles*, born in 1961. Turner received a divorce in London on November 11, 1965. On November 9, 1973, Finch married his companion of three years, Jamaican hairdresser *Eletha Barrett*, in Rome. At the time of their marriage, the couple had a daughter, *Diana*, born in 1970. Their marriage ended in Finch's death from a heart attack at age sixty in Los Angeles on January 14, 1977.

FINNEY, Albert
(1936-   )

In 1957, the British-born actor married actress *Jane Wenham*. A son, *Simon*, was born in 1958. The marriage ended in divorce in 1961. On August 7, 1970, Finney married French actress *Anouk Aimée* in London. The marriage ended in divorce in 1975.

FISHER, Carrie
(1956-   )

The actress, who is the daughter of *Eddie FISHER* and *Debbie REYNOLDS*, married rock singer and composer *Paul Simon* in August 1983 at his New York City apartment. They were divorced in 1984.

FISHER, Eddie
(1928-   )

On September 26, 1955, the singer-actor married film star *Debbie REYNOLDS* at the Catskill Mountain resort Grossinger's. Their daughter, actress *Carrie Frances FISHER*, was born on October 21, 1956, in Los Angeles. Their son, *Todd* (named for producer *Mike Todd*, a close family friend), was born in Burbank, California, on February 24, 1958. Mike Todd was killed in a plane crash on March 22, 1958, leaving actress *Elizabeth TAYLOR* a widow. Fisher was among those comforting the grieving Taylor, and a romance blossomed as Fisher's marriage to Reynolds began to fail. Debbie Reynolds received a divorce in Los Angeles on February 19, 1959. She testified that "another woman" had ruined their marriage but did not mention Taylor by name. Fisher and Taylor were married at Temple Beth Sholom in Las Vegas on May 12, 1959. Fisher adopted her daughter, *Liza Todd*. But in 1963, Taylor fell in love with actor *Richard BURTON*. She divorced Fisher in Puerto Vallarta, Mexico, on March 5, 1964, taking custody of Liza. In February 1967, Fisher married singer-actress *Connie Stevens*. The couple had two daughters: *Joely*, born October 29, 1967, and singer *Tricia Leigh Fisher*, born December 26, 1968. The marriage ended in divorce in Santa Monica on June 12, 1969. Fisher wed *Terry Richard* (a former "Miss Louisiana") in Puertecitos, Mexico, on October 29, 1975. They were divorced on April 1, 1976.

FITZGERALD, Geraldine
(1914-)

Fitzgerald wed Irish horseman *Edward Lindsay-Hogg* in London on November 18, 1936. Their son, film director *Michael Lindsay-Hogg*, was born in 1940. The actress received a Reno divorce on August 30, 1946, after a three-year separation. On September 10, 1946, Fitzgerald and New York publisher and theatre owner *Stuart Scheftel* were married in a judge's chambers in Los Angeles. Their daughter, *Susan*, was born in 1951.

FLEMING, Rhonda
(1923-)

In 1940, at seventeen, the actress married interior decorator *Thomas Wade Lane*. A son, *Kent*, was born in 1941. The marriage ended in divorce in 1947. On July 11, 1952, Fleming wed Beverly Hills physician *Dr. Lewis V. Morrill*. She filed for divorce in Santa Monica on June 9, 1958. The decree was granted later that same year. Fleming married actor *Lang Jeffries* on April 3, 1960, at the Little Church of the West in Las Vegas. Less than two years later, on January 11, 1962, the actress received a divorce in Santa Monica on the grounds of extreme cruelty. In October 1965, Fleming wed producer-director *Hall Bartlett* in Mexico. The couple was remarried on March 26, 1966, at the Los Angeles home of the *Robert Taylors*. Fleming received a divorce from Bartlett (and a million-dollar property settlement) in Los Angeles on February 17, 1972. Since 1978, Fleming has been married to her fifth husband, theatre chain owner *Ted Mann*.

FLYNN, Errol
(1909-1959)

On June 19, 1935, Flynn eloped to Yuma, Arizona, with French-born actress *Lili DAMITA*. The couple had one son, *Sean*, born in Los Angeles on May 31, 1941. Their marriage ended in divorce in Los Angeles on March 31, 1942. Damita, who testified that Flynn paid more attention to his yachts than to her, was given custody of Sean. In court facing a charge of statutory rape, Flynn met *Nora Eddington*, who worked behind the cigar counter in the Los Angeles County Hall of Justice. They were married in Acapulco in August 1943, after Flynn was acquitted. Two daughters were born: *Deirdre*, on January 10, 1945, in Mexico City, and *Rory*, on March 12, 1947, in Los Angeles. Eddington obtained a Nevada divorce on July 7, 1949. She married singer-actor *Dick HAYMES* a few days later. On October 23, 1950, four thousand spectators gathered outside the Lutheran Chapel in Nice, France, when he wed actress *Patrice WYMORE*. Flynn's fourth child, *Arnella Roma*, was born in Rome on Christmas Day, 1953. Although separated, the couple remained married until Flynn's death from a heart attack at the age of fifty on October 14, 1959, in Vancouver, Canada. His son Sean became an actor but disappeared in 1970 while working as a correspondent in Vietnam.

FOCH, Nina
(1924-   )

Foch married television actor *James Lipton* in 1954. The couple was divorced in 1958. In 1959, she wed writer *Dennis Brite*. Their son, *Schuyler Dirk Brite*, was born in Los Angeles on October 30, 1962. The marriage ended in divorce in 1963. Since 1967, Foch has been the wife of *Michael Dewell*.

FONDA, Henry
(1905-1982)

On Christmas Day, 1931, the actor married *Margaret SUL-LAVAN* at the Kernan Hotel in Baltimore, Maryland. The couple separated four months later and was divorced in 1933. Fonda married widowed socialite *Frances Seymour Brokaw* on September 16, 1936, at Christ Church in New York City. Their daughter is film star *Jane FONDA*, born on December 21, 1937, in New York City. Their son is actor, director, and producer *Peter FONDA*, born on February 23, 1939, also in New York City. In December 1949, Fonda announced that he and his wife would soon divorce. Brokaw suffered a nervous breakdown and was placed in a sanitarium in Beacon, New York, where, on April 14, 1950, she committed suicide. She was forty-two. Later that same year, on December 28, 1950, Fonda married *Susan Blanchard*, the step-daughter of *Oscar Hammerstein II*, at the Hammerstein's New York City home. In 1954, they adopted an eight-week-old daughter, *Amy*, from a foster home in Connecticut. Blanchard divorced Fonda in May 1956. On March 9, 1957, Fonda was wed for the fourth time, to *Baronessa Afdera Franchetti*. The ceremony took place at Fonda's New York City home. Franchetti received a divorce in Mexico in 1961, on the grounds of incompatibility. *Shirlee Mae Adams* a former airline stewardess and model, became Fonda's fifth wife on December 3, 1965, in Mineola, New York, on Long Island. *George Peppard* and his wife, *Elizabeth Ashley*, attended the couple at the wedding. Their seventeen happy years of marriage ended in Fonda's death from heart disease on August 12, 1982, in Los Angeles. He was seventy-seven.

FONDA, Jane
(1937-)

The actress is the daughter of *Henry FONDA* and the sister of *Peter FONDA*. She married French director *Roger Vadim* on August 14, 1965, in the Dunes Hotel in Las Vegas. Vadim was divorced from *Brigitte BARDOT*. Their daughter, *Vanessa*, was born in Paris on September 28, 1965. Fonda divorced Vadim in Santo Domingo in January 1973. A few days later, on January 21, 1973, Fonda married *Tom Hayden* at her home in the Laurel Canyon area of Los Angeles. Their son, *Troy Garity*, was born on July 7, 1973. The couple separated on February 15, 1989, after sixteen years of marriage. They filed for divorce in Los

Angeles on December 1, 1989, and the divorce was granted in June 1990.

FONDA, Peter
(1939-   )

The actor, producer, and director is the son of *Henry FONDA* and the brother of *Jane FONDA*. He wed *Susan Brewer*, whom he had met in drama school, on October 8, 1961, at St. Bartholomew's Protestant Episcopal Church in Beverly Hills. Their daughter, actress *Bridget Fonda*, was born in 1963, and their son, *Justin*, was born in 1966. The Fondas were divorced on April 16, 1974, after a two-year separation. Fonda lost his suit to prevent his former wife from using her married name when the judge declared that he had shown no reason why she should have to use her maiden name. Since 1976, Fonda has been married to *Portia Crockett*.

FONTAINE, Joan
(1917-   )

The actress, who is the younger sister of *Olivia DE HAVIL-LAND*, has been married four times. On August 20, 1939, Fontaine married actor *Brian AHERNE* in Del Monte, California. The marriage ended in divorce in Los Angeles on June 2, 1944, on the grounds of extreme cruelty. She wed producer *William Dozier* on May 2, 1946, at the Mexico City home of friends, *Mr. and Mrs. George Conway*. Their daughter, *Deborah Leslie*, was born in Santa Monica on November 4, 1947. The couple separated in 1949, and Fontaine received a divorce in Santa Monica on January 25, 1951, after testifying that Dozier had walked out on her life and had not come back. Dozier later married actress *Ann RUTHERFORD*. A year later, on November 12, 1952, Fontaine married producer and screenwriter *Collier Young*, who was divorced from *Ida LUPINO*. The wedding took place at Villa Montalva, the former home of *Senator James D. Phelan*, in Saratoga, California. The couple separated in May 1960, and

Fontaine received a divorce in Los Angeles on the grounds of cruelty on January 3, 1961. Since January 27, 1964, Fontaine has been married to *Alfred Wright, Jr.*, editor of *Sports Illustrated* magazine. The couple was married in the courthouse in Elkton, Maryland. In 1952, the actress adopted a Peruvian daughter, *Martita Pareja Caldron*.

FORBES, Ralph
(1902-1951)

On December 20, 1924, Forbes and actress *Ruth CHATTER-TON*, Broadway co-stars, were married in the Church of the Beloved Disciple in New York City. The union ended in divorce in Minden, Nevada, on August 12, 1932. They remained friends. Forbes eloped to Yuma, Arizona, on August 29, 1934, with British-born film actress *Heather Angel*. Angel obtained a divorce in Los Angeles on July 18, 1941, after testifying that Forbes "slapped her, belittled her in the presence of friends, ran up bills, and stayed away from home all night." In January 1946, Forbes married actress *Dora L. Sayers*, in New York State. The marriage ended in his death in New York City on March 31, 1951.

FORD, Glenn
(1916-   )

On October 24, 1943, Ford married dancer-actress *Eleanor PO-WELL* at her Beverly Hills home. They had met while working in the first Hollywood war-bond cavalcade. Their son, *Peter Newton Ford*, was born in 1945. Powell received an interlocutory divorce decree in Santa Monica on November 23, 1959, after testifying that Ford was "very moody." Ford wed actress *Kathryn Hays* at the Westwood Community Church in Los Angeles on March 28, 1966. Peter Ford was best man. The couple separated in 1968 and was divorced later that same year. On September 10, 1977, Ford married *Cynthia Hayward*, his companion of three years, at his Beverly Hills home. The Fords separated in June 1984, and were divorced later that year in Los Angeles on the grounds of irreconcilable differences. In May 1990, Ford wed *Karem Johnson*.

FORD, Harrison
(1942-)

Ford met his first wife, identified simply as *Mary*, when they were both students at Ripon College in Wisconsin. The couple had two sons: *Benjamin*, born in 1967, and *Willard*, born in 1969. The marriage ended in divorce in 1978. Since March 1983, Ford has been married to screenwriter *Melissa Mathison*.

FOX, Michael J.
(1961-)

On July 17, 1988, Fox married actress *Tracy Pollan* in Arlington, Vermont. Their son, *Sam Michael*, was born on May 30, 1989.

FRANCIS, Kay
(1903-1968)

In December 1922, Kay Gibbs married *James Dwight Francis*, of a prominent Pennsylvania family, at St. Thomas Church in New York City. She received a divorce in Paris in 1924. In 1925, she was briefly married to lawyer *Wiliam A. Gaston*. They were quickly divorced. In 1929, she wed dialogue director *John Meehan*. That marriage also quickly ended in divorce. Actor *Kenneth MacKenna* became her fourth husband on January 17, 1931, in Avalon, on Catalina Island, California. The marriage ended in divorce in Los Angeles on February 21, 1934. Francis told the judge that MacKenna nagged and harassed her. She never remarried.

FREDERICK, Pauline
(1883-1938)

In 1909, the actress married New York architect *Frank M. Andrews*. They were divorced in 1913. On September 24, 1917, she wed actor-playwright *Willard Mack* in Washington, D.C. Three years later, on August 13, 1920, Frederick filed for divorce in New York City charging Mack with misconduct. She wed Seattle physician *Dr. Charles A. Rutherford* in Santa Ana, California, on February 4, 1922. They separated less than a year later, and the actress filed for divorce in Los Angeles on December 16, 1924, charging desertion. Wealthy hotel executive *Hugh Chisolm Leighton* became her fourth husband on April 20, 1930. The couple was married at his New York City apartment. Leighton was granted an annulment eight months later on December 18, 1930, in Los Angeles. He charged fraud and failure on the part of the actress to be a "wife in anything but name." Frederick and *Col. Joseph A. Marmon* were married in Scarsdale, New York, on January 21, 1934. A year later, on December 4, 1934, Marmon, age fifty-nine, died after a long illness in Washington, D.C.

FURNESS, Betty
(1916-   )

On November 26, 1937, the actress wed orchestra leader and composer *Johnny Green*. Their daughter, *Barbara*, was born in 1939. The couple was divorced in 1942, and the decree became final in 1943. In 1944, Furness wed radio producer *Hugh "Bud" Ernst*. The couple was divorced in 1946. On June 1, 1946, a month after their divorce, Furness and Ernst were remarried in Las Vegas. Ernst committed suicide, at the age of thirty-nine, on April 11, 1950, in New York City. On August 15, 1967, the actress, who became a consumer advocate, married CBS television producer *Leslie G. Midgley* in the Mirror Room of the Regency Hotel in New York City. The couple had first met at the home of *Walter Cronkite*.

GABLE, Clark
(1901-1960)

Gable married his drama teacher, *Josephine Dillon*, in Hollywood on December 13, 1924. The union ended in divorce in 1930. On June 19, 1931, the actor married *Maria (Ria) Franklin Prentiss Lucas Langham*, a Houston socialite seventeen years his senior, in Santa Ana, California. The couple separated in 1935, and the following year Gable met film star *Carole LOMBARD*. Three years later, on March 7, 1939, Ria Gable received a divorce in Las Vegas, charging desertion. Gable and Lombard eloped to Kingman, Arizona, on March 29, 1939. Less than three years later, on the night of January 16, 1942, Lombard's plane crashed into Table Rock Mountain, near Las Vegas, killing everyone on board. Gable's last two wives would remind him of Lombard. His fourth wife, *Lady Sylvia Ashley* (the widow of *Douglas FAIRBANKS*), bore a strong physical resemblance to Lombard. Gable married Ashley on a ranch near Solvang, California, on December 20, 1949. Sylvia Gable received a divorce in Santa Monica, on April 21, 1952, after testifying that Gable had told her: "I wish to be free. I don't want to be married to you or anyone else." On July 11, 1955, Gable married *Kay Williams Spreckels*, the divorced wife of sugar heir *Adolph B. Spreckels II*, at the Minden, Nevada, home of Justice of the Peace *Walter Fischer*. The actor died at the age of fifty-nine from a heart ailment in Los Angeles on November 16, 1960. Five months later, on March 20, 1961, *John Clark Gable*, the actor's only child, was born in Los Angeles.

GABOR, Eva
(1924?-)

The youngest of the Gabor sisters, she married *Dr. Eric V. Drimmer*, an osteopath, in London in 1939. She divorced Drimmer in Los Angeles on February 24, 1942, charging him with cruelty. Gabor, who had just arrived in the United States to begin her acting career, testified that she had wanted a "simple family life," but her husband objected to children. Later that year, she wed *Charles Isaacs*, a Beverly Hills real estate millionaire. The couple was separated long before their divorce in California on April 5, 1949. On April 9, 1956, she married *Dr. John E. Williams*, a plastic surgeon, at her New York City home. They separated six months later and were divorced in 1957. *Richard Brown*, a textile manufacturer, became her fourth husband at the Flamingo Hotel in Las Vegas on October 4, 1959. Divorced from Brown in 1969, she soon married for the fifth and last time. Gabor and business executive *Frank Gard Jameson* were married at his Beverly Hills home on September 27, 1973. The Jamesons were divorced in Santa Monica in the summer of 1983. Her oldest sister, *Magda*, was briefly married to actor *George SANDERS*. The middle sister is actress *Zsa Zsa GABOR*.

GABOR, Zsa Zsa
(1920?-   )

At seventeen, Zsa Zsa married *Burhan Belge*, a Turkish foreign affairs minister, in her native Budapest. She divorced him shortly after she came to the United States in 1941. In April 1942, she married hotelier *Conrad Hilton* at the LaFonda Hotel in Santa Fe, New Mexico. The Hiltons were divorced in 1946. Their daughter, *Francesca*, was born in 1947, after the divorce had become final. She is the only child of any of the Gabor sisters. On April 2, 1949, Gabor and actor *George SANDERS* were married in a Las Vegas wedding chapel. Gabor received an interlocutory divorce decree in Los Angeles on April 1, 1954. She married corporation head *Herbert L. Hutner* in the New York City chambers of a state supreme court justice on November 5, 1962. The union, her fourth, ended in divorce in Juarez, Mexico, on March 3, 1966. Six days later, on March 9, 1966, she wed Texas oilman *Joshua Cosden, Jr.* in West Los Angeles. On October 18, 1967, Gabor received a divorce from Cosden in Juarez, Mexico. Millionaire inventor *Jack Ryan* became her sixth husband on October 6, 1976, in the bridal suite of Caesar's Palace Hotel in Las Vegas. Divorced from Ryan in 1977, she wed her divorce lawyer, *Michael O'Hara*, that same year. The marriage ended in divorce in 1982. In August 1986, she was married for the eighth time, to *Frederick von Anhalt*. In 1970, Gabor's older sister *Magda* was briefly married to Zsa Zsa's ex-husband, *George SANDERS*. Her younger sister is actress *Eva GABOR*.

GALLAGHER, Richard, "Skeets"
(1891-1955)

Gallagher wed his vaudeville partner, *Pauline Mason*, in the summer of 1929. The couple was happily married for thirty-six years, until the actor's death from a heart attack, at age sixty-four, on May 22, 1955, in Santa Monica, California.

GARDNER, Ava
(1922-1990)

On January 10, 1942, Gardner married film star *Mickey ROONEY* in Ballard, California. The marriage was given much publicity, but was shortlived. Gardner was granted an interlocutory divorce decree in Los Angeles on May 20, 1943, after testifying that Rooney had "told her repeatedly that he considered their marriage a mistake." Her second husband, bandleader *Artie Shaw*, is as equally famous as Rooney for his number of marriages. Shaw was divorced from *Lana TURNER* and later married *Evelyn KEYES*. Gardner and Shaw were married October 17, 1945, at the Hollywood home of *Judge Stanley Mosk*. The couple was divorced in 1947. After a well-publicized courtship, she married *Frank SINATRA* at the Philadelphia home of friends, *Mr. and Mrs. Lester Sacks*, on November 7, 1951. Separated in 1954, Gardner received a divorce on July 5, 1957, in Mexico City, on the grounds of desertion. She never remarried.

GARFIELD, John
(1913-1952)

In 1932, early in his career, the actor married *Roberta Siedman*, his high school sweetheart. A daughter, *Katharine*, was born in

1939 but died of a strep throat infection at the age of six in 1945. Their son, *David Patton Garfield*, an actor, was born in 1942. Their second daughter, *Julie*, was born on January 10, 1946, shortly after Katharine's death. The Garfields were separated at the time of the actor's death from a heart ailment on May 21, 1952, in New York City. He was thirty-nine.

GARLAND, Judy
(1922-1969)

Her first of five marriages was to *David Rose*, a composer and arranger who had formerly been married to actress *Martha RAYE*. Garland and Rose eloped to Las Vegas where they were married by a justice of the peace on July 28, 1941. The couple separated soon after, and they were divorced in early June of 1945. On June 15 of that year, she wed film director *Vincente Minnelli* at the Los Angeles home of her mother, *Ethel Gilmore*. *Ira Gershwin* was best man. Their daughter, *Liza May MINNELLI*, was born on March 12, 1946, in Los Angeles. Garland testified in divorce court that Minnelli "secluded himself and wouldn't explain why he would be away and leave me alone so much." The divorce was granted in Los Angeles on March 22, 1951. Her third husband was producer *Sid Luft* (formerly married to actress *Lynn BARI*), whom she wed on June 8, 1952, at the ranch of a friend, *Robert Law*, near Hollister, California. The Lufts had two children: singer *Lorna Luft*, born November 21, 1952, and *Joseph Wiley Luft*, born March 29, 1959. The couple was divorced in Santa Monica on May 19, 1965. The children became the objects of a bitter custody fight which Judy won. On November 14, 1965, she married actor *Mark Herron* in the Little Church of the West wedding chapel in Las Vegas. They separated six months later and were divorced on April 11, 1967, in Los Angeles. Garland testified that Herron drank excessively, beat her, and kicked her. She was wed for the fifth time on March 15, 1969, in London, to discothèque manager *Mickey Dean*. Three months later, on June 22, 1969, Garland was found dead in her London apartment from an overdose of sleeping pills. She was forty-seven.

GARNER, James
(1928-)

Garner and *Lois Clarke* were married at the courthouse in Beverly Hills on August 17, 1956. At the time of their marriage, Clarke had an eight-year-old daughter, *Kimberly*. A second daughter, *Greta*, was born in 1958.

GARNER, Peggy Ann
(1931-1984)

On February 22, 1951, Garner wed singer-actor *Richard Herbert Hayes* in a small wedding at the Hotel Delmonico in New York City. The union ended in divorce in 1953. In 1956, she married actor *Albert Salmi*, whom she met while on tour. Their daughter, *Cassandra*, was born in 1960. The couple was divorced in March 1963. On August 7, 1964, she married *Kenyon Foster Brown*, a Los Angeles real estate executive, at the Syracuse, New York, home of Justice of the Peace *Albert Gordon*. Divorced in the late sixties, Garner never remarried.

GARRETT, Betty
(1919-)

The actress-singer-dancer wed *Larry PARKS* on September 9, 1944, at St. Thomas Episcopal Church in Hollywood. Two sons were born: *Garrett Christopher* in 1950, followed by *Andrew Lawrence* in 1951. The couple was married thirty years until Parks died from a heart attack in their Studio City, California, home on April 13, 1975, at the age of sixty. Garrett has not remarried.

GARSON, Greer
(1908-)

The Irish-born actress married *Edward Alec Abbot Snelson*, a British government attaché, on September 28, 1933. The couple separated only five weeks later when Snelson's work took him to India, and Garson did not accompany him. She received a divorce in America on May 12, 1941. She married actor *Richard NEY* in Santa Monica on July 24, 1943. She received an uncontested divorce from Ney in Los Angeles on September 25, 1947. On July 15, 1949, the actress married *Edward E. (Buddy) Fogelson*, a Texas rancher and sportsman who later served on President Eisenhower's staff. The wedding was held at the Santa Fe, New Mexico, home of a friend, *Fletcher Catron*. The couple resided on a ranch outside of Santa Fe. Fogelson died in December 1987.

GAYNOR, Janet
(1906-1984)

Gaynor wed *Lydell Peck*, a San Francisco attorney, on September 11, 1929. She received an interlocutory decree of divorce from Peck in 1933. The decree became final on April 10, 1934, in Los Angeles. The actress testified that her husband was unreasonably jealous and often rude and discourteous to her. On August 14, 1939, she eloped to Yuma, Arizona, with costume designer *Gilbert Adrian*. Their son, *Robin Gaynor Adrian*, was born on July 6, 1940. Their twenty years of marriage ended in Adrian's death from a stroke at the age of fifty-six on September 13, 1959. Gaynor wed her third husband, Paramount Pictures production executive *Paul Gregory*, on December 24, 1964, in Las Vegas. They resided in Palm Springs, California, until, on September 14, 1984, Gaynor died of complications from injuries she had received in a car accident in September 1982. She was seventy-seven.

GAYNOR, Mitzi
(1930-)

Since 1954, the actress-dancer has been married to *Jack Bean*, an industrial public relations executive. The couple resides in Beverly Hills.

GEORGE, Gladys
(1900-1954)

In 1922, George married actor *Ben Erway*. They were divorced in 1929. On December 16, 1933, she married manufacturer *Edward H. Fowler* of Springfield, Massachusetts. Fowler divorced her in New York City in the summer of 1935, naming actor *Leonard Penn* as co-respondant. George and Penn were married in New Haven, Connecticut, on September 18, 1935. They were divorced in 1944. On July 1, 1946, she wed bellhop *Kenneth C. Bradley* at the First Methodist Church in Riverside, California. Three years later, on January 23, 1950, George divorced Bradley in Los Angeles.

GIBSON, Hoot
(1892-1962)

In 1913, the cowboy star married *Helen Rose Wenger* who became film star *Helen Gibson*. Divorced in 1921, he wed *Helen Johnson* that same year. Their daughter, *Lois*, was born in 1923. Helen Johnson Gibson received a divorce in Los Angeles on February 5, 1929. She testified that after he left her, she asked him to come back, but he refused to listen. He wed film star *Sally EILERS* at his Saugus, California, ranch on June 27, 1930. Eilers received a divorce in Chihuahua, Mexico, on September 24, 1933. Gibson married singer *Dorothy Dunstan* in 1941. They were married until his death from cancer at the age of seventy on August 23, 1962, in Woodland Hills, California.

GIBSON, Mel
(1956-   )

On June 7, 1980, Gibson wed *Robyn Denise Moore* in Forestville, New South Wales, Australia. The Gibsons have six children: *Hannah*, born in 1981; twin sons, *Edward* and *Christian*, born in 1982; *William*, born in 1984; and *Louis*, born in 1987; and *Milo*, born in December 1989.

GILBERT, John
(1895-1936)

On August 26, 1918, Gilbert married *Olivia Burwell* in a Hollywood church. They were divorced in 1921 after a long separation. That year, he married actress *Leatrice JOY* in Tijuana, Mexico. They were remarried on March 3, 1922, at the Los Angeles home of Judge *A.R. Summerfield*. Leatrice Joy sued for divorce in Los Angeles on August 19, 1924, charging Gilbert with intemperence, cruelty, and ill temper. A daughter, *Leatrice Joy II*, was born on September 6, 1924. The divorce decree was granted on May 29, 1925, and became final in June 1926. Gilbert eloped to Las Vegas with actress *Ina CLAIRE* on May 9, 1929. The union was shortlived. Claire received a divorce in Los Angeles on August 4, 1931, after testifying that it was ''impossible to live with him anymore.'' On August 10, 1932, he married actress *Virginia BRUCE* in a Los Angeles film studio. *Irving Thalberg* was best man and *Mrs. Donald Ogden Stewart* was matron-of-honor. The couple had a daughter, *Susan Ann*, born in Los Angeles on August 2, 1933. The marriage quickly ended in divorce in Los Angeles on May 25, 1934. Married for one year and eight months, Bruce testified that Gilbert was often intoxicated and had been abusive. Gilbert's daughter, *Leatrice Gilbert Fountain*, published a biography of her father in 1985.

GISH, Dorothy
(1898-1968)

Gish married her leading man, actor *James Rennie*, on December 26, 1920, in Greenwich, Connecticut. The ceremony was a double wedding in which *Constance TALMADGE* was also married to *John T. Pialoglu*. Gish divorced Rennie, charging intolerable cruelty, on October 11, 1935, in Bridgeport, Connecticut. She never remarried. Her older sister, actress *Lillian Gish*, has never married.

GLEASON, Jackie
(1916-1987)

The comedian married dancer *Genevieve Halford* in Newark, New Jersey on September 20, 1936. The couple had two daughters: *Linda*, born in 1940, and *Geraldine*, born in 1942. The Gleasons separated in 1941 but were reconciled in 1948. They separated again in 1951, and the separation became permanent in 1954. They were not divorced until June 22, 1970, when Gleason received a decree in New York City. A few days later, on July 4, 1970, he married secretary *Beverly McKittrick*. Four years later, on November 5, 1974, Gleason received a divorce in Fort Lauderdale, Florida. He wed *Marilyn Taylor* on December 16, 1975. Their eleven years of marriage ended in the comedian's death from cancer at the age of seventy-one in Fort Lauderdale, Florida, on June 24, 1987.

GODDARD, Paulette
(1911-1990)

In November 1927, Goddard married *Edgar James*, whom she had met while appearing in the Ziegfeld Follies in Palm Beach, Florida. He followed her to New York City where they were married. Goddard received a divorce in Reno in 1929. In June 1936, she married *Charlie CHAPLIN* in Canton, China. The Chaplins separated in 1940, and the actress received a divorce in Juarez, Mexico, on June 4, 1942, on the grounds of incompatibility of characters. Her third marriage was to actor *Burgess MEREDITH*, whom she wed on May 21, 1944, in the garden of *David O. Selznick's* Beverly Hills home. Goddard received a divorce in Cuernavaca, Mexico, on June 6, 1949. She married novelist

Erich Maria Remarque on February 25, 1958, in Branford, Connecticut. They divided their time between New York City and Switzerland, settling for the latter just before Remarque's death on September 25, 1970, in Lucarno, Switzerland. Goddard never remarried.

GOLDBERG, Whoopi
(1950-   )

The actress was briefly married (and divorced) in the early seventies. She has a daughter, *Alexandrea*, from this marriage. On September 1, 1986, Goldberg wed Dutch cinematographer *David Claessen* in Las Vegas. She filed for divorce in Santa Monica on the grounds of irreconcilable differences in October 1988.

GOLDBLUM, Jeff
(1952-   )

Goldblum wed actress *Patricia Gaul* in 1980. The marriage ended in divorce in 1985. On November 1, 1987, Goldblum married actress *Geena DAVIS* in Las Vegas. Davis filed for divorce in Los Angeles on the grounds of irreconcilable differences in October 1990.

GORDON, Ruth
(1896-1985)

In 1918, she wed well-known Broadway actor *Gregory Kelly*. Six years later, on July 9, 1927, Kelly died at the age of thirty-six from a heart disease in a New York City sanitarium. On October 16, 1929, a son, *Jones Harris*, was born to Gordon and Broadway producer *Jed Harris* in Paris. The actress married director and writer *Garson Kanin* at the Willard Hotel in Washington, D.C., on December 4, 1942. The forty-two year marriage, considered rewarding both personally and professionally, ended in Gordon's death on August 28, 1985, at their summer home in Edgartown, Massachusetts. The actress was eighty-eight.

GOUDAL, Jetta
(1901-1985)

On October 13, 1930, the French-born actress married *Harold Grieve*, an art director and interior decorator, in Yuma, Arizona. Their fifty-four years of marriage ended in Goudal's death at the age of eighty-four on January 15, 1985, in Los Angeles.

GOULD, Elliott
(1938-   )

On March 21, 1963, Gould and singer-actress *Barbra STREISAND* were married in Baltimore, Maryland. Their son, *Jason Emanuel*, was born on December 29, 1966, in New York City. Gould and Streisand filed jointly for divorce in Santo Domingo on July 1, 1971, and were divorced within seven days. That same year, Gould's daughter, *Molly*, was born to *Jennifer Bogart*. In 1972, the couple had a son, *Samuel*. Gould and Bogart were married in Las Vegas in December 1973. Bogart was granted a divorce in Los Angeles on October 6, 1975. In 1978, Gould and Bogart were remarried.

GRABLE, Betty
(1916-1973)

Grable married actor *Jackie COOGAN* at St. Brendan's Catholic Church in Los Angeles on November 20, 1937. Financial difficulties led to their divorce on October 11, 1939, in Los Angeles. Coogan did not contest the divorce. Her second husband was trumpeter and bandleader *Harry James*, whom she wed in Las Vegas on July 5, 1943. The couple had two daughters: *Victoria*, born March 3, 1944; and *Jessica*, born May 20, 1947. The marriage ended in divorce on October 8, 1965, in Las Vegas, after twenty-two years of marriage. Grable never remarried.

GRANGER, Stewart
(1913-)

On September 10, 1938, Granger and actress *Elspeth March* were married in a church wedding in the Boltons, England. Their son, *James (Jamie) Vale*, was born on July 22, 1944. Their daughter, *Lindsay*, was born in 1945. March was granted a divorce in England on April 13, 1948, and given custody of the children. Granger went to Hollywood in 1950, the same year as actress *Jean SIMMONS*. On December 21, 1950, Granger and Simmons were married in Tucson, Arizona. A daughter, *Tracy* (named for actor *Spencer Tracy*), was born in June 1956. Simmons was granted a divorce in Nogales, Arizona, on August 12, 1960. She charged Granger with mental cruelty and was given custody of Tracy. The actor wed Belgian-born *Caroline Lecerf* on June 12, 1964. Their daughter, *Samantha*, was born on March 11, 1968. Divorced in 1969, Granger has not remarried.

GRANT, Cary
(1904-1986)

Grant was married five times. His first wife was actress *Virginia Cherrill*, a protégé of Charlie Chaplin. The couple was married at Westminster registry office in London on February 9, 1934. Cherrill was granted a divorce in Los Angeles on March 26, 1935. Grant married heiress *Barbara Hutton* on July 8, 1942, at the Lake Arrowhead, California, home of his agent, *Frank Vincent*. Hutton obtained a divorce in Los Angeles on August 30, 1945, on the grounds of mental cruelty. She testified that Grant's conduct made her ''ill and nervous.'' On Christmas Day, 1949, Grant married actress *Betsy Drake* near Phoenix, Arizona. Separated in 1958, the couple was divorced in 1959. On July 22, 1965, Grant secretly married actress *Dyan CANNON* in Nevada. Their daughter, *Jennifer*, was born on February 26, 1966, in Burbank, California. Cannon received a divorce in Los Angeles on March 21, 1968. In her divorce suit, Cannon testified that Grant was a habitual LSD user and asked for custody of Jennifer, allowing Grant only daytime visits with a nurse present. The court gave her custody but concluded that Grant was no longer an LSD user and gave him visiting rights. In April 1981, Grant announced that he had been married to British publicity woman *Barbara Harris* for "quite some time." The marriage ended in his death from a heart attack on November 30, 1986, in Davenport, Iowa. He was eighty-two.

GRANVILLE, Bonita
(1923-1988)

On February 5, 1947, the film actress married Dallas oilman *John (Jack) Devereaux Wrather* at the Bel-Air Hotel. *Ann Rutherford* was matron-of-honor. The Wrathers had four children: *Molly*, born in 1948; *Jack*, born in 1949; *Linda*, born in 1950; and *Christopher*, born in 1952. The couple was married thirty-seven years until, on November 12, 1984, Wrather, age sixty-six, died of cancer in Santa Monica, California.

GRAYSON, Kathryn
(1922-   )

Grayson eloped to Las Vegas on July 12, 1941, with actor *John Shelton*. The couple was divorced in 1946. On August 22, 1947, she wed singer-actor *Johnny Johnston* at the Church of the Wayfarer on Monterey Peninsula, near Carmel, California. Their daughter, *Patricia Kathryn* (nicknamed Patti Kate), was born on October 7, 1948. Grayson received a divorce in Santa Monica on October 3, 1951, charging her husband with cruelty. She has not remarried.

GREER, Jane
(1924-)

On December 2, 1943, she wed *Rudy VALLEE* in the Westwood Village Community Chapel in Los Angeles. Eight months later, on July 27, 1944, the couple was divorced in Los Angeles. She married attorney-producer *Edward Lasker* on August 21, 1947. The Laskers had three sons: *Albert*, born June 23, 1948; *Lawrence*, born October 7, 1949; and *Steven*, born May 9, 1954. Greer received a divorce in Juarez, Mexico, on November 6, 1963. She has not remarried.

GRIFFITH, Corinne
(1896-1979)

In 1917, Griffith married actor-director *Webster Campbell*. She filed for divorce in New York City on August 1, 1923, and the decree was granted later that year. In 1924, she married producer *Walter Morosco*. They were divorced in Juarez, Mexico, on May 2, 1934. On June 27, 1936, Griffith married *George Preston Marshall*, owner of the Washington Redskins football team, in White Plains, New York. The Marshalls were divorced in 1958, after twenty-two years of marriage. On Valentine's Day, 1965, the actress married singer *Danny Scholl*. Thirty-three days later, on March 19, 1965, the union was annulled in Los Angeles. Griffith never remarried.

GRIFFITH, Melanie
(1957-)

On her eighteenth birthday, the actress, who is the daughter of *Tippi HEDREN*, became engaged to actor *Don Johnson*. They were married in Las Vegas in February 1976, and divorced in 1977. In 1983, Griffith wed actor *Steve Bauer* They were divorced in 1985, the same year their son, *Alexander*, was born. On June 26, 1989, Griffith and Johnson were remarried in Woody

Creek, Colorado. Their daughter, *Dakota*, was born in Austin, Texas, on October 4, 1989.

GUINNESS, Sir Alec
(1914-)

Following a three-year courtship, Guinness married actress *Merula Salaman* in June 1938, at Reigate registry office in London. Their son, *Matthew*, was born in 1941.

GURIE, Sigrid
(1911 - 1969)

The actress wed San Francisco businessman *Thomas W. Stewart* in 1935. The couple was divorced in 1938. On August 6, 1939, Gurie and physician *Laurence C. Spangard* were married in his Hollywood home. The Spangards were married thirty years until her death, at age fifty-eight, on August 14, 1969, in Mexico City, Mexico.

HACKMAN, Gene
(1931-)

On January 1, 1956, the actor married bank secretary *Fay Maltese*. The Hackmans have three children: *Christopher*, born in 1960; *Elizabeth*, born in 1962; and *Leslie*, born in 1966.

HAGMAN, Larry
(1931-)

The actor, who is the son of *Mary MARTIN*, wed Swedish-born clothing designer *Maj Axelsson* in England in 1954. The couple has a daughter, actress *Heidi Hagman*, born in 1958, and a son, *Preston*, born in 1962.

HALE, Barbara
(1921-)

Hale wed actor *Bill Williams* in her childhood home in Rockford, Illinois, on June 22, 1946. They have three children: *Barbara Willa Johanna*, born July 24, 1947; *William*, an actor, born February 16, 1951; and *Laura Lee*, born December 22, 1953.

HALEY, Jack
(1899-1979)

Haley married Ziegfeld Follies dancer *Florence McFadden* on February 25, 1921. The Haleys had two children: *Gloria*, born in 1928, and producer-director *Jack Haley, Jr.*, born on October 25, 1933, who married *Liza MINNELLI*. Their fifty-two years of marriage ended in Haley's death from a heart attack on June 6, 1979, in Los Angeles. He was seventy-nine.

HAMILTON, George
(1939-   )

On October 29, 1972, the actor married *Alana Collins*. The couple had one son, *Ashley*, born on October 1, 1974. Divorced from Collins since 1976, Hamilton has not remarried.

HAMILTON, Neil
(1899-1984)

The actor married *Elsa Whitmer* on November 27, 1922. The couple lived in Escondido, California, during their sixty-one years of marriage, which ended in his death from complications of asthma in Escondido, California, on September 24, 1984. He was eighty-five.

HAMMERSTEIN, Elaine
(1897-1948)

The actress was the daughter of stage producer *Arthur Hammerstein*, who married *Dorothy DALTON*. On June 10, 1926, she wed Los Angeles fire commissioner and insurance executive *James Walter Kays* at St. Basil's Church in Los Angeles. Their twenty-two years of marriage ended in her death in a car accident near Tijuana, Mexico, on August 13, 1948.

HANKS, Tom
(1956-   )

Hanks married actress and producer *Samantha Lewes* in 1978. The couple had a son, *Colin*, born in 1978, and a daughter, *Elizabeth*, born in 1982. They separated in 1985 and were divorced in 1987. On April 30, 1988, Hanks married his film co-star, actress *Rita Wilson*. Their son was born on August 4, 1990.

HARDING, Ann
(1901 - 1981)

Harding married actor *Harry Bannister* in New York City on October 21, 1926. Their daughter, *Jane*, was born on July 24, 1928. The actress received a divorce in Reno on May 7, 1932. On January 17, 1937, she wed composer and conductor *Werner Janssen* at Caxton Hall registry office in London. Twenty-five years later, in 1962, Harding obtained a divorce in Bridgeport, Connecticut, charging intolerable cruelty. She never remarried.

HARDWICKE, Sir Cedric
(1883 - 1964)

On January 8, 1928, Hardwicke married actress *Helena Pickard* in his native England. Their son, actor *Edward Hardwicke*, was born in 1932. Lady Hardwicke received a divorce in London on the grounds of adultery on May 11, 1950. She died in 1959. On July 27, 1950, the actor married starlet *Mary Scott* in Coronado, California. Their son, *Michael*, was born in 1951. Mary Hardwicke received a divorce in Santa Monica on November 14, 1961, after testifying that her husband had told her "marriage is for the bourgeoise." He never remarried. His son Michael committed suicide in 1983.

HARDY, Oliver
(1892 - 1957)

In 1913, the comedian married pianist *Madelyn Saloshin*. The marriage ended in divorce in 1921. That same year, on November 24, he wed *Myrtle Lee* in Los Angeles. There were many separations and reconciliations and, in 1933, Hardy filed for divorce. He later withdrew his suit. Finally, on May 18, 1937, Hardy received a divorce in Los Angeles. In 1940, Hardy wed *Virginia Lucille Jones*, who had worked as a script girl on his films. They were married seventeen years until, on August 7,

1957, the comedian died, after a series of strokes, in North Hollywood. Hardy was sixty-five.

HARLOW, Jean
(1911 - 1937)

At the age of sixteen, while a student at Ferry Hall in Lake Forest, Illinois, she eloped to Waukegan, Illinois, with *Charles Mc-Grew III* of Chicago. They were divorced two years later, in 1929, when Harlow was just beginning her film career. On July 2, 1932, she married MGM executive *Paul Bern* at her mother's Beverly Hills home. Two months later, on the night of September 5, 1932, Bern shot himself in the basement of their Benedict Canyon home. Harlow surprised friends by eloping to Yuma, Arizona, on September 18, 1933, with cameraman *Harold G. (Hal) Rosson*. They separated only a few months later, and Harlow obtained a divorce in Los Angeles on March 11, 1935, charging Rosson with cruelty. At the time of her death, from uremic poisoning, on June 7, 1937, Harlow was engaged to actor *William POWELL*.

HARMON, Mark
(1951 -   )

Harmon wed actress *Pam Dawber* in Los Angeles on March 21, 1987. Their son, *Sean Thomas*, was born on April 25, 1988.

HARRIS, Julie
(1925 -   )

In August 1946, Harris wed lawyer *Jay I. Julien*. The marriage ended in divorce in the summer of 1954. She married stage manager *Manning Gurian* on October 21, 1954. Their son, *Peter Alston Gurian*, was born on July 25, 1955. The marriage ended in divorce in 1967. Since April 27, 1977, the actress has been married to writer *William Erwin Carroll*.

HARRIS, Mildred
(1901-1944)

Harris became the first wife of *Charlie CHAPLIN* at the age of sixteen on October 23, 1918, in Los Angeles. Their son, *Norman Spencer Chaplin*, was born in Los Angeles on July 7, 1919, but died three days later. The marriage ended in divorce in Los Angeles, on the grounds of cruelty, on November 12, 1920. In 1924, she wed *Everett Terrence McGovern*, a widower from Florida. Their son, *Everett, Jr.*, was born in 1925. On November 26, 1929, Harris sued for divorce in Los Angeles, charging McGovern with desertion. In 1934, Harris married *William P. Fleckenstein* in Asheville, North Carolina. The couple remained married, although separated, until her death. The actress died on July 20, 1944, from pneumonia, following surgery, in Los Angeles. She was forty-two.

HARRIS, Phil
(1906-)

Harris and *Alice FAYE* surprised their friends when, on May 12, 1941, they eloped to Ensenada, Mexico, after a short courtship. The couple has two daughters: *Alice*, born May 19, 1942, and *Phyllis*, born April 26, 1944.

HARRISON, George
(1943-)

Harrison became the third Beatle to get married when he wed *Patti Boyd* in a London registry office on January 21, 1966. The Beatles' manager, *Brian Epstein*, was best man. After a two-year separation, the couple was divorced in London on June 9,

1977. On August 1, 1978, a son, *Dhani*, was born to Harrison and *Olivia Arrias* in London. Five weeks later, on September 9, 1978, Harrison and Arrias, who had been a secretary for his record company, were married.

HARRISON, Sir Rex
(1908-1990)

In 1934, the actor wed *Marjorie Thomas* in his native England. Their son, actor *Noel Harrison*, was born in London on January 29, 1936. The couple was divorced in 1942. Harrison married Viennese actress *Lilli PALMER* in London on January 25, 1943. Their son, playwright *Carey Harrison*, was born in 1947. After a year-long separation, the marriage ended in divorce in Juarez, Mexico, on February 6, 1957. Five months later, on June 22, 1957, Harrison married actress *Kay KENDALL* at the Universalist Church of the Divine Paternity in New York City. Kendall died two years later, on September 6, 1959, from leukemia at the age of thirty-three in London. Harrison was remarried three years later, on March 21, 1962, to British actress *Rachel Roberts*. The marriage ended in divorce in 1971. Later that same year, on August 26, 1971, Harrison married *Elizabeth Rees Harris*, the divorced wife of actor *Richard Harris*, in the United States. They were divorced in 1976. On December 17, 1978, Harrison married his sixth wife, *Mercia Mildred Tinker*. Twelve years later, on June 2, 1990, the actor died of cancer at their New York City home. He was eighty-two.

HART, William S.
(1870-1946)

On December 7, 1921, the Western star married his leading lady, *Winifred Westover*, in a Los Angeles church. Their son, *William, Jr.*, was born in Los Angeles on September 6, 1922. There were many separations and reconciliations which ended on February 11, 1927, when Westover was granted a divorce in Reno on the grounds of desertion. The couple remained friends, and she was at his bedside when he died in June 1946. Winifred Westover died in 1978.

HARVEY, Laurence
(1928-1973)

In August 1957, the actor married British actress *Margaret LEIGHTON*. Leighton filed for divorce in London on November 11, 1960. On October 16, 1968, Harvey and *Joan Perry Cohn* (the widow of producer *Harry Cohn*) were married at the Lyford Cay Club in Nassau, the Bahamas. She divorced him in 1972. Later that same year, on December 31, 1972, Harvey wed model *Paulene Stone*, by whom he had had a daughter, *Domino*, in 1969. Less than a year later, on November 25, 1973, Harvey died of cancer at their London home. He was forty-five.

HAVER, June
(1926-   )

She eloped to Las Vegas on March 9, 1947, with trumpeter *Jimmy Zito*. The marriage ended in divorce a little over a year later, on March 25, 1948, with Haver charging extreme mental cruelty. Haver married *Fred MACMURRAY* on June 28, 1954, on a ranch near Ojai, California. On December 4, 1956, the couple adopted twin daughters, *Katie Marie* and *Laurie Anne*. The MacMurrays reside in Brentwood, California.

HAVER, Phyllis
(1899-1960)

Haver and businessman *William Seeman* were married by *Mayor Jimmy Walker* at the New York City home of cartoonist *Rube Goldberg* on April 24, 1929. The wedding celebration included a serenade by *Paul Whiteman's* Band and fireworks, followed by a three-month honeymoon in Europe. The couple was divorced in 1945, and Haver never remarried.

HAVOC, June
(1916-)

At thirteen, the actress, who is the younger sister of *Gypsy Rose LEE*, eloped to North Platte, Nebraska, with a performer in her act, identified simply as *Bobby*. Her husband died from an illness when she was eighteen. On April 1, 1935, two months after her husband's death, their daughter, *April*, was born. The actress married *Donald S. Gibbs*, a New York advertising executive, late in 1935. Havoc obtained a divorce from Gibbs in Santa Monica on December 2, 1942. On January 25, 1948, Havoc married Los Angeles radio producer *William Spier*. Their twenty-five years of marriage ended in Spier's death from a heart attack at the age of sixty-six on June 1, 1973, at their home in Weston, Connecticut.

HAWKINS, Jack
(1910-1973)

In 1932, the British-born actor married actress *Jessica TANDY*. A daughter, *Susan*, was born in 1934. The marriage ended in divorce in 1940. On October 31, 1947, Hawkins married actress *Doreen Lawrence*. The couple had three children: *Nicholas*, born in 1948; *Andrew*, born in 1950; and *Caroline*, born in 1954. Their twenty-five years of marriage ended in the actor's death in London on July 18, 1973. He was sixty-two.

HAWN, Goldie
(1945-)

Hawn married actor and producer *Gus Trinkonis* on May 16, 1969. The couple separated in 1973 and filed for divorce in California in 1975. The decree was granted in 1976. On July 3, 1976, Hawn wed *Bill Hudson*, of the Hudson Brothers singing comedy troupe. The couple was married in the backyard of Hawn's childhood home in Takoma Park, Maryland. Their son, *Oliver Rutledge*, was born in September 1976. Their daughter, *Kate*, was born in 1979. They separated in 1980, and Hudson filed for divorce in August of that year. Hawn has a son, *Wyatt*, born July 10, 1986, in Los Angeles, with actor *Kurt Russell*.

HAYDEN, Sterling
(1916-1986)

On June 30, 1942, Hayden and film star *Madeleine CARROLL* announced that they had been married four months earlier, on Valentine's Day, 1942, in Peterboro, New Hampshire. Four years later, on May 8, 1946, Carroll divorced Hayden in Reno, charging him with cruelty. The actor wed Pasadena socialite *Betty Ann DeNoon* at the Montecito Presbyterian Church in Santa Barbara, on April 25, 1947. The couple had three sons: *Christian*, born in 1948; *Dana*, born in 1950; and *Matthew*, born in 1951, and a daughter, *Gretchen*, born in 1952. DeNoon received an interlocutory decree of divorce (and custody of their children) in Santa Monica on April 23, 1953. In March 1960, Hayden wed *Catherine Devine McConnell*. McConnell had a son, *Scott*, from a former marriage. A son, *David*, was born to the couple on February 11, 1961. The couple separated in 1969, but they were never divorced. Hayden died from cancer in his Sausalito, California, home on May 23, 1986. He was seventy.

HAYDON, Julie
(1910-   )

The actress married drama critic *George Jean Nathan* on June 19, 1955. The couple was married by the captain of the cruise ship *Santa Rosa* off Cape Hatteras, North Carolina. It was Nathan's first marriage. Three years later, on April 8, 1958, he died, after a long illness, at their New York City home. Haydon has not remarried.

HAYES, Helen
(1900-)

Hayes married playwright, screenwriter, and director *Charles MacArthur* on August 17, 1928, at the New York City law office of *Charles A. Oberwager*. Their daughter, *Mary,* was born in New York City on February 15, 1930. The couple also adopted a six-month-old son, actor *James MacArthur*, born in Los Angeles on December 8, 1937. Mary MacArthur became an actress, but she died in 1949 at the age of nineteen from polio. The MacArthurs were married twenty-seven years, until his death from an internal hemorrhage in New York City on April 21, 1956. Hayes has not remarried.

HAYMES, Dick
(1916-1980)

The singer-actor was married seven times. In 1939, he wed singer *Edith Harper*. The marriage was annulled in Little Rock, Arkansas, only a few weeks later. Haymes married dancer *Joanne Marshall* in September 1941. She later became an actress, using the professional name of *Joanne Dru*. The couple had three children: singer *Richard (Dick) Haymes, Jr.*, born in 1942; *Helen*, born in 1944; and *Barbara*, born in 1947. The marriage ended in divorce in July 1949. Dru later married actor *John Ireland*. Later that month, on July 17, 1949, Haymes wed *Nora Eddington Flynn*, the divorced wife of *Errol FLYNN*, at his Los Angeles home. Haymes received a divorce in Las Vegas on September 23, 1953, on the grounds of mental cruelty. An hour later, Haymes returned to the courthouse with *Rita HAYWORTH* and obtained a marriage license. Haymes and Hayworth were married in Las Vegas the following day. Two years later, on December 12, 1955, Hayworth received an uncontested in absentia divorce in Reno. Singer *Frances Ann Makris* became his fifth wife on November 14, 1958, in Arlington, Virginia. The marriage ended in divorce in 1959. Later that same year, Haymes married singer *Fran Jeffries* and their daughter, *Stephanie*, was born. The union ended in divorce in 1964. On March 18, 1966, Haymes married English model *Wendy Smith*. For many years the couple lived in Ireland with their son, *Sean*, born June 19, 1966, and their daughter, *Samantha*, born March 16, 1969. They had been married fourteen years when Haymes died from cancer in Los Angeles on March 28, 1980. He was sixty-three.

HAYWARD, Susan
(1918-1975)

Hayward married actor *Jess Barker* on July 23, 1944, at St. Thomas Episcopal Church in Los Angeles. Twin sons, *Timothy* and *Gregory*, were born on February 17, 1945. Her marriage to Barker ended in divorce on August 17, 1954, in Burbank, California. The decree became final the following year. Hayward was given custody of their sons and all property except a station wagon. Hayward wed lawyer *Floyd Eaton Chalkley* in Phoenix, Arizona, on February 8, 1957. Nine years later, on January 9, 1966, Chalkley died of hepatitis in Fort Lauderdale, Florida. Hayward never remarried.

HAYWORTH, Rita
(1918-1987)

Hayworth was married five times. On May 29, 1937, she married oil man *Edward Judson*. The marriage ended in divorce in 1943. Later that same year, on September 7, 1943, she married *Orson WELLES* in Santa Monica. Their daughter, *Rebecca*, was born on December 17, 1944. Hayworth received a divorce in November 1948. On May 27, 1949, the actress married *Prince Aly Khan*, son of Indian Potentate *Aga Khan*. A large crowd gathered outside the town hall in Vallauris, France, where the couple was married by the mayor. *Princess Yasmin (Jasmine)* was born in Lausanne, Switzerland, on December 28, 1949. Early in September 1953, Hayworth divorced Khan in Reno. She then went to Las Vegas where, on September 24, 1953, she married singer-actor *Dick HAYMES*. Two years later, on December 12, 1955, Hayworth was granted an uncontested in absentia divorce in Reno. She was married for the fifth time, to producer *James Hill*, on February 2, 1958, at her Beverly Hills home. Testifying that Hill was no longer interested in being married, Hayworth was granted a divorce, on the grounds of extreme mental cruelty, on September 7, 1961, in Santa Monica.

HEDREN, Tippi
(1935-   )

In 1954, Hedren married actor *Peter Griffith*. Their daughter, actress *Melanie GRIFFITH*, was born in New York City on August 9, 1957. The marriage ended in divorce in 1959. On September 27, 1964, she wed her manager, *Noel Marshall*, at her Sherman Oaks, California, home. The couple was divorced in 1982.

HEFLIN, Van
(1910-1971)

Heflin married an actress, *Esther Ralston*, in the summer of 1934. Separated six months later, they were divorced in October 1936. On May 16, 1942, Heflin wed actress *Frances Neal* at Westwood Congregational Church in Los Angeles. The couple had two daughters, *Vana*, born in 1943, and *Cathleen*, born in 1946, and a son, *Tracy*, born in 1954. After twenty-five years of marriage, Frances Heflin obtained a divorce in Santa Monica on August 4, 1967.

HEMINGWAY, Mariel
(1961-   )

Hemingway married *Steve Crisman*, manager of New York's Hard Rock Café, at St. Thomas Episcopal Church in New York City in December 1984. Their daughter, *Dree Louise*, was born in December 1987.

HENDRIX, Wanda
(1928-1981)

On February 8, 1949, the actress married WW II hero-turned-actor *Audie MURPHY*. The couple separated seven months later, and Hendrix received a divorce in Los Angeles on the grounds of mental cruelty on April 14, 1950. The decree became final on April 20, 1951. In 1954, she wed millionaire sportsman *James L. Stack, Jr.*, the brother of actor *Robert STACK*. She received a divorce (and a large financial settlement) in Reno on November 3, 1958, charging her husband with cruelty. Hendrix wed oil company executive *Steve LaMonte* in Las Vegas in 1969. The marriage ended in divorce ten years later.

HENIE, Sonja
(1912-1969)

On July 4, 1940, the ice skater and actress married *Daniel Reid Topping* (who had just been divorced by *Arline JUDGE*) at the Chicago home of a friend, *Arthur Wirtz*. The couple separated in January 1945, and Henie obtained a divorce in Chicago on February 13, 1946, after she told the judge that Topping had told her: "Go your way, and I'll go mine." Henie and aviation executive *Winthrop Gardiner, Jr.* were married at the Park Avenue Methodist Church in New York City on September 15, 1949. A reception at the Plaza Hotel followed the ceremony. Charging her with desertion and mental cruelty, Gardiner divorced Henie in West Palm Beach, Florida, on May 14, 1956. Less than a month later, a Norwegian minister married her to shipowner *Neils Onstad* in her New York City apartment. The couple, who had been childhood sweethearts in their native Norway, became avid art collectors. They were married until her death from leukemia on October 12, 1969, aboard an ambulance plane flying from Paris to Oslo. She was fifty-seven.

HENREID, Paul
(1908-)

Henreid married dress designer *Elizabeth Camilla Julia Gluck* (called Lisl) in Vienna on January 1, 1936. The couple adopted two daughters: *Monika Elizabeth* (an actress) in 1943 and *Mimi Maria* in 1945.

HEPBURN, Audrey
(1929-)

The actress married *Mel FERRER* in Burgenstock, Switzerland, on September 25, 1954. Their son, *Sean*, was born on January 17, 1960, in Lucerne, Switzerland. The couple was divorced in France in 1968, after fourteen years of marriage. She married Italian psychiatrist *Dr. Andrea Dotti* on January 18, 1969, in Morges (near Geneva), Switzerland. Their son, *Luca*, was born in Lausanne, Switzerland, on February 8, 1970. Hepburn and Dotti were divorced in 1982.

HEPBURN, Katharine
(1907-)

Her only marriage was to Philadelphia socialite and broker *Ludlow Ogden Smith* whom she married on December 21, 1928, at her parents' Hartford, Connecticut, home. Hepburn obtained a divorce from Smith in Merida, Mexico, on May 8, 1934.

HERSHEY, Barbara
(1948-)

Hershey has a son, *Free Seagull* (called "Tom"), born on October 6, 1972, with actor *David Carradine*, the son of *John CARRADINE*.

HERSHOLT, Jean
(1886-1956)

Hersholt married Danish-born *Via Anderson* in Montreal, Canada, circa 1913. Their son, *Allan*, who became a film critic, was born in December 1914. The marriage ended in the actor's death from cancer at the age of sixty-nine in Los Angeles on June 2, 1956.

HESTON, Charleton
(1923-   )

On March 17, 1944, Heston married *Lydia Clarke*, whom he had met when they were both students at Northwestern University, in Greensboro, North Carolina. The couple has a son, *Fraser Clarke*, born February 12, 1955, and a daughter, *Holly Ann*, born August 2, 1961.

HILLER, Dame Wendy
(1912-   )

The actress married English playwright *Ronald Gow* on February 25, 1937. The couple has a daughter, *Anne*, born in 1940, and a son, *Anthony*, born in 1943.

HODIAK, John
(1914-1955)

Hodiak married actress *Anne BAXTER* at the Burlingame, California, home of her parents on July 7, 1946. Their daughter, *Katrina*, was born on July 9, 1951. Baxter received a divorce, and custody of Katrina, in Los Angeles on January 27, 1953, after testifying that Hodiak had poor manners.

HOFFMAN, Dustin
(1937-)

Hoffman married ballet dancer *Anne Byrne* at Temple Beth El in Westchester County, New York, on May 4, 1969. He adopted her daughter, *Karina*. A second daughter, *Jennifer Celia*, was born on October 15, 1970. The marriage ended in divorce in 1975. Since October 21, 1980, Hoffman has been married to lawyer *Lisa Gottsegen*. The couple has four children: *Jacob*, born in March 1981; *Rebecca*, born March 20, 1983; *Max*, born in 1984; and *Alexandra*, born in October 1987.

HOLDEN, William
(1918-1981)

Just before dawn on July 13, 1941, Holden married actress *Brenda Marshall*, whom he had met on the set of the film *Golden Boy* (1939), at a resort near Las Vegas. Marshall had a daughter, *Virginia*, from a former marriage. The couple also had two sons: *Peter Westerfield*, born November 18, 1943, and *Scott Porter*, an actor, born May 2, 1946. Both of their sons were born in Los Angeles. Divorced from Marshall in 1973, Holden never remarried.

HOLLIDAY, Judy
(1922-1965)

Holliday married musician and Columbia Records executive *David Oppenheim* in New York City on January 4, 1948. A son, *Jonathan Lewis*, was born on November 11, 1952, in New York City. Oppenheim received an uncontested divorce in Juarez, Mexico, in March 1957.

HOLM, Celeste
(1919-)

She married film director *Ralph Nelson* in 1938. A son, *Theodore*, was born in 1939. Divorced, she married British-born

Francis E.H. Davies in January 1940. Divorced from Davies, she married *A. Schuyler Dunning*, an airline public relations executive, in 1946. A son, *Daniel*, was born in November 1946. The marriage ended in divorce in 1952. Since May 22, 1966, Holm has been married to actor *Wesley Addy*.

HOLT, Jack
(1888-1951)

The cowboy actor married *Margaret Wood* in 1916. Their son, *Charles John Holt, Jr.*, actor *Tim Holt*, was born in Beverly Hills on February 5, 1918. Their daughter, Elizabeth Marshall, actress *Jennifer Holt*, was born in Los Angeles on November 10, 1920. The couple separated in 1932, and Margaret obtained a Mexican mail order divorce later that same year. Jack Holt had the divorce declared void in 1940. The couple remained married, although separated, until his death at the age of sixty-two in Los Angeles on January 18, 1951.

HOPE, Bob
(1903-   )

The actor eloped with singer *Dolores Reade* to Erie, Pennsylvania, on February 19, 1934. In 1939, the Hopes adopted a daughter, *Linda Roberta Theresa*. They adopted a son, *Anthony Reade*, in 1940. Their two youngest children, *Honora Avis Mary* and *William Kelly Francis*, were adopted in 1946.

HOPKINS, Miriam
(1902-1972)

Hopkins married actor *Brandon Peters* on May 11, 1926. They were divorced in Chicago in 1927. On June 2, 1928, she eloped to Newark, New Jersey, with writer *Austin Parker*. The marriage ended in divorce in 1931. In 1932, the actress adopted an infant son, *Michael*, from the Evanston Cradle Society in Evanston, Illinois. She married film director *Anatole Litvak* in Yuma, Arizona, on September 4, 1937. Two years later, on October 11, 1939, Hopkins received a Reno divorce on the grounds of cruelty. Litvak filed a cross-complaint charging desertion, but gave no evidence. In the fall of 1945, Hopkins married *Ray Brock* a foreign correspondent for the *New York Times*. Divorced from Brock in 1951, she never remarried.

HOPPER, Hedda
(1890-1966)

She was *Elda Curry*, a Broadway chorine, when she married stage star *DeWolf Hopper* in Riverside, New Jersey, on May 8, 1913. Their son, *William DeWolf Hopper, Jr.*, was born on January 26, 1915, in New York City. She filed for divorce on July 21, 1922, in Long Island City, Queens County, New York, and the decree was granted later that year. It was DeWolf Hopper's fifth divorce. Hedda Hopper then became a successful Hollywood actress and gossip columnist. She never remarried.

HORNE, Lena
(1917-   )

The singer and actress wed New York printer *Louis J. Jones* in January 1937. A daughter, *Gail*, was born in December 1938, and a son, *Edwin (Teddy)*, was born in February 1940. Divorced form Jones in June 1944, Horne married *Leonard George "Lennie" Hayton*, a composer, conductor, and arranger, in December 1947. The couple had been married twenty-three years when Hayton died from a heart ailment at the age of sixty-three in Palm Springs on April 24, 1971. Her daughter, Gail Jones, married film director *Sidney Lumet* in 1963. That marriage ended in divorce in 1978.

HOUSEMAN, John
(1902-1988)

Houseman married actress *Zita Johann* in 1929. The couple separated in 1932, and Johann received a divorce in Juarez, Mexico, on September 12, 1933. In 1950, Houseman married *Joan Courtney*. The couple had two sons: *John Michael*, born in November 1951, and *Charles Sebastian*, born December 28, 1954. Both of their sons were born in Los Angeles. The Housemans had been married thirty-eight years when the actor, director, and screenwriter died from cancer in Malibu, California, on October 30, 1988. He was eighty-six.

HOWARD, Leslie
(1893-1943)

The actor married *Ruth Evelyn Martin*, daughter of a British Army officer, in England in 1916. Their son, actor *Ronald Howard*, was born on April 7, 1918, in Anerly, England. Their daughter, *Leslie Ruth Howard*, was born in the United States in October 1924. On June 1, 1943, the plane Howard was aboard was shot down by Nazi forces en route from Lisbon, Portugal, to London. Howard was fifty.

HUDSON, Rock
(1925-1985)

Hudson married his agent's secretary, *Phyllis Gates*, in November 1955. Gates received a divorce, charging mental cruelty, in Santa Monica on August 14, 1958. The actor never remarried.

HUME, Benita
(1906-1967)

Hume married writer *Eric Siepman* in her native England when she was nineteen. The marriage quickly ended in divorce. On September 30, 1938, Hume married film star *Ronald COLMAN* at his home, San Ysidro Ranch, near Santa Barbara, California.

Their daughter, *Juliet Benita*, was born in Los Angeles in July 1944. Known as one of Hollywood's happiest marriages, the union ended in Colman's death from a lung infection at the age of sixty-seven on May 19, 1958, at their ranch home. In February 1959, Hume married actor *George SANDERS* in Madrid, Spain. Eight years later, on November 1, 1967, the actress died at her sister's farm in England. She was sixty.

HUNT, Marsha
(1917-)

Hunt married film editor *Jerry Hopper* on November 23, 1938. The couple was divorced in 1945. Since February 3, 1946, she has been married to playwright, screenwriter, and novelist *Robert Presnell, Jr.* The couple was married in Los Angeles.

HUNTER, Jeffrey
(1925-1969)

In 1950, Hunter married actress *Barbara Rush*. A son, *Christopher,* was born in 1952. Rush received a divorce from the actor on March 29, 1955, in Los Angeles. Hunter wed actress *Dusty Bartlett* in 1957. Their son, *Todd*, was born in 1959. The marriage ended in divorce in 1967. On February 4, 1969, Hunter married actress *Emily McLaughlin*. Four months later, on May 27, 1969, Hunter died after surgery in Van Nuys, California, at the age of forty-three.

HURT, John
(1940-)

Hurt was briefly married to actress *Annette Robertson* in the early sixties. The marriage ended in divorce. On January 26, 1983, composer *Marie-Lise Volpeliere-Pierrot*, his companion for over twelve years, was killed in a horseriding accident. In September 1984, Hurt married American actress *Diana Peacock* in London. The couple was divorced in January 1990. Two weeks later, on January 24, 1990, Hurt married production assistant *Jo Dalton* in London. Their son, *Alexander John Vincent Hurt*, was born in London in February 1990.

HURT, William
(1950-)

In 1972, Hurt wed *Mary Beth Supinger*, better known as actress *Mary Beth Hurt*. The Hurts separated in 1978 and were divorced on December 3, 1982. On March 5, 1989, Hurt wed *Heidi Henderson*, daughter of bandleader *Skitch Henderson*, in Sneeden's Landing, New York. Their son, *Sam*, was born in August 1989. Hurt has a son, *Alexander Devon*, born in January of 1983, with dancer *Sandra Jennings*. In June 1989, Jennings sued Hurt for divorce, claiming to be his common-law wife. On October 3, 1989, a judge in New York City ruled that no common-law marriage had existed.

HUSTON, John
(1906-1987)

The actor, director, and screenwriter, the son of *Walter HUSTON*, was married six times. In 1925, he married *Dorothy Harvey*. The marriage ended in divorce less than a year later. He wed *Lesley Black* in 1937. The couple was divorced in 1945. On July 23, 1946, he married actress *Evelyn KEYES* in Las Vegas. They adopted a Mexican son, *Pablo Albarran*, in 1948. Huston received a divorce in Juarez, Mexico, on February 10, 1950. The following day, February 11, 1950, he wed ballerina and model *Enrica Soma*. Their son, *Walter Anthony (Tony)*, was born on April 16, 1950, in the United States. Their daughter, actress *Anjelica Huston*, was born in 1953, when the Hustons were living in Ireland. The couple separated in 1960, and Enrica Soma was killed in a car accident in 1969. He married his fifth wife, *Celeste Shane*, in 1972. Separated in 1975, Shane received a divorce in the winter of 1977. On February 16, 1986, Huston wed *Maricella Hernandez* in Puerto Vallarta, Mexico. They had been married eighteen months when Huston died from emphysema on July 28, 1987, in Fall River, Massachusetts, at the age of eighty-one.

HUSTON, Walter
(1884-1950)

In 1905, the actor married writer *Rhea Gore*. Their son, actor, director, and screenwriter *John HUSTON*, was born in Nevada, Missouri, on August 5, 1906. The couple separated in 1909, and they were divorced in 1913. Huston wed his vaudeville partner, *Bayonne Whipple*, in Little Rock, Arkansas, on December 4, 1914. After sixteen years of marriage, Whipple sued for divorce in Reno on October 13, 1931. A few weeks later, on November 9, 1931, Huston married actress *Ninetta Eugenia (Nan) Sunderland* at the Los Angeles office of his attorney, *Mark M. Cohen*. The Hustons were married eighteen years, until the actor's death from a heart attack in Beverly Hills on April 7, 1950. He was sixty-six.

HUTTON, Betty
(1921-   )

The actress married business executive *Theodore Briskin* in the Camellia House of the Drake Hotel in Chicago on September 2, 1945. The couple had two daughters: *Lindsay Dianne*, born November 23, 1946, and *Candice*, born April 14, 1948. Both of their daughters were born in Los Angeles. She divorced Briskin in Santa Monica on January 16, 1951, testifying that her husband was rude when they had dinner with studio executives. She was given custody of their daughters. On March 18, 1952, Hutton eloped to Las Vegas with movie dance director *Charles O'Curran*. The couple was married by *Judge Frank McNamee* in the chapel of the Last Frontier Hotel. Three years later, on February 21, 1955, Judge McNamee granted her a divorce from O'Curran in Las Vegas on the grounds of mental cruelty. Two weeks later, on March 8, 1955, she married *Alan W. Livingston*, a recording company executive, at the Desert Inn Hotel in Las Vegas. After their divorce in 1958, Livingston married actress *Nancy Olson*. Hutton wed jazz trumpeter *Pete Candoli* on December 24, 1960. A daughter, *Carolyn*, was born on June 19, 1962. Divorced from Candoli in Juarez, Mexico, in September of 1966, Hutton has not remarried. Candoli later married *Edie ADAMS*.

HYAMS, Leila
(1905-1977)

The actress married agent *Phil Berg* in 1927. The Bergs were married fifty years until her death on December 4, 1977, at the age of seventy-two.

HYER, Martha
(1924-   )

Hyer married film director *Ray Stahl* (the son of film director *John M. Stahl*) in 1951. The marriage ended in divorce in 1953. On December 31, 1966, the actress married producer *Hal B. Wallis*, who was the widower of *Louise FAZENDA*, in his Palm Springs, California, home. The couple was married nineteen years until, on October 5, 1986, Wallis died at their Palm Springs home at the age of eighty-eight. Hyer has not remarried.

IRONS, Jeremy
(1948-)

In the mid-seventies, Irons married and divorced actress *Julie Hallam*. Since 1978, Irons has been married to actress *Sinead Cusack*, the daughter of actor *Cyril Cusack*. She had been a fellow player at the Old Vic. The couple has two sons: *Sam*, born in 1979, and *Maximilian*, born in 1985.

IRVING, Amy
(1953-)

On November 27, 1985, the actress married director-producer *Steven Spielberg* in Santa Fe, New Mexico. At the time of their marriage, the couple had a son, *Max*, born in July 1985. In April 1989, the Spielbergs filed for divorce in Los Angeles. The divorce was granted later that year. The actress has a son, *Gabriel Davis Barreto*, born May 14, 1990, with Brazilian film director *Bruno Barreto*, whom she plans to marry.

—photo courtesy United Artists

Douglas Fairbanks and Mary Pickford in *The Taming of the Shrew*, 1929. Fairbanks and Pickford met during a World War I liberty bond tour.

Clara Bow and Rex Bell.

—photo courtesy Rex Bell

Charlie Chaplin and Paulette
Goddard at the premiere
of *Modern Times*, 1935.

Robert Taylor and Barbara Stanwyck
in *His Brother's Wife*.

Orson Welles and Rita Hayworth in *The Lady from Shanghai*. They were married in 1943, both for the second time.

Clark Gable and Carole Lombard in *No Man of Her Own,* 1933.

Above. Phil Harris and Alice
Faye surprised their friends
when they eloped in 1941.

Right. William Powell
and third-wife Diana Lewis
were married for forty-four years
until Powell's death in 1984.

Veronica Lake and film director-husband André DeToth had two
children during their six-and-a-half-year marriage.

Sir Laurence Olivier bids goodbye to wife Vivien Leigh, before she
leaves for Ceylon.

—photo courtesy BBC

Wedding of Rosalind Russell to producer Frederick Brisson at
Mission Santa Ynez, Solvang, California, 1941; Cary Grant is best man.

William Holden with his two sons, Scott (six years
old) and Peter (nine years old).

Above. Ingrid
Bergman with her
daughter Pia
in 1938. *Right.* Alan
Ladd and wife Sue
Carol with baby.

—photo courtesy San Francisco Examiner

Newlyweds Shirley Temple and Charles Black
in 1950.

Mario Lanza with wife Betty in New York in 1946. Their
fourteen-year marriage ended tragically with Lanza's fatal heart attack.

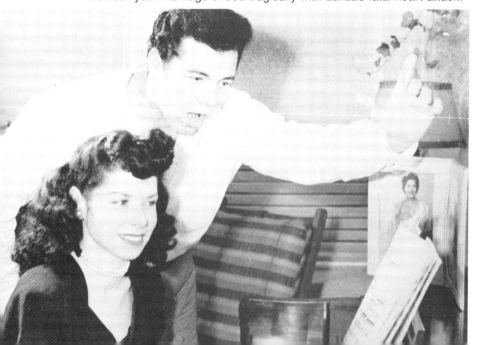

—photo courtesy Marshalltown Times-Republican

Jean Seberg wed French lawyer Francois Moreuil in her home town of Marshalltown, Iowa, in 1958.

Rex Harrison and Kay Kendall during the filming of *The Reluctant Debutante,* 1958.

Audrey Hepburn and Mel Ferrer were man and wife when they appeared together in *War and Peace,* 1956.

Left. Elizabeth Taylor and Eddie Fisher in a scene from *Butterfield 8,* 1960. They were married in 1959 after Fisher's divorce from Debbie Reynolds. *Right.* Dick Powell and June Allyson—their last photograph together before Powell died of cancer in 1963.

Her Royal Highness Princess Grace (Kelly) and Prince Rainier with their three children—Princess Caroline, infant Princess Stephanie, and Prince Albert, 1965.

Janet Leigh with daughters Jamie Lee Curtis and Kelly Lee Curtis on the set of *Three on a Couch,* 1965.

Three generations of Fondas—Peter Fonda, his father Henry Fonda, and Peter's son Justin in 1977.

—photo courtesy Michael Caine

Michael Caine with his oldest daughter Dominique in London.

Wedding Day—Jack Lemmon and Felicia Farr in Paris, 1962.

—photo courtesy The Museum of Modern Art/Film Stills Archive, New York.

Cary Grant with his first wife Virginia Cherrill. Their marriage lasted only thirteen months.

Actress Louise Brooks and director Eddie Sutherland were married in 1926.

—photo courtesy The Museum of Modern Art/Film Stills Archive, New York.

Betty Grable with her two daughters Victoria and Jessica.
—photo courtesy The Museum of Modern Art/Film Stills Archive, New York.

Judy Garland with her first child Liza May Minnelli.

JACKSON, Anne
(1926-   )

On March 5, 1948, Jackson married actor *Eli WALLACH*. The couple has three children: *Peter*, born February 20, 1951; *Roberta*, born in 1955; and *Katherine*, born July 13, 1958.

JACKSON, Glenda
(1936-   )

Jackson married *Roy Hodges*, who became the owner of an art gallery, at St. Marylebone registry office in London on August 2, 1958. In February 1969, their son, *Daniel*, was born in London. The Hodges were divorced in 1975.

JOHNS, Glynis
(1923-   )

In 1942, Johns married actor *Anthony Forwood*. Their son, *Gareth*, born in 1946, became an actor. The marriage ended in divorce in 1948. On February 2, 1952, the actress wed businessman *David Ramsey Foster* in New York City. Four years later, on May 17, 1956, Johns received a divorce from Foster in London. She married businessman *Cecil Peter Lamont Henderson* in London on October 10, 1960. The couple separated less than a year later, and Henderson divorced her in London on June 21, 1962, charging adultery. She wed novelist and screenwriter *Elliott Arnold* on October 1, 1964, in West Los Angeles. Divorced from Arnold since 1973, the actress has not remarried.

JOHNSON, Van
(1916-   )

On January 25, 1947, Johnson married *Eve Abbott Wynn*, just four hours after she had divorced comedian *Keenan WYNN*, Johnson's best friend. The couple was married in Juarez, Mexico. Their daughter, *Schuyler*, was born in 1948. Separated in 1964, the Johnsons were divorced in 1968. The actor has not re-married.

JOLSON, Al
(1886-1950)

In 1906, the entertainer married *Henrietta Keller*, daughter of a sea captain, in Oakland, California. She filed for divorce in Los Angeles on June 26, 1919, blaming wine, women, and racehorses for the break up of their marriage. The divorce was granted in July 1919. In August 1922, he married *Alma Osborne*, an actress known professionally as *Ethel Delmar*. She received a divorce in Paris in August 1926. Jolson wed a nineteen-year-old tap dancer named *Ruby KEELER* on September 21, 1928, in Port Chester, New York. The Jolsons adopted a seven-week-old son, *Al Jolson, Jr.*, on May 7, 1935, in Chicago. Keeler received a divorce in Los Angeles on December 28, 1940, charging Jolson with cruelty. She was given custody of their son. Jolson married *Erle Galbraith*, a film extra, on March 24, 1945, in Quartsite, Arizona. The Jolsons adopted two children: *Asa, Jr.* (Jolson's real name was *Asa Yoelson*) in 1948, and a daughter, *Alicia*, in 1949. The marriage ended in Jolson's death from a heart attack on October 23, 1950, in San Francisco. He was sixty-four.

JONES, Allan
(1908-   )

The singer-actor married *Marjorie Buel* in Asbury Park, New Jersey, on April 27, 1929. A son, *Theodore*, was born in 1930. Buel received a Reno divorce on the grounds of cruelty on July 25, 1936. The next day, July 26, 1936, Jones married film actress *Irene Hervey* in her Beverly Hills home. Their son, *John Allan* (singer *Jack Jones*), was born on January 14, 1938. Hervey obtained a divorce in Los Angeles in 1954, after eighteen years of marriage. The couple was reconciled, and the divorce never became final. But on December 27, 1954, Hervey obtained a second divorce in Las Vegas, charging Jones with cruelty. Jones wed *Mary Florsheim Pickering*, heiress to the Florsheim shoe fortune, early in 1958. They were divorced in 1964. Since 1967, Jones has been married to dancer *Esther Maria Villavincio*. His son, Jack Jones, married and divorced actress *Jill ST. JOHN*.

JONES, Jennifer
(1919-)

On January 2, 1939, exactly thirteen weeks after their first meeting, Jones, known at this time as *Phyllis Isley*, married actor *Robert WALKER* in New York City. The couple had two sons, both of whom became actors. *Robert Walker, Jr.* was born on April 15, 1940, and *Michael Walker* was born on March 13, 1941. Both of their sons were born in New York City. Soon after the Walkers arrived in Hollywood, Jones was signed to a long-term contract by producer *David O. Selznick*, who changed her name to Jennifer Jones. Selznick and Jones became romantically linked while Robert Walker's success in Hollywood at this time was moderate. On June 20, 1945, Jones divorced Walker in Los Angeles on the grounds of mental cruelty. Selznick received a divorce from his wife, *Irene Mayer*, the daughter of *Louis B. Mayer*. Jones and Selznick were married off the coast of Genoa, Italy, on July 13, 1949. Their twenty-five years of marriage ended in Selznick's death on June 22, 1965, at the age of sixty-three in Los Angeles following a coronary occlusion. Jones married industrialist *Norton Simon* on May 30, 1971, aboard a yacht off the coast of England.

JONES, Shirley
(1934-)

Jones married musical comedy singer *Jack Cassidy* in Cambridge, Massachusetts, on August 5, 1956. Cassidy had a son, pop singer *David Cassidy*, from a former marriage to actress *Evelyn Wood*, which ended in divorce. Actor *Shaun Paul Cassidy* was born on September 27, 1958. *Patrick Cassidy* was born January 4, 1962, followed by *Ryan Cassidy*, born on February 23, 1966. After eighteen years of marriage, Jones filed for divorce in Los Angeles on November 29, 1974. The decree was granted early in 1975. Jack Cassidy died in a fire the following year. Since November 13, 1977, Jones has been married to actor *Marty Ingels*.

JOURDAN, Louis
(1919-   )

On March 11, 1946, the French-born actor married *Berthe Frédérique*. She had worked with him in underground activities against the Nazis. They had one son, *Louis Henry Jourdan, Jr.*, born on October 6, 1951. He died from a drug overdose in 1981.

JOY, Leatrice
(1896-1985)

In 1921, Joy married *John GILBERT* in Tijuana, Mexico. They were remarried on March 3, 1922, in the Los Angeles home of *Judge A.R. Summerfield*. On August 19, 1924, Joy sued Gilbert for divorce in Los Angeles, charging Gilbert with intemperence, cruelty, and ill temper. Their daughter, *Leatrice Joy II*, was born on September 6, 1924. The divorce decree was granted on May 29, 1925, and became final in June 1926. The actress married Los Angeles businessman *William S. Hook* in Del Monte, California, on October 22, 1931. Separated from Hook in 1943, they were divorced in 1944. She married electrical engineer *Arthur K. Westermark* in Mexico City on March 5, 1945. Westermark received a divorce in Los Angeles on October 21, 1954, on the grounds of desertion after a four-year separation. Joy never remarried.

JOYCE, Alice
(1890-1955)

On May 11, 1914, the actress married film star *Tom MOORE* in Jacksonville, Florida. Their daughter, *Alice Joyce Moore*, was born in 1916. The marriage ended in divorce in 1920. That same year, on March 6, 1920, Joyce married *James B. Regan, Jr.*, the son of a Manhatten hotelier, at Holy Innocents Church in New York City. Their daughter, *Margaret*, was born on October 28, 1921. Joyce divorced Regan in Reno late in 1932. On March 31, 1933, she wed director *Clarence Brown* in Virginia City, Nevada. The couple was divorced on October 2, 1945. She never remarried.

JUDGE, Arline
(1912-1974)

The actress was married and divorced seven times. On October 15, 1931, she wed film director *Wesley Ruggles* at his Hollywood home. The director was the brother of actor *Charles RUGGLES*. Their son, *Wesley, Jr.*, was born in 1933. Judge divorced Ruggles in Reno on April 9, 1937. That afternoon, she married *Daniel Reid Topping*, heir to a tin plate fortune, in Virginia City, Nevada. Their son, *Daniel, Jr.*, was born in January 1938. Three years later, on May 3, 1940, Judge received a divorce from Topping in her hometown of Bridgeport, Connecticut, charging her husband with cruelty. Two days later, she wed New York hotel executive *James McKinley Bryant* in Kentucky. Later divorced, she wed *Capt. James Ramage Addams* on October 7, 1942, in Montecito, California. Addams was called on duty eight days later. Judge received a divorce in Chicago on July 24, 1945, charging that Addams had deserted her eight days after their marriage. A few days later, on August 3, 1945, the actress married Chicago advertising executive *Vincent Morgan Ryan* in Las Vegas. After divorcing Ryan, she wed *Henry J. (Bob) Topping* on April 29, 1947, at the Miami Beach home of a friend, *John Paul Riddle*. Topping, who later married *Lana TURNER*, was Judge's former brother-in-law. After her sixth divorce, she married New York City insurance executive *George Ross* in Fort Lee, New Jersey, on January 18, 1949. Divorced from Ross, she married inventor *Edward T. Heard* in 1955. On November 2, 1960, the actress received a divorce in Santa Monica, after testifying that he "left me last [January] and said divorce was our only answer." She never remarried.

KARLOFF, Boris
(1887-1969)

Karloff married dancer *Helen Vivian Soule* in 1923. The marriage ended in divorce in 1928. He married librarian *Dorothy (Dot) Stine* in 1930. A daughter, *Sara Jane*, was born in 1938. Karloff was granted an uncontested divorce in Las Vegas on April 9, 1946, on the grounds of mental cruelty. Stine was given custody of Sara Jane. Two days later, on April 11, 1946, he wed *Evelyn Hope Helmore*, a former story assistant to *David O. Selznick*, in Boulder City, Nevada. Their twenty-two years of marriage ended in the actor's death, at age eighty-one, on February 3, 1969 in London.

KAYE, Danny
(1913-1987)

The comedian married *Sylvia Fine* in Fort Lauderdale, Florida, on January 3, 1940. Their only child, *Dena*, was born in New York City on December 17, 1946. Sylvia Fine Kaye wrote much of her husband's material and songs. The couple had been married forty-seven years when Kaye died, at age seventy-four, in Los Angeles on March 3, 1987.

KEATON, Buster
(1895-1966)

Keaton and script girl *Natalie Talmadge* were married on May 31, 1921, at the Bayside, Long Island, home of her sister, screen star *Norma TALMADGE*. *Anita Loos* and actor *Ward Crane* attended the couple. The Keatons had two sons: *James*, born in June 1922, and *Robert* born in February 1924. Natalie Talmadge Keaton received an interlocutory decree of divorce in Los Angeles on August 9, 1932, on the grounds of mental cruelty. The decree would not become final for another year, but Keaton married *Mae Scribbins* in Ensenada, Mexico, on January 8, 1933. The couple was remarried in Ventura, California, on October 17, 1933. Scribbins obtained a divorce in Los Angeles on the grounds of cruelty on October 14, 1936. Keaton married dancer *Eleanor Norris* in the Los Angeles courthouse on May 29, 1940. This marriage was Keaton's happiest, ending only in his death from cancer at the age of seventy at their Woodland Hills, California home on February 1, 1966.

KEATON, Michael
(1951-)

Keaton married actress *Caroline MacWilliams* in 1982. Their son, *Sean*, was born in 1983. The couple separated in December 1988, but they were reunited in August 1989. They filed for divorce in April 1990.

KEEL, Howard
(1917-)

Keel married actress *Rosemary Cooper* in 1943. Cooper received a divorce in Las Vegas in October 1948. In January 1949, Keel married dancer *Helen Anderson*. The couple had three children: *Kaija Liane*, born in 1950; *Kristine*, born June 22, 1952; and *Gunnar Lewis*, born June 3, 1956. The marriage ended in divorce in 1970. Since December 21, 1970, the singer-actor has been married to his third wife, *Judith Ann (Judy) Magamoll*, a former airline stewardess. The couple has a daughter, *Leslie Grace*, born on September 1, 1974.

KEELER, Ruby
(1909-)

Keeler was nineteen when she married entertainer *Al JOLSON* in Port Chester, New York, on September 19, 1928. The couple adopted a seven-week-old son, *Al Jolson, Jr.*, in Chicago on May 7, 1935. Keeler obtained a divorce in Los Angeles on December 28, 1940, on the grounds of cruelty. She was given custody of their son. She retired from the screen when she married Pasadena, California, real estate broker *John Homer Lowe* on October 29, 1941, at St. Charles Catholic Church in North Hollywood. The Lowes had four children: *Kathleen,* born in 1943; *Christine,* born in 1945; *John, Jr.,* born in 1946; and *Theresa,* born in 1948. Their twenty-eight years of marriage ended in Lowe's death from a heart attack in February 1969.

KELLERMAN, Annette
(1888-1975)

In 1912, the Australian-born swimmer and actress married her manager, *James R. Sullivan,* secretly in Danbury, Connecticut. Their sixty-three years of marriage ended in Kellerman's death, at age eighty-two, in Southport, Australia, on October 30, 1975.

KELLERMAN, Sally
(1938-)

Kellerman married television director *Richard (Rick) Edelstein* on December 19, 1970. The marriage ended in divorce in 1971. Since 1980, she has been married to *Jonathan Krane.*

KELLY, Gene
(1912-)

Kelly married actress *Betsy Blair* on September 22, 1941. A daughter, *Kerry,* was born on October 16, 1942. Blair received a divorce in Las Vegas on April 3, 1957, charging mental cruelty. Kelly wed dancer and choreographer *Jeanne Coyne* on August 6, 1960. The couple had a son, *Timothy,* born March 3, 1962, and a daughter, *Bridget,* born June 10, 1964. Jeanne Coyne Kelly died of leukemia in Los Angeles on May 10, 1973. Seventeen years later, on July 24, 1990, Kelly wed *Patricia Ward,* his girlfriend of five years, in Santa Barbara, California.

KELLY, Grace
(1928-1982)

Her marriage to *Prince Rainier III* of the House of Grimaldi took place on April 18, 1956, when they were wed in the throne room of the royal palace in Monte Carlo. She became *Princess Grace* the following day when they were remarried according to the rites of the Roman Catholic Church in the Cathedral of Monaco. *Princess Caroline Louise Marguerite* was born on January 23, 1957, and *Prince Albert Alexandre Louis Pierre* was born fourteen months later, on March 14, 1958. *Princess Stephanie Marie Elisabeth* followed on February 1, 1965. On September 13, 1982, the car Princess Grace and Stephanie were traveling in plunged off a mountain road near Monte Carlo. Stephanie was treated for bruises and shock, but the following day, September 14, 1982, Grace died as a result of her injuries at the age of fifty-four. Her story has been called "The Last Fairy Tale."

KELLY, Nancy
(1921-   )

Kelly eloped to Yuma, Arizona, with actor *Edmond O'BRIEN* on February 19, 1941. Separated only a few months later, the actress received a divorce in Los Angeles on February 2, 1942. She married cameraman *Fred Jackman, Jr.*, on Valentine's Day, 1946 in Las Vegas. Kelly received an interlocutory divorce decree in Los Angeles on January 13, 1950. The decree became final on February 2, 1951. On November 26, 1955, the actress married *Warren Caro*, an executive with the New York Theatre Guild, aboard the SS *Ocean Monarch* in New York harbor. A daughter, *Kelly*, was born in New York City on January 7, 1957. Divorced from Caro in 1968, Kelly has not remarried.

KENDALL, Kay
(1926-1959)

The actress became the third wife of *Rex HARRISON* on June 22, 1957, at the Universalist Church of the Divine Paternity in

New York City. Two years later, on September 6, 1959, Kendall died of leukemia in London. She was thirty-three.

KENNEDY, Madge
(1892-1987)

On September 30, 1916, Kennedy married *Harold Bolster*, business manager of the American Vitagraph Company of America. She was widowed on August 3, 1927. Kennedy and *William B. Hanley* were married in Kingman, Arizona, on August 13, 1934. Hanley was a former Broadway actor and had been Kennedy's leading man. He became dramatic director of NBC radio. The Hanleys were married for twenty-five years until his death, at age fifty-nine, on October 2, 1959, in Los Angeles. Kennedy never remarried.

KENYON, Doris
(1897-1979)

The actress married film star *Milton SILLS* by the shores of Lake Silver at Ausable Forks, New York, on October 12, 1926. Their son, *Kenyon Clarence Sills*, was born in 1927. Less than four years later, on September 15, 1930, Sills died suddenly from a heart attack at the age of forty-eight while playing tennis at their Santa Monica home. Kenyon was remarried on June 14, 1933, to Syracuse, New York, real estate broker *Arthur E. Hopkins*. The wedding was held in the garden of her Brentwood home. The couple separated less than two months later, and the union was annulled early in 1934. In November 1938, Kenyon wed advertising agency executive *Albert D. Lasker*. Separated from Lasker only four months later, the actress received a Nevada divorce in June 1939. On January 28, 1947, Kenyon married *Bronislaw Mlynarski* a Polish composer and conductor (and brother-in-law of *Arthur Rubenstein*). The couple was married at the Second Presbyterian Church in New York City. The marriage lasted twenty-four years until Mlynarski's death in 1971. Her son Kenyon, a geologist, died that same year.

KERR, Deborah
(1921-   )

On November 28, 1945, Kerr wed *Anthony C. Bartley*, son of *Sir Charles and Lady Bartley*, and an air force squadron leader. The wedding took place at St. George's Church, in Hanover Square, London, and a reception at Claridge's followed. The couple had two daughters: *Melanie Jane*, born December 27, 1947, and *Francesca Ann*, born December 18, 1951. Both of their daughters were born in Los Angeles. The marriage ended in divorce in Los Angeles on July 19, 1960. Four days later, on July 23, 1960, Kerr married novelist *Peter Viertel*. The couple resides in Switzerland.

KEYES, Evelyn
(1919-   )

In 1938, Keyes eloped to Nevada with *Barton Leon Bainbridge*, an architect and owner of a swimming pool construction corporation. The couple separated in May 1940, and Bainbridge killed himself in his car in Los Angeles on July 20, 1940. On March 3, 1943, Keyes married film director *Charles Vidor* at his Bel-Air home. The couple separated in November 1944, and they were divorced in 1945. She married *John HUSTON* in Las Vegas on July 23, 1946. The couple adopted a Mexican son, *Pablo Alberran*, in 1948. Huston received a divorce in Juarez, Mexico, on February 10, 1950. He remarried the next day. Keyes became the eighth wife of bandleader *Artie Shaw* in Spain in 1956. Shaw was divorced from actresses *Lana TURNER* and *Ava GARDNER*. The couple was separated many years before their divorce in the early eighties.

KINGSLEY, Ben
(1943-   )

In 1966, Kingsley wed actress *Angela Morant*. The couple had a son, *Thomas*, and a daughter, *Jasmin*, but were divorced after six years of marriage. Since July 1, 1978, Kingsley has been married to British theatrical director *Alison Macaulay Sutcliffe*.

Their son, *Edmund*, born in July 1982, is named after the British stage actor Edmund Kean, whom Kingsley once portrayed on stage.

KINSKI, Nastassja
(1961-)

The daughter of Polish-born actor *Klaus Kinski*, the actress married Egyptian talent agent, film producer, and jeweler *Ibrahim Moussa* on September 12, 1984. At the time of their marriage, the couple had a son, *Aljosha*, born in July 1984. Their daughter, *Sonia*, was born in 1986.

KITT, Eartha
(1928-)

The singer-actress married *William O. MacDonald* in June 1960. The couple had one daughter, *Kitt*, born in 1961. Divorced in 1965, she has not remarried.

KLINE, Kevin
(1947-)

Kline married actress and model *Phoebe CATES* in New York City on March 5, 1989.

LADD, Alan
(1913-1964)

In October 1936, early in his career, Ladd married *Marjorie (Midge) Jane Harrold* in Los Angeles. Their son, producer and studio executive *Alan Ladd, Jr.*, was born in Los Angeles on October 22, 1937. Ladd and Harrold were divorced in 1941, shortly after he met actress-turned-agent *Sue CAROL*. They were married in Mexico on March 15, 1942. A daughter, child actress *Alana Ladd*, was born on April 21, 1943. Their son, actor *David Ladd*, was born on February 5, 1947. Both children were born in Los Angeles. Their marriage ended in Ladd's death from a heart attack in their Palm Springs home on January 29, 1964, at the age of fifty.

LAHR, Bert
(1895-1967)

The actor married his vaudeville partner, *Mercedes Delpino*, in Hoboken, New Jersey, in August 1929. Their son, *Herbert*, was born later that same year. His marriage to Delpino was annulled in White Plains, New York, on February 8, 1940. Lahr stated that soon after the birth of their son Delpino's mental condition had "become very poor." Three days later, on February 11, 1940, Lahr wed dancer *Mildred Schroeder* in a hotel lobby in Elkton, Maryland. The couple had a son, writer *John Lahr*, born July 12, 1941, and a daughter, *Jane*, born September 2, 1943. The Lahrs were married thirty-seven years until the actor's death, at age seventy-two, on December 4, 1967, in New York City. John Lahr published a biography of his father in 1975.

LAKE, Veronica
(1919-1973)

Lake married art director *John Detlie* in Santa Ana, California, on September 27, 1941. Their daughter, *Elaine*, was born on August 21, 1942, in Los Angeles. Lake divorced Detlie in Los Angeles in October 1943. On December 17, 1944, she wed director *André DeToth* at the Los Angeles home of friends, *Mr. and Mrs. Ed Gardner*. The couple had a son, *Michael*, born October 25, 1945, and a daughter, *Diana* born October 16, 1948. Both children were born in Los Angeles. Lake was granted a divorce in Los Angeles on June 2, 1952, on the grounds of cruelty. They were given joint custody of the children. She married music publisher *Joseph McCarthy* on August 28, 1955, at the First Congregational Church in Traverse City, Michigan. The marriage ended in divorce in 1960. In June 1972, Lake wed British sea captain *Robert Carlton-Monroe*. The couple was in the process of getting a divorce when, on July 7, 1973, the actress died of hepatitis in Burlington, Vermont. She was fifty-three.

LA MARR, Barbara
(1896-1926)

In 1914, the actress, then known as *Reatha Watson*, married a ranch hand, *Jack Lytell*, while visiting friends in Yuma, Arizona. Lytell died of pneumonia only months later. She wed Los Angeles lawyer *Lawrence Converse* in June 1914. Converse, however, was already a married man with three children. He was arrested on charges of bigamy, but died three days after their marriage, during an operation for a blood clot on the brain. In 1916, La Marr wed dancer *Phil Ainsworth*. Separated after seven weeks, the union ended in divorce in 1917. In 1918, the actress married for the fourth time. She wed vaudeville comedian *Ben Deely* The couple separated in April 1921, and later divorced. On February 16, 1923, La Marr adopted an infant son, *Marvin Carville La Marr*, from Hope Cottage in Dallas, Texas. In May of that year, she wed serial player *Jack Daugherty*. The couple was separated, and Daugherty had filed for divorce when, on January 30, 1926, La Marr died of a nervous condition in Altadena, California, at the age of twenty-nine. After her death, her son was adopted by actress *ZaSu PITTS* and her husband, *Thomas Gallery* who renamed him *Donald Michael Gallery*.

LAMARR, Hedy
(1913-)

On August 10, 1933, Lamarr wed *Fritz Mandl*, an Austrian munitions manufacturer, in the Church of St. Karl's in her native Vienna. In 1937, she fled from Mandl and went to Paris, where she divorced him on the grounds of desertion. She came to the United States in 1938. On March 4, 1939, she married screenwriter *Gene Markey*. Markey was divorced from *Joan BENNETT* and would later marry *Myrna LOY*. Lamarr and Markey were married in the Governor's Palace in Mexicali, Mexico. Fourteen months later, on September 27, 1940, Lamarr was granted a divorce in Los Angeles on the grounds of cruelty. The court advised her that next time she should spend longer than four weeks getting acquainted before she married. She adopted an infant son, after the child's mother died, on November 4, 1941. He was named *James Lamarr Markey*. On May 27, 1943, Lamarr and actor *John Loder* were married at the Beverly Hills home of a friend, *Mrs. Lily Veidt*. The couple had a daughter, *Denise*, born May 29, 1945, and a son, *Anthony*, born March 1, 1947. Both of their children were born in Los Angeles. Lamarr was granted an interlocutory divorce decree in Los Angeles on July 17, 1947. She was given custody of their children. On June 12, 1951, she married *Ernest (Ted) Stauffer*, a nightclub owner, at the West Los Angeles home of *Judge Stanley Mosk*. Less than a year later, on March 17, 1952, she obtained an interlocutory divorce decree in Los Angeles on the testimony that Stauffer had struck her several times without reason. The decree became final on March 23, 1953. Lamarr and Texas oilman *Howard Lee* were married in the Queens County courthouse in New York City on December 22, 1953. Her fifth marriage ended in divorce in Houston, Texas, on April 15, 1959. Lee later married *Gene TIERNEY*. On March 5, 1963, the actress and Los Angeles attorney Lewis W. Boies, Jr., were married in Fresno, California. Lamarr was divorced for the sixth, and last, time in Los Angeles on June 2, 1965.

LAMAS, Fernando
(1915-1982)

In 1940, Lamas married Argentine actress *Pearla Mux* in his native Buenos Aires. The brief marriage ended in divorce. The actor married Uruguayan heiress *Lydia Babachi* in Mexico in 1946. Their daughter, *Alexandra*, was born in 1947. The marriage ended in divorce in 1952, soon after Lamas began his Hollywood career. He married *Arlene DAHL* in 1954. Their son, actor *Lorenzo Lamas*, was born January 20, 1958. Dahl received a divorce in Santa Monica in August 1960, on the grounds of mental cruelty. In 1967, Lamas wed actress-swimmer *Esther WILLIAMS* in Europe. They were remarried on December 31, 1969, at the Founder's Church of Religious Science near Hollywood. The marriage ended in his death from cancer, at age sixty-seven, on October 8, 1982, in Los Angeles.

LAMOUR, Dorothy
(1914-   )

The actress married bandleader *Herbie Kaye* on May 10, 1935, in Waukegan, Illinois. Kaye received a divorce in Chicago on May 1, 1939, on the grounds of desertion. On April 7, 1943, Lamour wed *Capt. William Ross Howard III*, of a prominent Baltimore family, in Beverly Hills. They adopted a son, *Ridgely*, in 1945. Their second son, *Richard*, was born on October 20, 1949. The couple was married thirty-four years until Howard's death on February 15, 1978, at the age of seventy.

LANCASTER, Burt
(1913-   )

In 1935, Lancaster was briefly married to acrobat *June Ernst*. They were quickly divorced. He wed *Norma Anderson*, a stenographer and war widow, on December 28, 1946. At the time of their marriage, Anderson had a son, *James Stephen*, born in July

1946. The couple had four children together: *William Henry*, born in November 1947; *Susan Elizabeth*, born in July 1949; *Joanna*, born in July 1951; and *Sighle*, born in July 1954. Anderson divorced Lancaster in Santa Monica on the grounds of mental cruelty in July 1969, after twenty-two years of marraige. Lancaster did not remarry until September 10, 1990, when he wed film coordinator *Susie Scherer* in Los Angeles.

LANCHESTER, Elsa
(1902-1986)

Lanchester met actor *Charles LAUGHTON* while co-starring with him on the London stage. They were married on February 10, 1929. The marriage ended in Laughton's death from cancer in Los Angeles on December 16, 1962. He was sixty-three.

LANDI, Elissa
(1904-1948)

Landi wed attorney *John Cecil Lawrence* in London in 1928. The actress-writer divorced her husband in California on May 9, 1936, on account of his "unconventional views of marriage." She married author *Curtiss Kinney Thomas* on August 28, 1943, at Christ Church in New York City. Their daughter, *Caroline Maude*, was born on December 11, 1944. The marriage ended in Landi's death from cancer, at age forty-three, in a Kingston, New York, hospital on October 21, 1948.

LANDIS, Carole
(1919-1948)

At fifteen, in 1934, Landis married writer *Irving Wheeler*, while living with her family in San Bernadino, California. The couple separated after three weeks of marriage, but they were not divorced until May 1940. That same year, on July 4, 1940, Landis and yacht broker *Willis Hunt, Jr.,* were married in Nevada. Six months later, on November 12, 1940, Landis divorced Hunt in Los Angeles, saying that Hunt was "abusive and sullen." *Capt. Thomas C. Wallace,* a navy flier, and Landis were married at the Church of the Assumption in London on January 5, 1943. Landis did not disclose her reasons for divorcing Wallace in Las Vegas on July 19, 1945. Later that same year, on December 8, 1945, she married Broadway producer *Horace Schmidlapp* at the Carlton House Hotel in New York City. The couple was separated when Landis was found dead in her Los Angeles home, a suicide, on July 5, 1948. She was twenty-nine.

LANGDON, Harry
(1884-1944)

The comedian married *Rose Frances Mensolf,* who used the professional name *Rose Francis* on the vaudeville stage, in 1903. Mensolf received a divorce in 1928, which became final in 1929. That same year, Langdon married actress *Helen Walton.* They were divorced in 1932. On February 12, 1934, Langdon married *Mabel Georgena Sheldon.* The couple had a son, *Harry, Jr.,* born December 16, 1934, and a daughter, *Virginia.* The Langdons were divorced, remarried, divorced, and remarried for the last time in 1938. The marriage ended in the comedian's death from a cerebral hemorrhage, at age sixty, on December 22, 1944, in Los Angeles.

LANGE, Jessica
(1950-)

While studying fine arts at the University of Minnesota, she met Spanish-born photographer *Paco Grande,* whom she married in 1970. They were divorced in 1982. The actress has a daughter, *Alexandra,* born in March 1981, with ballet dancer *Mikhail Baryshnikov.* She also has two children with actor-playwright *Sam Shepherd: Hannah Jane,* born January 11, 1986, in Santa Fe, New Mexico, and *Samuel Walker,* born June 14, 1987, in Virginia.

LANSBURY, Angela
(1925-)

In 1945, the British-born actress married actor *Richard Cromwell*. They were divorced, after less than a year of marriage, in 1946. Since August 12, 1949, Lansbury has been married to agent *Peter Shaw*. The Shaws have two children: *Anthony Peter*, born in 1952, and *Deirdre Angela*, born in 1953.

LANZA, Mario
(1921-1959)

In January 1945, the singer-actor wed *Betty Hicks* in a civil ceremony performed at Beverly Hills City Hall. The couple had two daughters: *Colleen*, born December 9, 1948; and *Ellisa*, born December 3, 1950; and two sons, *Damon Anthony* (named for author *Damon Runyon* whom Lanza admired), born in December 1952; and *Marc*, born on May 19, 1954. Their fourteen years of marriage ended in Lanza's death from a heart attack at the age of thirty-eight in Rome on October 7, 1959. Betty Lanza died the following year.

LAPLANTE, Laura
(1904-)

On November 14, 1926, LaPlante married film director *William A. Seiter* in Los Angeles. The actress divorced Seiter in Riga, Latvia, on April 17, 1934. Two months later, on June 19, 1934, she wed British producer and director *Irving Asher* in Paris. *Jimmy Walker*, the former mayor of New York City, and his wife, actress *Betty Compton*, attended the couple. The Ashers have a daughter, *Jill*, born March 2, 1935, and a son, *Tony*, born in 1939. The couple now lives in Mill Valley, California.

LAROCQUE, Rod
(1896-1969)

Fans thronged the streets and nearly one hundred policemen were needed to control the crowd as *Rod LaRocque* and *Vilma BANKY* were married at the Church of the Good Shepherd in Beverly Hills on June 26, 1927. *Samuel Goldwyn*, who had planned the wedding, gave the bride away, and *Cecil B. DeMille* was best man. Their forty-two years of marriage ended in LaRocque's death following a short illness on October 16, 1969, at their Beverly Hills home.

LAUGHTON, Charles
(1899-1962)

Laughton met actress *Elsa LANCHESTER* when they played opposite each other on the London stage. They were married on February 10, 1929. The marriage ended in Laughton's death from cancer, at age sixty-three, in Los Angeles on December 16, 1962.

LAUREL, Stan
(1890-1965)

In 1916, singer-dancer *Mae Charlotte Dahlberg* became the comedian's common-law wife. They separated in the early twenties. On August 23, 1926, the comedian wed screen actress *Lois Neilson* in Los Angeles. The couple had a daughter, *Lois*, born in 1928, who later married actor *Rand Brooks*. A son, *Stan, Jr.*, was born in 1930 but died a few days later. The Laurels separated in 1933, and Lois Laurel received a divorce in California on September 10, 1935. Meanwhile, in 1934, the comedian had married widower *Virginia Ruth Rogers* in Agua Caliente, Mexico. After the divorce became final, Laurel and Rogers were remarried in Los Angeles on September 28, 1935. The marriage ended in divorce in 1937. Laurel wed Russian singer-dancer *Ivanova Shuvalova* (known professionally as *"Illeana"*) in

Yuma, Arizona, on January 1, 1938. The union ended in divorce in 1940. The comedian wed for the sixth time in 1941, when he remarried Virginia Ruth Rogers. They were divorced for the second time in Yuma, Arizona, on April 30, 1946. Laurel's seventh wife was actress *Ida Raphael*, whom he married in Yuma, Arizona, in May 1946, shortly after his divorce from Rogers. The Laurels were happily married for eighteen years, until his death from a heart attack on February 23, 1965, at their Santa Monica home. He was seventy-four.

LAURIE, Piper
(1932-)

The actress wed drama critic and writer *Joseph N. Morgenstern* on January 21, 1962, at the Long Beach, California, home of her sister, *Mrs. Sherye Wade*. The couple has a daughter, *Anna Grace*, born in 1971.

LAWFORD, Peter
(1923-1984)

On April 24, 1954, the British-born star married socialite *Patricia Kennedy*, the sister of *John F. Kennedy, Robert Kennedy,* and *Edward Kennedy*. The ceremony, held at the Roman Catholic Church of St. Thomas More in New York City, was followed by a reception at the Plaza Hotel. Their son, *Christopher*, was born on March 29, 1955, followed by three daughters: *Sydney Maleia*, born August 25, 1956; *Victoria Frances*, born November 4, 1958; and *Robin Elizabeth*, born July 2, 1961. All of their children were born in Santa Monica. After eleven years of marriage, Patricia Lawford was granted a divorce in Gooding, Idaho, on the grounds of mental cruelty on February 1, 1966. She was given custody of their children. The divorce was the first in the Kennedy family. Five years later, on November 1, 1971, the actor wed *Mary Ann Rowan,* daughter of comedian *Dan Rowan,* in Puerto Vallarta, Mexico. Rowan filed for divorce on June 15, 1973, after a year and a half of marriage. Lawford wed *Deborah Gould* on June 25, 1976. The couple separated a few months later, and they were divorced shortly after. In July 1984, Lawford wed model *Patricia Seaton*. Five months later, on December 24, 1984, Lawford died from a cardiac arrest in Los Angeles at the age of sixty-one.

LAWRENCE, Florence
(1886-1938)

In 1908, Lawrence married actor-director *Harry Salter*, who helped to build her into one of the most popular stars of the WWI era. The marriage ended in divorce in 1914. On May 12, 1921, Lawrence wed automobile salesman *Charles B. Woodring*. They were divorced in 1931. In November 1933, she married *Henry Bolton*. Five months later, Lawrence obtained a divorce from Bolton after testifying that he beat her. Lawrence committed suicide in her Beverly Hills home on December 28, 1938.

LEDERER, Francis
(1906-)

In 1935, the actor was divorced in his native Prague from opera singer *Ada Nejedly*. The couple had been married for eighteen months. He wed actress *MARGO* on October 16, 1937, in Las Vegas. Margo received a divorce in that city on December 21, 1940. On July 10, 1941, Lederer wed Canadian *Marion Irvine* at Immanuel Community Church in Las Vegas. The couple remains married.

LEE, Gypsy Rose
(1914-1970)

Lee, who is the older sister of actress *June HAVOC*, married New York manufacturer *Arnold Robert Mizzy* at sea on August 13, 1937. The couple was remarried three days later, on August 16, 1937, in Santa Ana, California. Lee filed for divorce in Chicago on January 27, 1941, charging that Mizzy had knocked her down on two occasions. She wed actor *Alexander Kirkland* on August 31, 1942, at her country home in Highland Mills, New York. The Kirklands were divorced in Reno in October 1944. On December 11, 1944, a son, *Erik,* was born to Lee in New York City. Erik was given the last name Kirkland, and it was not until he was seventeen that he learned the name of his real father— producer *Otto Preminger.* In December 1971, Preminger legally adopted his twenty-six-year-old son, and Erik changed his name to Preminger. He has published a memoir of his mother. Lee and artist *Julio de Diego* were married on March 19, 1948, at the Bronx Marriage License Bureau in New York City. The union ended in divorce on August 8, 1955, in Reno, on the grounds of their having been separated for over a year. She never remarried.

LEE, Lila
(1901 - 1973)

On July 25, 1923, Lee married actor-director *James Kirkwood* in Los Angeles. Their son, who became playwright, novelist, and actor *James Kirkwood, Jr.,* was born in March 1924. Kirkwood divorced Lee in Los Angeles on August 6, 1930, charging her with desertion. He was given custody of their son. They had been separated since 1928. Lee married Chicago stockbroker *John L. Peine* on December 5, 1934, in Harrison, New York. Eight months later, on July 1, 1935, she divorced Peine in Carson City, Nevada, on the grounds of extreme cruelty. In 1945, she wed New York stockbroker *John E. Murphy.* The couple separated a year later and, on September 9, 1949, Lee divorced him in Reno. She never remarried. James Kirkwood, Jr., died in 1989.

LEIGH, Janet
(1927 -   )

At fifteen, in 1942, she eloped to Reno, Nevada, with nineteen-year-old college student *John Kenneth Carlyle.* The union was annulled four months later. On October 5, 1945, she wed *Stanley*

Reames, who was serving in the navy. The marriage ended in divorce in July 1948, shortly after Leigh began her Hollywood career. She married actor *Tony CURTIS* on June 4, 1951, in Greenwich, Connecticut. The couple had two daughters: *Kelly Lee*, born June 17, 1956, and actress *Jamie Lee CURTIS*, born November 21, 1958. Curtis and Leigh were considered Hollywood's ideal couple, but on July 11, 1962, Leigh was granted a divorce in Santa Monica, charging Curtis with extreme cruelty. The decree would not be final for one year, so Leigh obtained a second decree in Juarez, Mexico, on September 14, 1962. The next day, she was married for the fourth time, in Las Vegas, to stockbroker *Robert Brandt*.

LEIGH, Vivien
(1913-1967)

On December 20, 1932, she wed barrister *Herbert Leigh Holman* at St. James's Church in London. The actress derived her professional name from her husband's name. Their daughter, *Suzanne*, was born in London in 1934. During the filming of *Fire Over England* (1937), Leigh met and fell in love with her costar, *Laurence OLIVIER*. His wife, *Jill Esmond*, divorced him on the grounds of adultery, naming Leigh as co-respondant. In January 1940, Holman filed for divorce in London and eventually won custody of Suzanne. On August 30, 1940, Leigh and Olivier were married at San Ysidro Ranch near Santa Barbara, California, the home of their fellow British actors, *Ronald COLMAN* and *Benita HUME*. Twenty years later, on December 2, 1960, Leigh divorced Olivier in London on the grounds of adultery, naming actress *Joan Plowright* as co-respondant. Leigh never remarried.

LEIGHTON, Margaret
(1922-1976)

In 1947, the British-born actress married publisher *Max Reinhardt*. The marriage ended in divorce on January 28, 1955, in London. In August 1957, she wed actor *Laurence HARVEY*. She sued for divorce in London on November 11, 1960. On July 15, 1964, she married *Michael WILDING* in Los Angeles. The Wildings were married for twelve years until her death after a long illness, at age fifty-three, on January 13, 1976, in Chichester, England.

LEMMON, Jack
(1925-)

He wed actress *Cynthia Boyd Stone* in Peoria, Illinois, on May 7, 1950. A son, *Christopher*, was born in Los Angeles on June 22, 1954. The marriage ended in divorce in 1956. Stone later married actor *Cliff ROBERTSON*. Lemmon married actress *Felicia Farr* in Paris on August 17, 1962. The couple has a daughter, *Courtney*, born on January 7, 1966.

LENNON, John
(1940-1980)

In August 1962, Lennon married art student *Cynthia Powell* in Liverpool, England. Their son, singer (*John*) *Julian Lennon*, was born in Liverpool on April 8, 1963. Powell received a divorce in London on November 8, 1968. On March 20, 1969, Lennon wed Japanese artist *Yoko Ono* in Gibraltar. Their son, *Sean*, was born on October 5, 1975. Their eleven years of marriage ended suddenly when, on the night of December 8, 1980, Lennon was assassinated outside their New York City apartment house.

LENZ, Kay
(1953-)

The actress married singer *David CASSIDY*, the step-son of *Shirley JONES*, in Las Vegas on April 3, 1977. Divorced from Cassidy in 1981, Lenz has not remarried.

LESLIE, Joan
(1925-   )

She wed *Dr. William Caldwell* on St. Patrick's Day, March 17, 1950, in Santa Barbara. Identical twin daughters, *Patrice* and *Ellen*, were born on January 5, 1951. The Caldwells live in the Las Feliz area of Los Angeles.

LEWIS, Jerry
(1926-   )

Lewis eloped to New York City on October 3, 1944, with singer *Patti Palmer*. Their oldest son, *Gary*, was born in 1945. The couple also adopted five sons: *Ronald, Scott, Christopher, Anthony*, and *Joseph*.

LINDFORS, Viveca
(1920-   )

In January 1943, the actress married lawyer *Folke Rogard* in her native Sweden. A son, *Jan*, was born that same year, and a daughter, *Lena*, was born in 1944. She was divorced from Rogard in 1949. Later that year, on August 10, 1949, Lindfors married film director *Donald Siegel* in Paris. Their son, *Christopher*, was born in Los Angeles in September 1952. Siegel received a divorce in Los Angeles on April 29, 1953, after testifying that Lindfors had told him that she was in love with another man. Since July 4, 1954, Lindfors has been married to Hungarian-born novelist *George Tabori*.

LITHGOW, John
(1945-   )

The actor married schoolteacher *Jean Taynton* on September 10, 1966. Their son, *Ian*, was born in 1972. The marriage ended in divorce in 1976. Since 1981, Lithgow has been married to history professor *Mary Yeager*. The couple has a daughter, *Phoebe*, born in 1982, and a son, *Nathan George*, born September 13, 1983.

LLOYD, Harold
(1893 - 1971)

On February 10, 1923, the comedian wed his leading lady, *Mildred DAVIS*, at St. John's Episcopal Church in Los Angeles. Their first daughter, *Mildred Gloria*, was born in May 1924. In the fall of 1930, they adopted four-year-old *Gloria Freeman* from a foundling home in Pasadena, California. She was renamed *Marjorie Elizabeth* and nicknamed "Peggy". A third child, singer and actor *Harold Clayton Lloyd, Jr.*, was born on January 25, 1931. Mildred Davis died of a heart attack, at age sixty-nine, on August 18, 1969, in Santa Monica, after forty-six years of marriage. Their son died in 1971.

LOGAN, Jacqueline
(1901 - 1983)

On June 3, 1925, the silent screen actress wed Los Angeles realty dealer *Robert Gillespie*. Logan received a divorce in Los Angeles on March 22, 1928, charging cruelty. She then married stockbroker *William Lawrence Winston* in Agua Caliente, Mexico. After the wedding, Logan learned that should she return to Los Angeles as Winston's wife she would be arrested on charges of bigamy because her divorce from Gillespie would not be final until March 1929. Logan announced that she and her husband would separate until they could be legally married. They never remarried. In 1934, Logan married an industrialist. Divorced in 1947, she never remarried.

LOLLOBRIGIDIA, Gina
(1927-   )

On January 15, 1949, the actress married Yugoslavian-born physician *Drago Milko Skofic*. Their son, *Andrea Milko*, was born on July 28, 1957. The Skofics were divorced in 1968. On December 19, 1969, Lollobrigidia married realtor *George Kaufman*.

187

LOMBARD, Carole
(1908-1942)

Lombard married *William POWELL* on June 26, 1931, at the Los Angeles home of her mother, *Elizabeth Peters*. Eighteen months later, on August 18, 1933, Lombard received a Reno divorce. Lombard and Powell remained close friends. After a well-publicized three-year courtship, Lombard and *Clark GABLE* were married in Kingman, Arizona, on March 29, 1939. Their marriage ended in Lombard's sudden death in a plane crash near Las Vegas on January 16, 1942.

LONG, Shelley
(1950?-)

In the mid-seventies, the actress was briefly married to a producer of industrial and educational films. The marriage ended in divorce. On October 16, 1981, Long wed stockbroker *Bruce Tyson* on the steps of the city hall in Beverly Hills. The couple was remarried in a religious ceremony in a city park in Santa Monica the following day. Their daughter, *Juliana*, was born on March 27, 1985.

LOREN, Sophia
(1934-)

On September 27, 1957, Loren and her producer, *Carlo Ponti*, were married by proxy in Juarez, Mexico. Now living in France, the couple has two sons: *Carlo, Jr.*, born December 30, 1968, and *Eduardo*, born January 6, 1973. Both of their sons were born in Geneva, Switzerland.

LORRE, Peter
(1904-1964)

In the spring of 1934, the Hungarian-born actor wed actress *Celia Lvovsky* at Westminster registry office in London. Lorre then traveled to the United States to begin his Hollywood career. The union ended in divorce on March 13, 1945. Two months later, he married German actress *Kaaren Verne* on May 25, 1945, in Las Vegas. They were divorced in the United States in 1950. On July 21, 1950, Lorre married *Annemarie Brenning* in Hamburg, Germany. Their daughter, *Catharine*, had been born a month before. The couple separated in October 1962, and the marriage ended in Lorre's death from a stroke on March 23, 1964, in Los Angeles. He was fifty-nine.

LOUISE, Anita
(1915-1970)

She wed actor *Buddy Adler* on May 17, 1940. The couple had two children: *Melanie*, born August 10, 1947, and *Anthony*, born in 1950. Their twenty years of marriage ended in Adler's death from cancer, at age fifty-one, in Los Angeles on July 12, 1960. Louise was remarried on April 21, 1962, to importer *Henry L. Berger*. Eight years later, on April 25, 1970, the actress died from a stroke at the age of fifty-five at their home in Holmby Hills, California.

LOVE, Bessie
(1898-1986)

The silent film star married Beverly Hills stockbroker *William Ballinger Hawks* (the brother of directors *Kenneth Hawks*, who married *Mary ASTOR*, and *Howard Hawks*), on December 27, 1929, at St. John's Episcopal Church in Hollywood. *Blanche Sweet* was matron-of-honor and bridesmaids were *Bebe DANIELS, Carmel MYERS, Edith and Irene Mayer* (the daughters of Louis B. Mayer), *Norma SHEARER*, and Mary Astor. A daughter, *Patricia*, was born in 1932. Divorced from Hawks in 1936, she never remarried.

LOY, Myrna
(1905-)

Loy married producer *Arthur Hornblow, Jr.* in Prado, Mexico, on June 27, 1936. Six years later, on June 1, 1942, Loy received a Reno divorce on the grounds of mental cruelty. Five days later, on June 6, 1942, she married advertising executive *John D. Hertz, Jr.* at the New York City home of his sister. Loy filed for divorce in Cuernavaca, Mexico, on August 21, 1944. Her third husband was screenwriter *Gene Markey* who was divorced from *Joan BENNETT* and *Hedy LAMARR*. Loy and Markey were married, while he was serving in the military, on January 3, 1946, at the chapel on Terminal Island, near San Diego, California. She divorced Markey in Mexico City in August 1950. On June 2, 1951, Loy married *Howland Sargeant*, Deputy Assistant Secretary of State (to Dean Acheson), in Fort Myer, Virginia. On May 31, 1960, following a two-year separation, Loy received a divorce from Sargeant in Juarez, Mexico. She has not remarried.

LUGOSI, Bela
(1882-1956)

On June 25, 1917, the Hungarian-born actor married *Ilona Szmik*, the daughter of a banker, at St. Anne's Church in Budapest. She received a divorce in Budapest in 1922 while Lugosi was pursuing a film career in Germany. It was the first of his five marriages. Later that year, in America, Lugosi wed Viennese actress *Ilona Montagh de Nagybanyhégyes*. They were quickly divorced. In the summer of 1929, Lugosi wed *Beatrice Woodruff*, a widow from San Francisco. This marriage also ended in divorce after only a short time. On January 31, 1933, he wed his secretary, *Lillian Arch*, in Las Vegas. Their son, *Bela, Jr.*, was born on January 5, 1938. Lillian Lugosi was granted a divorce in Los Angeles on July 17, 1953, after twenty years of marriage. She charged cruelty and testified that Lugosi was overly jealous. She later married actor *Brian DONLEVY*. Two years after the divorce, on August 25, 1955, Lugosi married *Hope Lininger* at the Los Angeles home of *Rev. Manuel Hall*. Lininger was a clerk at a film studio who had written the actor many letters when he had been hospitalized. The couple had been married nearly a year when, on August 16, 1956, the actor died in Los Angeles. He was seventy-one.

LUKAS, Paul
(1894-1971)

Lukas wed *Gizella "Daisy" Benes* in his native Hungary on June 4, 1927. Their thirty-five years of marriage ended in her death in 1962. The actor was remarried on November 7, 1963, to *Annette Driesens*. They were searching for a retirement home in Tangier, Morocco, when Lukas died from a heart attack on August 16, 1971, at the age of seventy-six. His cousin, *Edwin J. Lukas*, was married to *Betty FIELD*.

LUPINO, Ida
(1918-   )

The actress, director, and screenwriter is the daughter of British comedian *Stanley Lupino*. She married actor *Louis Hayward* in Los Angeles on November 17, 1938. They were divorced on May 11, 1945. Lupino wed producer and screenwriter *Collier Young* at LaJolla Presbyterian Church in LaJolla, California, on August 5, 1948. Three years later, on October 20, 1951, Lupino divorced Young in Minden, Nevada, on the grounds of mental cruelty. Young later married *Joan FONTAINE*. The day after the divorce was granted, on October 21, 1951, Lupino married her television co-star, actor *Howard Duff*, in Glenbrook, Nevada. Their daughter, *Bridget*, was born in Los Angeles on April 23, 1952. The couple separated in 1972, and they were divorced in Los Angeles in 1984.

LYNN, Diana
(1926-1971)

On December 18, 1948, the actress married architect *John C. Lindsay*. The couple separated in January 1953 and on June 5, 1953, Lynn was granted a divorce in Santa Monica. She wed Los

Angeles radio producer *Mortimer Hall* (divorced from *Ruth RO-MAN*) in Mexico on December 7, 1956. The Halls had four children: *Matthew*, born July 6, 1958; *Dorothy*, born April 26, 1960; *Mary*, born July 2, 1962; and *Margaret*, born August 6, 1964. Their fifteen years of marriage ended on December 18, 1971, when Lynn died of a stroke in Los Angeles at the age of forty-five.

LYON, Ben
(1901-1979)

On June 14, 1930, Ben Lyon and *Bebe DANIELS*, two of the silent screen's most popular stars, were married at a Hollywood hotel. *Louella Parsons* was matron-of-honor and bridesmaids included *Lila LEE, Constance TALMADGE, Betty COMPSON*, and *Adela Rogers Hyland*. The Lyons settled in London, where their daughter, *Barbara*, was born on September 9, 1931. Their adopted son, *Richard*, a child actor, was born in 1937. Their forty-year marriage ended in Daniels' death from a cerebral hemorrhage, at age seventy-two, in London on March 16, 1971. Lyon returned to America where, on April 1, 1972, he married widowed actress *Marian Nixon* at Westwood Methodist Church in Los Angeles. They had first met at the Coconut Grove nightclub in Los Angeles in 1927. Their marriage ended in Lyon's death from a heart attack, at age seventy-eight, on March 22, 1979, aboard the *Queen Elizabeth II* cruise ship. Nixon died in 1983.

LYTELL, Burt
(1885-1954)

The actor's first wife was his leading lady in a traveling stock company, *Evelyn Vaughn*. The couple was married in New Jersey on August 5, 1910. Fourteen years later, on October 20, 1924, Vaughn divorced him in Independence, Missouri. On May 14, 1925, Lytell and film star *Claire WINDSOR* were married in the Presidenca Room of the Juarez, Mexico, city hall. Windsor divorced him in Los Angeles on August 9, 1927, charging cruelty. In 1934, Lytell wed his Broadway co-star, actress *Grace Menken*. Her sister, actress *Helen Menken*, was married to *Humphrey BOGART*. The Lytells were married twenty years, until the actor's death from an illness at the age of sixty-nine in New York City on September 28, 1954.

MCAVOY, May
(1901 - 1984)

The silent film star married *Maurice J. Cleary,* a Los Angeles banker, at the Church of the Good Shepherd in Beverly Hills on June 26, 1929. Their son, *Patrick Garrett Cleary*, was born in 1932. Their forty-two years of marriage ended in Cleary's death in 1972.

MCCAMBRIDGE, Mercedes
(1918-)

In 1939, the actress married writer *William Fifield*. Their son, *John Lawrence*, was born on Christmas Day, 1941. The couple was divorced in 1946. On February 19, 1950, McCambridge married director-producer *Fletcher Markle*, who adopted her son. The actress received a divorce in Los Angeles on June 7, 1962. She has not remarried. Her son committed suicide in 1987.

MCCARTNEY, Paul
(1942-)

McCartney, the last Beatle to get married, wed photographer *Linda Eastman* at Marylebone registry office in London on March 12, 1969. At the time of their marriage, Eastman had a six-year-old daughter, *Heather*, from a former marriage to geologist *Melville See*. The McCartneys have three more children: *Mary*, born August 28, 1969; *Stella*, born September 13, 1971; and *James*, born September 13, 1977.

MCCREA, Joel
(1905 - 1990)

The actor wed film star *Frances DEE* on October 20, 1933, at White Methodist Church in Rye, New York. The couple had three sons: *Joel Dee*, born September 7, 1934; *David*, born November 15, 1936; and *Peter*, born in 1955. McCrea died from lung trouble on their fifty-seventh wedding anniversary, October 20, 1990, in Woodland Hills, California.

MACDONALD, Jeanette
(1901-1965)

Fifteen thousand people lined the streets to catch glimpses of the stars attending the wedding of MacDonald to actor *Gene RAYMOND* on June 16, 1937. The wedding, held at Wilshire Boulevard Church in Los Angeles, has been described as one of the most beautiful Hollywood has ever seen. The Raymonds were married twenty-six years until her death from a heart attack in Houston, Texas, on January 14, 1965, at the age of sixty-three.

MCDOWELL, Malcolm
(1943-   )

On April 21, 1975, McDowell married actress-publicist *Margot Bennett Dullea*, the divorced wife of actor *Keir Dullea*. McDowell and Dullea were divorced in September 1980. A few days later, on September 29, 1980, he married actress *Mary STEENBURGERN* in New York City. Their daughter, *Lilly*, was born in January 1981, and their son, *Charlie*, was born in 1983. Steenburgern filed for divorce on September 11, 1989, and the divorce was granted in 1990.

MCGILLIS, Kelly
(1958-   )

The actress married writer *Royd Black* about 1979. The couple was divorced three years later. After a romance with actor *Barry Tubb*, McGillis wed yacht broker *Fred Tillman* in January 1989.

MACGRAW, Ali
(1938-   )

As a student at Wellesley College, MacGraw was briefly married to a college sweetheart. The marriage ended in divorce. On October 24, 1969, the actress wed Paramount vice-president *Robert Evans* in Palm Springs, California. Their son, *Joshua*, was born on January 16, 1971, in New York City. The marriage ended in divorce on June 7, 1973, in Santa Monica, on the grounds of irreconcilable differences. She was given custody of their son. A month later, on July 12, 1973, she wed film star *Steve MCQUEEN* in a city park in Cheyenne, Wyoming. Divorced in 1978, she has not remarried.

MCGUIRE, Dorothy
(1918-   )

The actress married photographer *John Swope* on July 18, 1943, at the Brentwood home of *Leland Hayward* and *Margaret Sullavan*. The Swopes have two children: *Mary*, born February 14, 1949, and *Mark*, born May 14, 1953. Mary became an actress, using the professional name of *Topo Swope*.

MCLAGLEN, Victor
(1886-1959)

In 1919, the actor married *Enid Lamont*. Their son, film director *Andrew V. McLaglen*, was born on July 28, 1920. Their daughter, *Sheila*, was born in 1921. Both of their children were born in London. The McLaglens were married twenty-three years, until her death, at age forty-three, after a long illness at their home in Flintridge, California, on April 2, 1942. Enid McLaglen had been a well-known equestrienne in Southern California. In November 1943, McLaglen married his secretary, *Suzanne Breuggemann*. The marriage ended in divorce in 1948. Later that year, the actor married *Margaret Pumphrey* of Berkeley, California. Their eleven years of marriage ended in his death from heart failure at their Newport Beach, California home, on November 8, 1959, at the age of seventy-two.

MACLAINE, Shirley
(1934-)

On September 17, 1954, the actress married producer *Steve Parker*. Their daughter, *Stephanie Sachiko*, was born in 1956. After a long separation, the couple was divorced in 1982. Her younger brother, actor-producer *Warren Beatty*, has never married.

MACMAHON, Aline
(1899-)

On March 27, 1928, the actress married architect *Clarence S. Stein* in New York City. Their forty-six years of marriage ended in Stein's death, at age ninety-two, on February 7, 1975, at their Radburn, New Jersey, home.

MACMURRAY, Fred
(1911-)

The actor married dancer *Lillian Lamont* on June 20, 1936, in Las Vegas. In 1942, the MacMurrays adopted a one-year-old daughter, *Susan*. They adopted a one-year-old son, *Robert*, in 1945. The couple was married seventeen years until, on June 22, 1953, Lillian MacMurray died in Santa Monica after a long illness at the age of forty-five. One year later, on June 28, 1954, MacMurray married *June HAVER* in Ojai, California. They adopted twin daughters, *Katie Marie* and *Laurie Anne*, on December 4, 1956. The couple now lives in Brentwood.

MCQUEEN, Steve
(1930-1980)

On November 2, 1956, McQueen and singer-actress *Neile Adams* were married at Mission San Juan Capistrano in Mission Viejo, California. The couple had a daughter, *Terri Leslie*, born June 6, 1959, and a son, *Chadwick Stephen*, born December 28, 1960. The McQueens separated in June 1971. Neile McQueen filed for divorce in Los Angeles on the grounds of irreconcilable differences on September 10, 1971. McQueen and actress *Ali MACGRAW* were married on July 12, 1973, in a city park in Cheyenne, Wyoming. The marriage ended in divorce in 1978. In January 1980, McQueen married model *Barbara Minty*, but later that year, on November 7, 1980, the actor died from a heart attack in Juarez, Mexico. He was fifty.

MACRAE, Gordon
(1921-1986)

MacRae married British-born *Sheila Stephens* on May 21, 1941. The MacRaes had four children: actress *Meredith MacRae*, born in 1944; *Heather*, born in 1946; *Bruce,* born in 1948; and *Garr*, born in 1954. After twenty-five years of marriage, Sheila MacRae received a mutual-consent divorce (and custody of their children) in Juarez, Mexico, on April 15, 1967. Six months later, on September 25, 1967, MacRae wed socialite *Elizabeth Lambert Schrafft* in St. Peter's Lutheran Church in New York City. A daughter, *Amanda,* was born on May 2, 1968. Their eighteen years of marriage ended in MacRae's death from cancer in Lincoln, Nebraska, on January 24, 1986. He was sixty-four.

MADISON, Guy
(1922-   )

On July 31, 1949, the actor married *Gail RUSSELL*. Their marriage ended in divorce in Los Angeles on October 6, 1954. Madison testified that Russell "cared nothing for their home or marriage." He wed *Sheila Connolly* in 1955. The couple had three daughters: *Bridget*, born in 1955; *Erin*, born in 1956; and *Dolly*, born in 1957. They were divorced in 1963.

MAGNANI, Anna
(1908-1973)

In 1935, the actress wed director *Goffredo Alessandrini* in her native Italy. In October 1942, Magnani gave birth to a son, *Luca*, with actor *Massimo Serato*. After a lengthy separation, her marriage to Alessandrini was annulled in 1960. She never remarried.

MAIN, Marjorie
(1890-1975)

The actress married Chautaqua lecturer *Dr. Stanley LeFevre Krebs* on November 2, 1921. Thirteen years later, on September 27, 1935, Dr. Krebs died from cancer in New York City at the age of seventy-one. Main never remarried.

MALDEN, Karl
(1914-)

Malden married actress *Mona Graham* on December 18, 1938. The couple has two daughters: *Mila*, born in 1948, and *Carla*, born in 1953.

MALKOVICH, John
(1953-)

Malkovich married actress *Glenne Headly* on August 1, 1982. The couple was divorced in 1990. The actor has a daughter, *Amandine*, born October 9, 1990, with an Italian actress.

MALONE, Dorothy
(1925-)

On June 28, 1959, Malone wed French actor *Jacques Bergerac* (divorced from *Ginger ROGERS*) in Hong Kong. The couple had two daughters: *Mimi*, born April 3, 1960, and *Diane*, born February 20, 1962. Malone divorced Bergerac on the grounds of mental cruelty on December 8, 1964. In April 1969, Malone married New York businessman *Robert Tomarkin* in Las Vegas. The marriage was annulled four weeks later when Malone claimed that he had married her only for her money and had tried to swindle her out of her savings. Since October 2, 1971, the actress has been married to motel chain executive *Charles Huston Bell* of Dallas.

MANGANO, Silvana
(1930-1989)

On July 17, 1949, Mangano wed Italian-born producer *Dino De Laurentiis*. The couple had four children: *Veronica*, born in 1950; *Rafaella*, born in 1952; *Frederico*, born in 1955; and *Francesca*, born in 1961. Their son, Frederico, was killed in a plane crash in Alaska in 1981 while filming a movie on location. The couple separated in 1983, and the marriage ended with Mangano's death from cancer, at age fifty-nine, in Madrid on December 16, 1989.

MANSFIELD, Jayne
(1933-1967)

She was *Vera Jane Palmer* when, at sixteen, on May 6, 1950, she married college student *Paul Mansfield* in Forth Worth, Texas. Their daughter, *Jayne Marie*, was born in November 1950. The Mansfields moved to Los Angeles where, on January 8, 1958, they were divorced. Five days later, on January 13, 1958, the actress married weightlifter *Mickey Hargitay* at Portuguese Bend, California. A son, *Miklos Hargitay, Jr.*, was born on December

21, 1958. A second son, *Zoltan Anthony*, was born on August 1, 1960. A daughter, *Mariska Magdolna*, was born on January 23, 1964. All of the children were born in Santa Monica. The Hargitays were divorced in Juarez, Mexico, in 1964. That same year, on September 24, 1964, she married film director *Matt Cimber*, who became her manager, in Baja, Mexico. Their son, *Anthony Richard Cimber*, was born in Los Angeles on October 18, 1965. The marriage ended in divorce in 1966.

MARCH, Fredric
(1897-1975)

March wed actress *Florence ELDRIDGE* in Mexico on May 30, 1927. The couple adopted a daughter, *Penelope*, in 1932, and a son, *Anthony*, in 1935. Their forty-seven years of marriage ended in March's death from cancer in Los Angeles on April 14, 1975, at the age of seventy-seven.

MARGO
(1917-1985)

The Mexican-born actress married *Francis LEDERER* on October 16, 1937, in Las Vegas. Three years later, on December 21, 1940, she returned to Las Vegas and was granted a divorce from the actor in a brief hearing. She wed *Eddie ALBERT* on December 5, 1945, at St. Patrick's Cathedral in New York City. Their son, actor *Eddie Albert, Jr.*, was born on February 20, 1951, in Los Angeles. In 1954, the Alberts adopted a four-year-old Spanish orphan, *Maria del Carmen*, in Madrid. The couple was married nearly forty years until Margo's death on July 17, 1985, after a long illness, at their home in Pacific Palisades, California.

MARKEY, Enid
(1896-1981)

On October 15, 1942, the actress married *George W. Cobb, Jr.*, an executive of the American Can Company. Five years later, on

March 14, 1948, Cobb died after a long illness in New York City. He was fifty-one. She never remarried.

MARSH, Mae
(1895-1968)

In 1918, the actress married *Louis Lee Arms*, a publicity man for *Samuel Goldwyn*. A daughter, *Mary Marsh*, was born in September 1919. Their son, *Brewster*, was born on December 18, 1925. A second daughter, *Marguerite*, was born in 1928. She was named for Marsh's older sister, actress *Marguerite Loveridge*, who died in 1925. The couple was married until Marsh's death from a heart attack, at age seventy-two, on February 13, 1968, in Hermosa Beach, California.

MARSHALL, Herbert
(1890-1966)

In 1915, Marshall married actress *Mollie Maitland*. They were divorced in 1928. That same year, on November 26, 1928, he wed actress *Edna Best* in Jersey City, New Jersey. A daughter, *Sarah Best Marshall*, was born on May 25, 1933, in London. Best was granted a divorce in Las Vegas on February 7, 1940, on the grounds of cruelty. She testified that Marshall had deserted her in 1934. She was given custody of their daughter. Nineteen days later, on February 26, 1940, Marshall married actress *Lee Russell* in Las Vegas. The marriage ended in divorce in 1946. He married his fourth wife, actress *Boots Mallory*, on August 3, 1947, at the First Presbyterian Church in Santa Barbara, California. Mallory died at the age of forty-five on December 1, 1958, from a chronic throat ailment in a Santa Monica hospital. Marshall was remarried on April 25, 1960, to department store buyer *Dee Ann Kahmann*. The marriage ended in his death from a heart attack at his Beverly Hills home on January 22, 1966. He was seventy-five.

MARTIN, Dean
(1917-   )

On October 2, 1940, the actor-singer wed *Elizabeth MacDonald* in St. Anne's Church in Cleveland. The Martins had four children: *Craig*, born in 1942; *Claudia*, born in 1944; *Gail*, born in 1945; and *Deana*, born in 1948. Elizabeth Martin was granted a divorce on August 24, 1949. A week later, on September 1, 1949, Martin married model *Jeanne Beiggers* in Beverly Hills. Their son, *Dean, Jr.* (called Dino), was born in 1951. A second son, *Ricci*, was born in 1953, and a daughter, *Gina*, was born in 1956. The marriage ended in divorce in 1972. Martin was married for the third time, to beautician *Catherine Mae Hawn*, on April 24, 1973, at his Bel-Air home. He adopted her daughter, *Sasha*. The stormy union ended in divorce in 1977. Martin has not remarried. His son Dino married actress *Olivia Hussey*.

MARTIN, Mary
(1913-1990)

In 1935, the actress-singer wed lawyer *Bernard Hageman* in her hometown of Weatherford, Texas. Their son, actor *Larry HAGMAN*, was born in Weatherford in September 1936. Martin and Hageman were divorced in 1937. On May 5, 1940, she wed literary agent *Richard Halliday*. Their daughter, *Mary Heller Halliday*, was born in 1941. The couple was married thirty-two years, until his death after surgery at the age of sixty-seven on March 3, 1973, in Brasilia, Brazil. Martin never remarried.

MARTIN, Steve
(1945-   )

The comedian married actress *Victoria Tennant* in Rome on November 20, 1986.

MARTIN, Tony
(1913-)

Martin eloped to Yuma, Arizona, on September 4, 1937, with film star *Alice FAYE*. They separated early in 1940 and on March 22, 1940, Faye was granted a divorce in Los Angeles on the grounds of mental cruelty. On May 9, 1948, Martin married actress-dancer *Cyd CHARISSE*. He adopted her son, *Nicky*, from her former marriage to dance instructor *Nico Charisse*. A second son, *Tony, Jr.*, was born on August 28, 1950. The couple resides in Beverly Hills.

MARVIN, Lee
(1924-1987)

The actor married *Betty Edeling* on February 5, 1952, in Las Vegas. The Marvins had four children: *Christopher*, born in 1952; *Courtenay*, born in 1954; *Cynthia*, born in 1956; and *Claudia*, born in 1958. Separated in 1964, Betty Marvin obtained a divorce in Santa Monica on January 4, 1967, and custody of their children. On October 19, 1970, Marvin married *Pamela Freeley* in Las Vegas. Their sixteen years of marriage ended in the actor's death at the age of sixty-three from a heart attack in Tucson, Arizona, on August 29, 1987.

MARX, Chico
(1886-1961)

Born *Leonard Marx* in New York City, he was the oldest of the Marx Brothers. In 1910, Marx wed dancer *Betty Karp*. Their daughter, *Maxine*, was born in 1911. The couple separated in 1941 and divorced the following year. On August 22, 1958, he wed actress *Mary DeVithas* at the Beverly Hills home of a friend. Three years later, on October 11, 1961, Marx died from a heart ailment at his Los Angeles home at the age of seventy-five.

MARX, Groucho
(1890-1977)

He was born *Julius Henry Marx*, the youngest of the three Marx Brothers. He married dancer *Ruth Johnson* in Chicago on February 4, 1920. The couple had a son, *Arthur*, born July 21, 1921, and a daughter, *Miriam*, born in 1927. The couple separated in December 1941, and Ruth Marx received a divorce in Los Angeles on July 15, 1942. On July 21, 1945, he married *Catherine Marvis Gorcey*, the divorced wife of actor *Leo Gorcey*, at the Los Angeles home of *Arthur Sheekman* and *Gloria Stuart*, who attended the couple. A daughter, *Melinda*, was born on August 14, 1946, in Los Angeles. Gorcey received a divorce on May 15, 1951. Marx wed *Eden Marie Hartford* in a private ceremony in Sun Valley, Idaho, on July 17, 1954. Hartford obtained a divorce (and a one-million dollar property settlement) in Santa Monica on December 3, 1969. Marx never remarried.

MARX, Harpo
(1888-1964)

Arthur "Harpo" Marx, the second oldest Marx Brother, married actress *Susan Fleming* on September 12, 1936. The marriage was not announced until that November, in a telegram the comedian sent to President Franklin D. Roosevelt. The Marxs adopted four children: *Billy Woollcott, Alexander*, and twins, *Minnie* and *Jimmy*. The couple was married twenty-eight years, until, on September 28, 1964, Marx died following surgery in Los Angeles.

MASON, James
(1909-1984)

In February 1941, the actor married *Pamela Ostrer Kellino*. The Masons had a daughter, *Portland*, born in 1948, named after their friend, actress *Portland Hoffa* (the wife of *Fred ALLEN*).

Their son, *Alexander*, was born in 1953. After twenty-three years of marriage, Pamela Mason obtained a divorce in Santa Monica on August 31, 1964. She charged the actor with desertion and extreme mental cruelty. On August 13, 1971, Mason married *Clarissa Kaye*. The Masons were married twelve years, until the actor's death, at age seventy-five, on July 27, 1984, in Lausanne, Switzerland.

MASON, Marsha
(1942-   )

Mason wed actor and painter *Gary Campbell* in 1966. The marriage ended in divorce in 1971. On October 25, 1973, the actress married widowed playwright and screenwriter *Neil Simon*. The couple was divorced ten years later, in October 1983.

MASSEY, Ilona
(1910-1974)

While singing at the Vienna State Opera, circa 1925, the Hungarian-born actress-singer married landowner *Nicholas Szavozd*. The couple was divorced less than a year later. She then married film actor *Alan Curtis* on March 26, 1941, in Hollywood. "Terrific domestic quarrels" were blamed as the cause of their divorce in Los Angeles on December 16, 1942. On January 6, 1952, Massey and New York jeweler *Charles A. Walker* were married by *Mayor Stanley W. Church* in New Rochelle, New York. Divorced in 1955, she wed *Donald S. Dawson*, a former advisor to *President Truman,* that same year. The couple settled on an estate in Maryland. The marriage ended in Massey's death after a short illness in Bethesda, Maryland, on August 20, 1974. She was sixty-two.

MASSEY, Raymond
(1896-1983)

In 1921, the Canadian-born actor wed *Margery (Peggy) Fremantle* in England. Their son, *Geoffrey*, was born in England in October 1924. The couple was divorced in 1929. That same year, on November 12, 1929, Massey wed actress *Adrienne Allen*. The couple had two children, both of whom became actors. *Daniel* was born on October 10, 1933, followed by *Anna*, born in 1937. Both children were born in London. Allen divorced Massey on July 6, 1939, in Carson City, Nevada, on the grounds of mental cruelty. She was given custody of their children. Four days later, on July 10, 1939, Massey wed *Dorothy Ludington Whitney*, a divorced lawyer. The couple was married by a judge at the New York City home of friends, *Mr. and Mrs. Charles Garside*. Whitney had a daughter, *Dorothy*, from a former marriage. Their forty-three years of marriage ended in Whitney's death in July 1982. Massey died the following year, on July 29, 1983, from pneumonia at the age of eighty-six in Los Angeles. His daughter, Anna, married British actor *Jeremy Brett* in 1958. His son, Daniel, married British actress *Penelope Wilton* in 1976.

MASTROIANNI, Marcello
(1923-)

Mastroianni married Italian actress *Flora Carabella* in 1950. Their daughter, *Barbara*, was born in 1951. The actor also has a daughter, *Chiara-Charlotte,* born in 1972, with French actress *Catherine DENEUVE.*

MATTHAU, Walter
(1920-)

The actor prefers to remain quiet about his first marriage, in 1948, to *Grace Geraldine Johnson*. The couple had one son, *David*, and a daughter, *Jenny*, before the divorce in 1958. On August 21, 1959, Matthau married actress and author *Carol Wellington-Smythe Marcus*, the divorced wife of writer *William Saroyan*. Their son, *Charles*, was born in 1963.

MATTHEWS, Jessie
(1907-1981)

The actress-singer-dancer wed actor *Henry (Harry) Lytton*, the son of actor *Sir Henry Lytton*, at Hammersmith registry office in London in 1926. The marriage ended in divorce in 1929. On January 24, 1931, Matthews married her stage and screen co-star, *Sonnie Hale*, at Hampstead registry office in London. The couple adopted an infant daughter, *Catherine*, in 1933. The Hales were considered one of show business's most happily married couples until their divorce in 1944. The following year, on August 9, 1945, Matthews wed British *Lieut. Brian Lewis* at Chelsea registry office in London. Divorced from Lewis in October 1954, she never remarried.

MATURE, Victor
(1915-   )

Mature has been married five times. On January 30, 1938, the actor wed a fellow student at the Pasadena Playhouse, *Frances Evans*. The marriage was annulled the following year. He married *Martha Stephenson Kemp*, the widow of bandleader *Hal Kemp*, on June 18, 1941, at her New York City apartment. Kemp received a divorce in Las Vegas on February 10, 1943. The actor wed *Dorothy Stanford Berry* on February 28, 1948, in Yuma, Arizona. Seven years later, on November 8, 1955, Berry received a divorce in Santa Monica. British actress *Joy Urwick* became Mature's fourth wife in Capri on September 27, 1959. They were divorced in 1969. Mature married his fifth wife, *Lorey*, in 1974. Their daughter, *Victoria*, was born on March 16, 1975. The couple is now divorced.

MAXWELL, Marilyn
(1921-1972)

In 1944, Maxwell married actor *John Conte* in The Little Church Around the Corner in New York City. They were divorced in 1946. On January 1, 1949, she wed restaurateur *Anders (Andy) MacIntyre*. Maxwell received a divorce in Santa Monica on

March 22, 1951, charging MacIntyre with cruelty. She married producer and screenwriter *Jerome (Jerry) Davis* on November 21, 1954. Their son, *Matthew Paul Davis*, was born on April 28, 1956. The couple was divorced on December 21, 1960. Maxwell never remarried.

MAYO, Virginia
(1920-)

On July 6, 1947, Mayo and actor *Michael O'Shea* were married in The Little Church of the Flowers in Glendale, California. Their daughter, *Mary Catherine O'Shea*, was born on November 12, 1953, in Los Angeles. Their twenty-seven years of marriage ended in O'Shea's death from a heart attack at the age of sixty-seven in Dallas, Texas, on December 4, 1974. The actress has not remarried.

MEIGHAN, Thomas
(1879-1936)

In 1908, Meighan wed his Broadway co-star, actress *Frances Ring* in Jersey City, New Jersey. Ring's sister, actress *Blanche Ring*, married actor *Charles WINNINGER*. The Meighans were married twenty-eight years, until the actor's death from a bronchial ailment at the age of fifty-seven on July 8, 1936, at their Long Island home.

MENJOU, Adolphe
(1890-1963)

In April 1920, the actor married *Katherine Tinsley* in New York City. They separated in November 1925, and an interlocutory decree of divorce became final in Los Angeles on October 20, 1927. Tinsley charged Menjou with desertion. He married actress *Kathryn Carver* in Paris on May 16, 1928. Carver received a divorce in Los Angeles on August 14, 1933, after testifying that the actor would fly into fits of rage. A year later, on August 25, 1934, Menjou and actress *Verree TEASDALE* were married in the Los Angeles chambers of *Judge James H. Pope*. The couple adopted a son, *Peter Adolphe Menjou*, in 1937. The couple was married until the actor's death from chronic hepatitis on October 29, 1963, at their Beverly Hills home. He was seventy-three.

MERCOURI, Melina
(1923-)

At nineteen, in 1942, Mercouri wed businessman *Panayiotis Gharocopos* in her native Greece. The marriage ended in divorce in 1965. Since 1966, Mercouri has been married to American filmmaker *Jules Dassin*.

MEREDITH, Burgess
(1908-)

The actor married *Helen Berrian Derby* in 1932. The marriage ended in divorce in 1935. Meredith wed *Margaret Perry*, the daughter of actress-director *Antoinette Perry*, on January 10, 1936, at his Sneeden's Landing, New York, home. Perry received a Reno divorce on July 19, 1938. On May 21, 1944, Meredith wed film star *Paulette GODDARD* in the garden of *David O. Selznick*'s Beverly Hills home. Goddard obtained a divorce in Cuernavaca, Mexico, on June 6, 1949. In 1950, Meredith married ballet dancer *Kaja Sundsten*. Their son, *Jonathan*, was born later that same year. Their daughter, *Tala Beth*, was born in 1952. The couple separated in 1979.

MERKEL, Una
(1903-1985)

On January 1, 1932, the actress married aviation designer *Ronald L. Burla*. Divorced in 1945, she never remarried.

MERMAN, Ethel
(1909-1984)

On November 15, 1940, she married agent *William R. Smith* in Elkington, Maryland. Smith divorced her in Mexico a year later charging desertion. Later that same year, 1941, Merman married Hearst Publications executive *Robert D. Levitt*. Their daughter, *Ethel*, was born on July 20, 1942, in New York City. Their son, *Robert Daniels Levitt, Jr.*, was born on August 11, 1945, also in New York City. Merman obtained a mutual-consent divorce in Juarez, Mexico, on June 10, 1952. On March 9, 1953, she wed *Robert F. Six*, the president of Continental Airlines, in Mexicali, Mexico. Merman received a divorce from Six in Mexico in December 1960. On June 27, 1964, Merman married actor *Ernest BORGNINE* at his Beverly Hills home. Thirty-eight days later, the couple separated. Merman received a divorce in Santa Monica on November 18, 1964, on the grounds of extreme cruelty. She never remarried.

MIDLER, Bette
(1945-   )

On December 16, 1984, Midler wed *Martin Rochus Sebastian von Haselberg*, a commodities trader, at the Candlelight Wedding Chapel in Las Vegas. Their daughter, *Sophie*, was born in Los Angeles on November 14, 1986.

MILLAND, Ray
(1905-1986)

The actor wed *Muriel "Mal" Weber* on September 30, 1932, at the Mission Inn in Riverside, California. Their son, *Daniel David*, was born on March 6, 1940. The couple adopted a six-year-old daughter, *Victoria Francesca*, on November 18, 1949. The Millands had one trial separation in 1945, but were reconciled. Their marriage ended in the actor's death from cancer in Torrance, California, on March 10, 1986.

MILLER, Ann
(1923-)

The actress-dancer married *Reese Milner*, on February 16, 1946, at All-Saints-by-the-Sea Church in Montecito, California. Less than a year later, on January 22, 1947, she was granted an interlocutory decree of divorce in Los Angeles. On August 22, 1958, Miller married oilman and film producer *William Moss* in LaJolla, California. Moss was divorced form actress *Jane WITH-ERS*. Miller received an interlocutory decree of divorce in Los Angeles on May 12, 1961. The decree would become final in one year. On May 25, 1961, she married another Texas oil million-aire, *Arthur Cameron*, at the Tecali Hotel in Mexico City. Only days after her California divorce from Moss became final, Miller and Cameron were divorced. She has not remarried.

MILLER, Marilyn
(1898-1936)

In June 1919, Miller married *Frank Carter*, a fellow performer in the Ziegfeld Follies of 1918. Eleven months later, on May 9, 1920, Carter was killed in a car accident near Grantsville, Mary-land. On July 30, 1922, Miller married actor-director *Jack PICK-FORD* at Pickfair in Beverly Hills. *Mary PICKFORD*, sister of the groom, served as matron-of-honor and director-screenwriter *Victor Heerman* was best man. Miller received a Parisian divorce on November 2, 1927. On October 1, 1934, Miller married dancer *Chester L. (Chet) O'Brien* at the Harrison town hall in Harrison, New York. O'Brien, several years her jun-ior, was widowed on April 7, 1936, when Miller died after a long illness in New York City at the age of thirty-seven.

MILLS, Hayley
(1946-)

The actress, who is the daughter of *John MILLS*, married film director *Roy Boulting* at a villa on the French Riviera on June 11, 1971. Their son, *Jonathan Crespian*, was born on January 18, 1973. Separated in 1975, the couple was divorced in 1976. Mills has a son, born on July 30, 1976, with British actor *Leigh Lawson*.

MILLS, John
(1908-)

Mills married actress *Aileen Raymond* in 1931. They were divorced in 1940. On January 16, 1941, he wed actress-playwright *Mary Hayley Bell* in London. The couple has three children: actress *Juliet Mills*, born November 21, 1941; actress *Hayley MILLS*, born April 18, 1946; and assistant director *Jonathan Mills*, born December 3, 1949. All three of their children were born in London.

MIMIEUX, Yvette
(1939-)

The actress married filmmaker *Stanley Donen* on November 22, 1972, at his sister's home in Columbia, South Carolina.

MINNELLI, Liza
(1946-)

The actress-singer was born *Liza May Minnelli* in Los Angeles to film director *Vincente Minnelli* and *Judy GARLAND*. On March 3, 1967, she wed Australian singer-songwriter *Peter Allen* at the New York City home of friends, *Mr. and Mrs. Richard*

Friedberg. The couple was divorced in 1972. She became engaged to actor *Desi Arnaz, Jr.*, later that same year, but the couple never married. Minnelli married film director *Jack Haley, Jr.*, the son of *Jack HALEY*, in Santa Barbara, California, on September 15, 1974. The marriage ended in divorce in April 1979. Since December 4, 1979, Minnelli has been married to actor-producer *Mark Gero*.

MINTER, Mary Miles
(1902-1984)

In 1957, the actress married Santa Monica real estate agent *Brandon O'Hildebrandt*. The marriage ended in O'Hildebrandt's death on August 13, 1965. Minter never remarried.

MIRANDA, Carmen
(1909-1955)

The Brazilian-born singer, dancer, and comedienne married producer *David Sebastian* on March 17, 1947, at the Church of the Good Shepherd in Beverly Hills. The marriage was cut short by her untimely death, at the age of forty-six, on August 5, 1955, after collapsing on the set of the *Jimmy Durante Show*. Sebastian was at her side when she died at their Beverly Hills home.

MITCHUM, Robert
(1917-)

On March 16, 1940, Mitchum married *Dorothy Spencer* in Dover, Delaware. The couple has three children: actor *Jim Mitchum*, born May 8, 1941; actor *Chris Mitchum*, born October 16, 1943; and *Petrine*, born March 3, 1952.

MIX, Tom
(1880-1940)

The cowboy wed *Grace I. Allin* in 1902. The marriage ended in divorce later that same year. He married *Kitty Perrine* in 1905, but the marriage ended in divorce in 1906. In 1909, Mix married *Olive Stokes*. A daughter, *Ruth*, was born in 1913. The couple was divorced in 1917. He married film actress *Victoria Forde* in 1918. Their daughter, *Thomasina*, was born in 1922. Forde received a divorce from Mix in Los Angeles on December 4, 1930, charging him with extreme mental cruelty. Mix was then briefly married to *Mary Mabel Morgan*. The couple had a daughter, *Betty*, born in San Antonio, California. The union ended in divorce. On February 15, 1932, Mix married *Mabel Hubbard Ward*, a circus performer, in Mexicali, Mexico. The marriage ended in divorce in 1934. In 1935, he remarried Olive Stokes. A daughter, *Bessie Mae*, was born soon after. The couple was divorced for the second time in 1939.

MONROE, Marilyn
(1926-1962)

In 1942, at the age of sixteen, she married aircraft worker *James Dougherty* to escape returning to a foster home. They were divorced in 1946. On January 14, 1954, Monroe and baseball player *Joe DiMaggio* were married in San Francisco's city hall. The celebrated marriage, a union of the sports and entertainment worlds, ended in divorce nine months later, on October 27, 1954, in Santa Monica. Monroe testified that she had offered to give up her career to save her marriage. On June 29, 1956, she wed playwright *Arthur Miller* in the Westchester County courthouse in White Plains, New York. The couple was divorced in Juarez, Mexico, on January 24, 1961.

MONTEZ, Maria
(1920-1951)

Montez wed French film star *Jean-Pierre Aumont* on July 13, 1943. Their daughter, *Maria Christina*, was born on February

14, 1946, in Los Angeles. She became an actress, using the professional name *Tina Marquand*. The marriage ended in Montez's sudden death, at age thirty-one, from a heart attack on September 7, 1951, at their home in Paris.

MONTGOMERY, Elizabeth
(1933-   )

The actress, who is the daughter of *Robert MONTGOMERY*, married Harvard graduate and socialite *Frederic Gallatin Cammann* at St. James Protestant Episcopal Church in New York City on March 27, 1954. The couple was divorced the following year. On December 28, 1956, she married actor *Gig YOUNG*. The marriage ended in divorce in January 1963. On October 26, 1963, Montgomery married her television director, *William Asher*, in Juarez, Mexico. The marriage was not announced until January 1964. The Ashers had three children: *William,* born July 24, 1964; *Robert,* born October 4, 1965; and *Rebecca*, born in 1969. Divorced in 1973, Montgomery has not remarried.

MONTGOMERY, George
(1916-   )

On December 5, 1943, the actor wed *Dinah SHORE* in Las Vegas. Their daughter, *Melissa Ann,* was born in 1948. In 1954, the couple adopted a son, *John David.* The marriage was considered one of Hollywood's happiest, but on May 9, 1962, Shore was granted a divorce in Santa Monica after eighteen years of marriage. Montgomery has not remarried.

MONTGOMERY, Robert
(1904-1981)

The actor married socialite *Elizabeth Bryan Allen* on April 14, 1928. Their daughter, actress *Elizabeth MONTGOMERY*, was born on April 15, 1933. A son, *Robert, Jr.*, was born on January 6, 1936. His wife received a divorce in Las Vegas on December 5, 1950, after twenty-two years of marriage. She charged Montogmery with mental cruelty and was given custody of their children. Four days later, on December 9, 1950, Montgomery married *Elizabeth Harkness* in Sag Harbor on Long Island. The couple was married thirty years until his death from cancer on September 27, 1981, in New York City. He was seventy-seven.

MOORE, Colleen
(1900-1988)

Moore wed studio executive *John E. McCormick* on August 18, 1923, in Beverly Hills. She received a divorce in Los Angeles on May 13, 1930, on the grounds of mental cruelty. She married stockbroker *Albert P. Scott* in Fort Pierce, Florida, on February 15, 1932. Three years later, on July 21, 1935, Moore divorced Scott in Los Angeles after testifying that his conduct had made her a nervous wreck. In 1937, she married stockbroker *Homer Hargrave* in Chicago. Hargrave was a widower with two children, *Homer, Jr.*, and *Judy*. The couple was married thirty years, until Hargrave's death in 1967. In December 1983, Moore married California contractor *Paul Maginot*. Four years later, on January 25, 1988, Moore died on her ranch near Templeton, California, at the age of eighty-seven.

MOORE, Demi
(1962-)

She married actor *Bruce WILLIS* in Las Vegas on November 21, 1987. The couple has a daughter, *Rumer Glenn Willis,* born on August 16, 1988, in Paducah, Kentucky.

MOORE, Dudley
(1935-)

In June 1986, the actor-musician married British actress *Suzy Kendall*. The marriage ended in divorce in 1970. In 1975, Moore married actress *Tuesday WELD*. Their son, *Patrick*, was born in March 1976. The couple was divorced in 1980. On February 21, 1988, Moore wed model *Brogan Lane* in Las Vegas. The marriage ended in divorce, on the grounds of irreconcilable differences, on July 26, 1990.

MOORE, Grace
(1901-1947)

The opera singer and actress met actor *Valentin Parera*, known as the "John Gilbert of Spain," while on a European concert tour. They were married in Cannes, France, on July 22, 1931. Parera described himself as "terribly shocked" after hearing the news that Moore had been killed in a plane crash on January 26, 1947, near Copenhagen, Denmark. She was forty-five.

MOORE, Mary Tyler
(1937-)

In August 1955, Moore wed salesman *Richard Meeker*. Their son, *Richard Carlton Meeker, Jr.*, was born on July 3, 1956. The couple was divorced in February 1962. On June 1, 1962, she married advertising agency executive *Grant Tinker* in Las Vegas. They were divorced in 1981. Moore married *Dr. Robert Levine* in New York City on November 23, 1983. Her son, Richard, committed suicide in 1980.

MOORE, Owen
(1886-1939)

On January 7, 1911, the actor, who was the brother of actors *Tom MOORE* and *Matt Moore* (1888–1960), wed *Mary PICKFORD* in a Jersey City, New Jersey, courtroom. In 1917, Pickford fell in love with *Douglas FAIRBANKS*, who was divorced from his wife in 1919. On March 3, 1920, Pickford divorced Moore in Minden, Nevada, on the grounds of desertion. She wed Fairbanks later that month. Moore eloped to Greenwich, Connecticut, on July 16, 1921, with stage and screen actress *Kathryn Perry*. The union was a stormy one, filled with separations and reconciliations, ending in Moore's death, at age fifty-two, on June 7, 1939, at his Beverly Hills home.

MOORE, Terry
(1929-)

On February 9, 1951, the actress married football player *Glenn Davis* in Glendale, California. The marriage ended in divorce in 1952. In 1956, she wed Panamanian businessman *Eugene C. McGrath*. The couple was divorced in Panama in November 1958. The actress wed socialite and oilman *Stuart Cramer III* (divorced from *Jean PETERS*) on June 29, 1959, at the Church of the Hills in Glendale. The Cramers had two sons: *Stuart, Jr.*, born July 28, 1960, and *Grant*, born November 10, 1961. They were divorced in 1972. In 1979, she married businessman *Richard Carey* in Mexico. They are separated. In September of 1983, Moore won a seven-year legal battle to be acknowledged as the widow of billionaire producer *Howard Hughes* (also at one time married to Jean Peters), who died in 1976. Moore states that she married Hughes in the fall of 1949 on his yacht off the coast of California. A daughter was born to the couple in December 1952 in Munich, Germany, but died at birth. Hughes destroyed the ship's log containing the record of their marriage, and the couple was never divorced.

MOORE, Tom
(1885-1955)

The silent film star was the brother of actors *Owen MOORE* and *Matt Moore* (1888–1960). On May 11, 1914, Moore wed film actress *Alice JOYCE* in Jacksonville, Florida. Their daughter, *Alice Joyce Moore*, was born in 1916. The couple was divorced in 1920. On February 12, 1921, he married actress *Renée ADOREE*. *Jack PICKFORD* and *Mabel NORMAND* were their attendants. Adorée filed for divorce in Los Angeles on July 21, 1923, charging Moore with cruelty. Their divorce became final in October 1924. In 1931, Moore wed actress *Eleanor Merry*. A son, *Tom, Jr.*, was born in 1933. Their twenty-four years of marriage ended in Moore's death from cancer in Santa Monica, California, on February 13, 1955. He was seventy-one.

MOOREHEAD, Agnes
(1906-1974)

In 1930, Moorehead married actor *John Griffith Lee*. The couple adopted a son, *Sean*. The marriage ended in divorce in 1952. She married actor *Robert Gist* in 1953. Divorced in 1958, she never remarried.

MORENO, Antonio
(1887-1967)

On January 27, 1923, the actor wed socialite and divorcée *Daisy Canfield Danzigan* in Los Angeles. Moreno had three step-children: *Robert, Frances*, and *Daisy Danzigan*. The couple had many separations and reconciliations ending suddenly on February 23, 1933, when Danzigan was killed in a car accident in Los Angeles at the age of forty-five. The actor never remarried.

MORENO, Rita
(1931-)

On June 18, 1965, Moreno married *Dr. Leonard I. Gordon* in the New York City chambers of *Judge Samuel M. Gold*. The Gordons have one daughter, *Fernanda Lu* born on October 28, 1966.

MORGAN, Dennis
(1910-)

The actor-singer married *Lillian Vedder*, whom he had met in high school, in Wisconsin on September 5, 1933. Their son, *Stanley, Jr.* (Morgan's real name is Stanley Morner), was born in 1934. A daughter, *Kristin*, was born in 1937 and a second son, *James Irving*, was born in 1943. The Morgans live in Awahnee, California, near Yosemite National Park.

MORGAN, Helen
(1900-1941)

On May 15, 1933, the singer-actress married Cleveland attorney *Maurice Maschke, Jr.*, son of the Cleveland Republican Party leader, in New Castle, Pennsylvania. Two years later, on June 19, 1935, Morgan was granted an interlocutory decree of divorce in Los Angeles on the grounds of cruelty. The decree became final the following year. She married Los Angeles automobile dealer *Lloyd Johnson* on July 27, 1941. Three months later, on October 8, 1941, Morgan died of a liver ailment in Chicago at the age of forty-one.

MORGAN, Michéle
(1920-)

On September 15, 1942, the French-born actress married actor-director *William Marshall* in Los Angeles. Their son, *Michael*, born in 1946 in Los Angeles, became an actor. The marriage ended in divorce in 1949. Marshall later married *Ginger ROG-ERS*. The following year, Morgan wed French film star *Henri Vidal*. On December 10, 1959, Vidal died suddenly of a heart attack in Paris at the age of forty. Morgan has not remarried.

MOSTEL, Zero
(1915-1977)

In 1939, the actor married college student *Clara Sverd*. The couple was divorced in 1941. On July 2, 1944, Mostel married *Kathryn (Kathy) Harkin*, a former Radio City Music Hall Rockette, in Long Branch, New Jersey. The couple had two sons: *Joshua*, born in 1946, and *Tobias*, born in 1948. The Mostels were married thirty-three years, until, on September 8, 1977, the actor died from cardiac arrest in New York City. He was sixty-two.

MUNI, Paul
(1895-1967)

On May 8, 1921, the actor married *Bella Finkel* in New York City. The Munis, who had no children, were one of Hollywood's most happily married couples. Their forty-six years of marriage ended in the actor's death from a heart ailment at the age of seventy-one on August 25, 1967, at their home in Santa Barbara, California. Bella Muni died in 1971.

MURPHY, Audie
(1924-1971)

Murphy, WW II's most decorated GI-turned-film actor, married actress *Wanda HENDRIX* on February 8, 1949. The couple separated seven months later. Hendrix received a divorce in Los Angeles on the grounds of mental cruelty on April 14, 1950. The decree became final on April 20, 1951. Three days later, on April 23, 1951, Murphy married *Pamela Archer*, a former airline hostess, at Highland Park Methodist Church in Dallas, Texas. The couple had two sons: *Terry Michael*, born in 1952, and *James Shannon*, born in 1954. Their twenty-year marriage ended suddenly when, on May 31, 1971, Murphy was killed in a plane crash twelve miles northwest of Roanoke, Virginia, at the age of forty-six.

MURPHY, George
(1902-   )

On December 28, 1926, he wed *Juliette Henkel*, a dancer whose professional name was *Julie Johnson*. She had taught Murphy how to dance and became his vaudeville dancing partner. The couple had one son, *Dennis Michael*, born in 1939, and a daughter, *Melissa Elaine*, born in 1943. Their forty-seven years of marriage ended in Henkel's death from a heart ailment on September 28, 1973. Murphy has not remarried.

MURRAY, Bill
(1950-   )

The comedian wed television talent coordinator *Mickey Kelly* in a civil ceremony on January 21, 1981. The couple was remarried in a religious ceremony on March 25, 1981. A son, *Homer Banks Murray*, was born in 1982. The couple resides in New York City.

MURRAY, Mae
(1885-1965)

In September 1908, Murray wed *William M. Schwenker, Jr.*, of a socially prominent family, in Hoboken, New Jersey. The couple was divorced in 1909. On December 18, 1916, the actress married stockbroker *Jay O'Brien*, who was also known as the "Beau Brummel of Broadway," in Pasadena, California. The marriage ended in divorce a year later. Film director *Robert Z. Leonard* became Murray's third husband in June of 1918 in Los Angeles. Seven years later, on May 26, 1925, she received a divorce in Paris, testifying that the union had very quickly become unhappy. Her husband, she stated, had treated her with "insulting coldness, marked disdain, and haughty contempt." Leonard later married silent film actress *Gertrude Olmstead*, a marriage which lasted until his death in 1968. After a three-week courtship, Mae Murray, film star, and *Prince David Mdivani* of the Republic of Georgia, were married in a Beverly Hills church on June 27, 1926. *Rudolph VALENTINO* and *Pola NEGRI* (who would marry David Mdivani's brother, *Serge*) were the attendants at their wedding. In February 1927, their son, *Koran*, was born in Los Angeles although the birth was kept a secret until June 1928. Murray was granted her fourth, and last, divorce decree in Los Angeles on October 26, 1933. She charged Mdivani with nagging her and objecting to her friends. The interlocutory decree became final on November 2, 1934. She never remarried.

MYERS, Carmel
(1899 - 1980)

The actress married attorney and songwriter *Isadore Kornblum* in New York City on July 19, 1919. Four years later, on July 6, 1923, Myers obtained a divorce in Los Angeles on the grounds of desertion. She married lawyer *Ralph H. Blum* on June 9, 1929, at Temple B'nai B'rith in Los Angeles. The Blums had three children: *Ralph, Jr.*, born in 1931; *Susan*, born in 1939; and *Mary*, born in 1941. Their twenty years of marriage ended in Blum's death in Los Angeles in April of 1950. On October 30, 1951, Myers married studio executive *Alfred W. Schwalberg* in New York City. The Schwalbergs were married twenty-three years, until his death in 1974.

NAGEL, Conrad
(1897-1970)

The actor wed *Ruth Helms*, daughter of a flautist, in Chicago on June 24, 1919. Their daughter, *Ruth Margaret Nagel*, was born in 1921. After fifteen years of marriage, the Nagels were divorced in Juarez, Mexico, on the grounds of incompatibility on August 7, 1934. Nagel married starlet *Lynn Merrick* at the Municipal Building in Fort Lee, New Jersey, on December 21, 1945. The union ended in divorce in 1947. On August 31, 1955, Nagel married widowed *Michael Coulson Smith* at the Rumson, New Jersey, home of friends, *Mr. and Mrs. Shepherd Alexander*. Divorced from Smith less than a year later, the actor never remarried.

NAZIMOVA, Alla
(1879-1945)

At twenty-five, circa 1904, she married actor *Paul Orleneff*, star of the Nemetti Theatre in St. Petersburg, Russia. The theatre group traveled to New York, and the couple separated when Orleneff returned to Russia and Nazimova remained in the United States. On December 5, 1912, she married actor *Charles Bryant* in her New York City apartment. The marriage was not legal because Nazimova had never been divorced from Orleneff. Orleneff refused to give her a divorce, and she lived as Bryant's common-law wife. She divorced Bryant in Paris in July of 1925. She never remarried.

NEAGLE, Dame Anna
(1904-1986)

After a long professional association and eighteen films together, Neagle wed her producer and director, *Herbert Wilcox*, on August 9, 1943, at Caxton Hall registry office in London. The couple continued to make films together during their thirty-three years of marriage. Wilcox died after a long illness on May 15, 1977, in London. He was eighty-five.

NEAL, Patricia
(1926-   )

On July 2, 1953, the actress married British writer *Roald Dahl* in a church wedding in New York City. The Dahls had five children: *Olivia Twenty*, born in 1955; actress *Tessa Sophia Dahl*, born in 1957; *Theo Matthew Roald*, born August 3, 1960; *Ophelia Magdalene*, born May 12, 1964; and *Lucy Neal*, born August 4, 1965. Their oldest daughter, Olivia, died of encephalitis at the age of eight in 1962. Neal received a divorce from Dahl in London on July 5, 1983, after thirty years of marriage.

NEFF, Hildegarde
(1925-   )

In 1947, the German-born actress married United States information officer Kurt Hirsch in England. The couple was divorced in America in 1952. On June 30, 1962, Neff wed writer *David Anthony Palastanga (Cameron)*. Their daughter, *Christina*, was born on May 17, 1968. The actress was divorced from Palastanga. She married Paul von Schell zu Bauschlott on June 1, 1977.

NEGRI, Pola
(1894-1987)

At nineteen, the actress married *Count Eugene Dambski* in Sosnoweic, Poland. After a lengthy separation, Dambski received a divorce in 1923, the same year Negri arrived in the United States. She was engaged to both *Charlie CHAPLIN* and *Rudolph VALENTINO*, but never married either, the latter because of his untimely death. On May 14, 1927, Negri and *Prince Serge Mdivani* of the Republic of Georgia were married in a religious ceremony performed in the chapel of Negri's Château de Rueil in Seraincourt, France, near Paris. A civil ceremony, performed by the mayor of the city at the town hall, followed that afternoon. Mdivani's brother, *Prince David*, wed *Mae MUR-RAY* in 1929. Negri was granted a divorce from Mdivani in Paris on the grounds of abandonment on April 2, 1931. She never remarried.

NEWMAN, Paul
(1925-)

In December 1949, Newman wed actress *Jackie Witte*. Three children were born: *Scott*, in 1950; *Susan*, in 1953; and *Stephanie*, in 1954. The marriage ended in divorce in 1957. On January 29, 1958, Newman married actress *Joanne WOODWARD* in Las Vegas. The couple has three daughters: *Elinor*, born in 1959; *Melissa*, born in 1961; and *Claire*, born in 1965. They have often co-starred together, and Newman directed his wife in one film. His son, Scott, died in 1978 from an accidental overdose of alcohol and valium. In his memory, Newman established the Scott Newman Foundation to finance anti-drug films.

NEWTON-JOHN, Olivia
(1948-)

On December 15, 1984, Newton-John wed actor *Matt Lattanzi* at her Malibu Canyon home. Their daughter, *Chloe*, was born on January 17, 1986, in Los Angeles.

NEY, Richard
(1918-)

On July 24, 1943, the actor married *Greer GARSON* in Santa Monica, California. Four years later, on September 25, 1947, Garson received an uncontested divorce from Ney in Los Angeles. Since June 16, 1949, Ney, who is now a Wall Street financier, has been married to *Pauline Settle McMartin*. The couple was married in San Diego.

NICHOLSON, Jack
(1937-)

Nicholson married actress *Sandra Knight* in 1962. Their daughter, *Jennifer*, was born in 1964. Divorced in 1967, the actor has not remarried. He has a daughter, *Lorraine*, born in Los Angeles on April 16, 1990, with actress Rebecca Broussard.

NILSSON, Anna Q.
(1890-1974)

In 1916, the actress was briefly married to her film co-star, actor *Guy Coombs*. The couple was quickly divorced. Nilsson married shoe manufacturer *John Marshall Gunnerson* in 1923. Divorced from Gunnerson in 1925, she never remarried.

NIMOY, Leonard
(1931-)

He wed actress *Sandi Zober* on February 21, 1954. A daughter, *Julie*, was born in 1955, and a son, *Adam*, was born in 1956. The Nimoys separated in 1986 and are now divorced.

NIVEN, David
(1909-1983)

Niven wed *Primula Rollo*, the daughter of an officer in the Royal Air Force, on September 21, 1940, in Huish, a village near Marlborough, England. The Nivens had two sons: *David, Jr.*, born December 15, 1942, and *James Graham*, born November 6, 1945. Both of their sons were born in London. Tragedy struck on May 21, 1946, when Primula Niven died as a result of injuries incurred in a fall. On January 14, 1948, Niven was married to Swedish model *Hjördis Tersmeden* at South Kensington registry office in London. In the late fifties, the couple adopted a daughter, *Kristina* and, two years later, a second daughter, *Fiona*. Their thirty-five years of marriage ended in the actor's death from a muscular disorder on July 29, 1983, at their alpine chalet, Château d'Oex, in Switzerland. He was seventy-three.

NORMAND, Mabel
(1897 - 1930)

For seven years the comedienne was the professional associate and fiancée of actor, director, and producer *Mack Sennett*, but the couple was never married. Mack Sennett remained a bachelor, but on September 17, 1926, Normand and actor *Lew CODY* eloped to Ventura, California. Three years later, on February 23, 1930, Normand died of tuberculosis in a Monrovia, California, sanitarium. The marriage occurred at the end of a series of scandals which, combined with her illness, had put an end to her career. After breaking with Sennett, Normand became known for her wild parties and there were rumors about her supposed addictions to drugs and alcohol. In 1922, she was one of the last people to see murdered film director William Desmond Taylor alive, although she was later cleared of having any connection with his death. Soon after, her chauffeur murdered a Hollywood millionaire with a pistol thought to belong to Normand.

NORTH, Sheree
(1933-)

At fifteen, in 1948, North married *Fred Bessire*, a draftsman, in Los Angeles. The couple had one daughter, *Dawn*, born in 1949. They separated after eighteen months of marriage and were divorced in Los Angeles in September 1953. On February 20, 1955, North married music publisher *John "Bud" Freeman* in Quartzide, Arizona. Two years later, in July of 1957, the marriage ended in divorce. North wed her psychiatrist, *Dr. Gerhardt Sommer*, on December 17, 1958. Their daughter, *Erika*, was born on July 7, 1959. The couple was divorced on May 27, 1963.

NOVAK, Kim
(1933-)

On March 15, 1965, Novak wed British actor *Richard Johnson*, her co-star in the film *The Adventures of Moll Flanders* (1965), in an outdoor setting in Beaver Dam, Colorado. The couple was divorced a little over a year later, on May 26, 1966. On March 12, 1976, Novak wed veterinarian *Dr. Robert Malloy* at her home in the Big Sur area of California.

OAKIE, Jack
(1903-1978)

The actor married *Venita Varden* in 1936. Nine years later, on February 16, 1945, Varden received a divorce. In the early fifties, Oakie married actress *Victoria Horne*. They were married until his death, at age seventy-four, at their Northridge, California, home on January 23, 1978.

OBERON, Merle
(1911-1979)

The actress wed director *Alexander Korda* on June 3, 1939, in Antibes, France. The marriage ended in divorce in Juarez, Mexico, on June 4, 1945. Later that month, on June 26, 1945, Oberon and cinematographer *Lucien K. Ballard* were married by proxy in Juarez. The couple was divorced in Juarez in the summer of 1949. On July 28, 1957, Oberon married Italian industrialist *Bruno Pagliai* in Rome. That same year, the couple adopted a son, *Bruno, Jr.* In 1958, they adopted a daughter, *Francesca*. Both children were adopted from orphanages in Italy. The Pagliais resided in Mexico City until their divorce in 1973. Oberon married her fourth husband, Dutch actor *Robert Wolders*, on January 31, 1975. Their marriage ended in her death from a stroke in Los Angeles on November 23, 1979. She was sixty-eight.

O'BRIEN, Edmond
(1915-1985)

On February 19, 1941, O'Brien eloped to Yuma, Arizona, with actress *Nancy KELLY*. Separated only four months later, Kelly obtained a divorce in Los Angeles on February 2, 1942. O'Brien married actress *Olga San Juan* at the Santa Barbara County courthouse on September 26, 1948. The O'Briens had two daughters: *Maria*, born in 1950; and *Bridget*, born in 1951; and a son, *Brendan*, born May 9, 1962. The couple was divorced in 1976, after twenty-eight years of marriage.

O'BRIEN, George
(1900-1985)

On July 15, 1933, the actor married actress *Marguerite Churchill* at Santa Ynez Mission, near Solvang, California. A son, *Brian O'Brien*, was born in June of 1934, but died nine days after birth. A daughter, *Orin Ynez*, was born in 1935, followed by a son, *Darcy George*, born in 1939. Marguerite O'Brien received an interlocutory divorce decree in Los Angeles on July 15, 1948, their fifteenth wedding anniversary. The decree became final on July 20, 1949. The actor never remarried.

O'BRIEN, Margaret
(1937-)

The former child actress married *Harold Robert Allen, Jr.*, on August 8, 1959, at St. Martin of Tours Roman Catholic Church in Hollywood. Allen divorced her in 1968, saying that she preferred her career to marriage. O'Brien wed electrical engineer and business executive *Roy T. Thorsen* on June 8, 1974. Their daughter, *Mara Tolene*, was born on July 14, 1976, in Los Angeles.

O'BRIEN, Pat
(1899-1983)

O'Brien wed actress *Eloise Taylor* in California on January 23, 1931. In 1934, the O'Briens adopted an infant daughter, *Mavourneen*, from The Cradle in Evanston, Illinois. They also adopted two sons from The Cradle: *Patrick Sean* in 1936 and *Terrence Kevin* on October 28, 1941. A daughter, *Kathleen Bridget*, was born to the couple on June 3, 1946. The O'Briens were married fifty-three years, until the actor's death from a heart attack on October 15, 1983, in Santa Monica, California. He was eighty-three.

O'CONNOR, Donald
(1925-   )

On February 6, 1944, O'Connor married *Gwendolyn Carter* in Tijuana, Mexico. A daughter, *Donna*, was born in 1946. The marriage ended in divorce in July 1954. Gwendolyn O'Connor married *Dan DAILEY* in 1955. Since November 1956, the actor has been married to *Grace Noble*. The couple has three children: *Alicia*, born in 1957; *Donald, Jr.*, born August 21, 1960; and *Kevin*, born January 31, 1962.

O'HARA, Maureen
(1920-   )

In 1939, the actress married British film director *George Hanley Brown*. They were divorced two years later, in 1941. That same year, on December 29, 1941, she wed dialogue director *Will Price*. Their daughter *Bronwyn Bridget* (named for O'Hara's oldest sister), was born on June 30, 1944. The Prices were divorced on August 4, 1952, and she was given custody of their daughter. On March 11, 1968, she wed air force *Brig. Gen. Charles Blair*, the first person to make a solo flight over the Arctic Ocean and the North Pole, in Charlotte-Amalie, the Virgin Islands. Blair was killed in a plane crash at the age of sixty-nine on September 1, 1978, in the Virgin Islands. O'Hara, who still resides on St. Croix, has not remarried.

O'KEEFE, Dennis
(1908-1969)

During the thirties, O'Keefe was briefly married to actress *Louise Stanley*. The marriage ended in divorce. On October 18, 1940, O'Keefe married Hungarian-born actress *Steffi Duna* in Phoenix, Arizona. Duna had a daughter, *Julianna*, from a former marriage to actor *John Carroll* that had ended in divorce. A son, *Edward James (Jimmy)*, was born to the O'Keefes in 1943. Their twenty-seven years of marriage ended in the actor's death, at age sixty, from cancer in Santa Monica on August 31, 1968.

OLIVIER, Sir Laurence
(1907-1989)

Lord Olivier was first married to actress *Jill Esmond*, whom he married at All Saints Church in Marylebone, London, on July 25, 1930. Their son, *Simon Tarquin*, was born in 1937. During the filming of *Fire Over England* (1937), Olivier fell in love with his leading lady, *Vivien LEIGH*. On January 29, 1940, Esmond received a divorce in London on the grounds of adultery, naming Leigh as corespondant. She was given custody of their son. Leigh was divorced from her husband, a barrister, and on August 30, 1940, Olivier and Leigh were married at San Ysidro Ranch in Montecito, California. *Garson Kanin* and *Katharine HEPBURN* attended the couple. After twenty years of marriage, Olivier was again divorced on the grounds of adultery. Leigh received a divorce in London on December 2, 1960, naming actress *Joan PLOWRIGHT* as corespondant. On March 17, 1961, Olivier and Plowright were married in Wilton, Connecticut, at the offices of Justice of the Peace *Edward S. Rimer, Jr.* A son, *Richard Kerr*, was born in London on December 3, 1961. A daughter, *Tamsin Agnes Margaret*, was born on January 10, 1963, followed by a second daughter, *Julie Kate*, born in Brighton, England, on July 27, 1966. The marriage ended in the actor's death on July 11, 1989, in Steyning, West Sussex, England. He was eighty-two.

O'NEAL, Ryan
(1941-)

O'Neal married actress *Joanna Moore* on April 3, 1963. Their daughter, actress *Tatum Beatrice O'NEAL*, was born on November 5, 1963. Their son, *Griffin Patrick*, was born on October 28, 1964. Divorced from Moore in February of 1967, O'Neal married actress *Leigh Taylor-Young* later that month on February 28, 1967. A son, *Patrick*, was born on September 14, 1967. Divorced from Taylor-Young, the actor married actress-model *Farrah FAWCETT* in Paris on June 18, 1988. At the time of their marriage, the couple had a son, *Redmond James Fawcett O'Neal*, born on January 30, 1985, in Los Angeles.

O'NEAL, Tatum
(1963-)

On August 1, 1986, the actress, who is the daughter of *Ryan O'NEAL*, married professional tennis player *John McEnroe* in Oyster Bay, New York. At the time of their marriage, the couple had a son, *Kevin*, born on May 25, 1986. A second son, *Sean*, was born in 1987.

O'SULLIVAN, Maureen
(1911-)

On September 12, 1936, the Irish-born actress married director *John Farrow* at St. Monica's Church in Santa Monica. The Farrows had seven children: *Michael Damien*, born May 30, 1939; *Patrick Joseph*, born November 27, 1942; *Maria de Lourdes*, born February 10, 1945; *John Charles*, born September 6, 1946; *Prudence*, born January 21, 1948; *Stephanie Margarita*, born June 4, 1949; and Theresa Magdalena, born July 22, 1951. Michael Farrow was killed in an aviation accident in 1958. Maria became better known as actress *Mia FARROW* and Theresa as actress *Tisa Farrow*. Stephanie Farrow also became an actress. The Farrows were married twenty-six years, until Farrow's death, from a heart attack on January 28, 1963, at their Beverly Hills home. He was fifty-six. On August 22, 1983, O'Sullivan married contractor *James Cushing* in Loudonville, New York.

O'TOOLE, Peter
(1932-)

O'Toole married actress *Sian Phillips* in Dublin, Ireland, in December of 1959. The couple had two daughters: *Kate*, born in March 1960 in England, and *Pat*, born in June 1963 in Dublin. Phillips received a divorce in London in August 1979, on the grounds of irretrievable breakdown. O'Toole has not remarried.

PAGE, Geraldine
(1924-1987)

Page married violinist *Alexander Schneider* in 1954. The brief marriage ended in divorce in 1957. On September 11, 1963, she announced that she had been married to actor *Rip TORN* for nine months, but in later years both Page and Torn confessed that they could not remember exactly when they had been married. Their daughter, *Angelica*, was born on February 17, 1964. Twin sons, *Anthony* and *Jonathan*, were born on June 9, 1965. The marriage ended in Page's death on June 13, 1987, in New York City at the age of sixty-two.

PAGET, Debra
(1933-   )

On January 14, 1958, Paget married actor-singer *David Street*. Four months later, on April 10, 1958, the actress received an uncontested divorce in Juarez, Mexico, on the grounds of incompatibility. She wed film director *Bud Boetticher* on March 28, 1960, in Tijuana, Mexico. They separated twenty-two days later, and Paget received a divorce in Juarez on August 24, 1961. On June 19, 1962, Paget married oilman *Louis C. Kung, Jr.,* a nephew of *Madame Chiang Kai-Shek*. Their son was born on June 22, 1964. The Kungs resided on an estate near Houston, Texas, until their divorce in 1971. Paget has not remarried.

PAIGE, Janis
(1922-   )

Paige married *Frank Martinelli, Jr.,* the son of a San Francisco restaurateur, on December 27, 1947. They were divorced in 1950. On January 18, 1956, she married *Arthur Matthew Stander*, a television writer and producer, in Las Vegas. Eighteen months later, on June 4, 1957, Paige received a divorce in Santa Monica after stating that Stander was jealous and temperamental. She married songwriter and music publisher *Ray Gilbert* (the composer of "Zip-a-Dee-Doo-Dah") on August 30,

1962. The Gilberts were married thirteen years, until his death in Los Angeles on March 4, 1976, at the age of sixty-three. The actress has not remarried.

PALANCE, Jack
(1919-)

Palance married actress *Virginia Baker* in 1949. The couple had three children: actress *Holly Palance*, born in 1952; a second daughter, *Brook*, born in 1954; and a son, *Cody John*, born in 1956. Divorced from Baker in 1968, the actor has not remarried.

PALMER, Lilli
(1914-1986)

The Viennese actress wed *Rex HARRISON* in London on January 25, 1943. Their son, *Carey*, a playwright, was born in 1947. The couple was divorced so that Harrison could marry actress *Kay KENDALL*. The decree was granted on February 6, 1957, in Juarez, Mexico, after the couple had been separated more than a year. On September 21, 1957, Palmer wed Argentine actor *Carlos Thompson* near Zurich, Switzerland. The marriage ended in Palmer's death from a heart attack at their Los Angeles home on January 27, 1986.

PARKER, Eleanor
(1922-)

Parker married navy dentist *Dr. Fred Losee* in 1943. The marriage ended in divorce in 1944. In 1946, she married producer *Bert Friedlob*. The couple had three children: *Susan*, born in 1948; *Sharon*, born in 1950; and *Richard*, born in 1952. Parker filed for divorce from Friedlob in Santa Monica on July 2, 1953, charging that he had caused her "grievous mental suffering." The decree was granted later that year. Parker married artist

Paul Clemens in 1956. A son, *Paul, Jr.,* was born in 1957. The marriage ended in divorce in 1964. Since April 17, 1966, the actress has been married to Chicago businessman *Raymond N. Hirsch.* The couple was married in Las Vegas.

PARKS, Larry
(1914-1975)

On September 9, 1944, Parks wed actress-singer-dancer *Betty GARRETT* at St. Thomas Episcopal Church in Los Angeles. The couple had two sons: *Garrett Christopher*, born in 1950, and *Andrew Lawrence*, born in 1951. Their thirty years of marriage ended in the actor's death from a heart attack at the age of sixty on April 13, 1975, at their home in Studio City, California.

PATRICK, Gail
(1911-1980)

The actress married *Robert Howard Cobb*, manager of the Brown Derby restaurant, in Tijuana, Mexico, on December 16, 1936. They were divorced less than four years later, on November 14, 1940, on the grounds of mental cruelty. Patrick wed *Lieut. Arnold Dean White* in 1944 at the naval air station in Jacksonville, Florida. The union ended in divorce in 1946. On July 25, 1947, she married literary agent *Thomas Cornwall Jackson* at her Los Angeles home. The Jacksons adopted two children, *Jennifer* and *Thomas, Jr.*, in 1954. The couple was divorced in 1969. Patrick married business executive *John E. Velde, Jr*, on September 28, 1974. The marriage ended in her death from leukemia at their Los Angeles home on July 6, 1980. The actress was sixty-nine.

PAYNE, John
(1912-1989)

Payne married film actress *Anne SHIRLEY* on August 22, 1937, in Santa Barbara, California. Their daughter, *Julie Anne*, was born on August 10, 1940. On February 19, 1942, Shirley divorced him in Los Angeles on the grounds of cruelty. She told the judge that she had been "desperately unhappy." The actor married *Gloria DE HAVEN* in Beverly Hills on December 28, 1944. The couple had two children: *Kathie*, born in 1945, and *Thomas*, born in 1948. De Haven divorced Payne in Los Angeles on February 9, 1950, stating that their careers clashed. She was given custody of their children. In 1953, Payne married *Alexandra "Sandy" Curtis*. The thirty-six year marriage ended in Payne's death from heart failure at the age of seventy-seven at their Malibu home on December 6, 1989.

PECK, Gregory
(1916-)

In October 1942, Peck wed *Greta Konen*, a Finnish-born hairdresser and make-up artist for *Katherine Cornell*. The couple had three sons: *Jonathan*, born July 20, 1944; *Stephen*, born August 16, 1946; and *Carey Paul*, born June 17, 1949. The couple was divorced in California on December 30, 1954. A year and a day later, on December 31, 1955, the actor married French journalist *Veronique Passani*. The couple was married at the Lompoc, California, home of friends, *Mr. and Mrs. Channing Peake*. The Pecks have two children: *Anthony*, born in October 1956, and *Cecilia*, born in May 1958. His oldest son, Jonathan, committed suicide in 1975.

PENN, Sean
(1960-)

Penn married singer and actress *Madonna* on August 16, 1985, at real estate developer *Dan Unger's* Malibu home. The couple filed for divorce in January of 1988, but withdrew their suit. They again filed for divorce in Los Angeles on January 5, 1989, on the grounds of irreconcilable differences. The decree was granted later that year. Penn is engaged to actress *Robin Wright*.

PEPPARD, George
(1928-   )

Peppard married actress *Helen Bradford Davies* in 1954. The couple had a son, *Bradford Davies*, born in 1955, and a daughter, *Julie Louise*, born in 1956. They were divorced in 1964, and the decree became final in January 1965. On April 17, 1966, Peppard married actress *Elizabeth ASHLEY* at the Bel-Air Hotel. Their son, *Christian Moore Peppard*, was born on March 12, 1968. Six years later, on April 30, 1972, Ashley received a divorce (and custody of Christian) in Los Angeles on the grounds of irreconcilable differences. Peppard married *Sherry Boucher* on January 30, 1975. Later divorced from Boucher, he married actress-artist *Alexis Adams* in Studio City, California, in December 1984.

PERKINS, Anthony
(1932-   )

On August 9, 1973, the actor married photographer *Berinthia (Berry) Berenson* on Cape Cod. The couple has two sons: *Osgood*, born February 2, 1974, and *Elvis*, born in 1976.

PETERS, Jean
(1926-   )

The actress married socialite and oilman *Stuart Cramer III* in 1945. Divorced in 1947, Cramer later married actress *Terry MOORE*. On May 29, 1957, Peters wed producer *Howard Hughes* (who also had been married to Terry Moore) in Washington, D.C. After a lengthy separation, Peters received a divorce on June 15, 1971. Since August 1971, she has been married to producer *Stanley Hough*.

PFEIFFER, Michelle
(1958-   )

Pfeiffer married actor *Peter Horton* in 1982. The couple was divorced in 1988.

PICKFORD, Jack
(1896-1933)

The actor-director was the younger brother of *Mary PICK-FORD*. In May 1917, he married *Olive THOMAS*, *Florenz Ziegfeld*'s beautiful star, in New York City. Thomas quickly became a top Hollywood star, second only to her sister-in-law. On September 20, 1920, Thomas died in the American Hospital in Neuilly, France, after swallowing a bottle of bichloride of mercury tablets. Her death remains a mystery. Ziegfeld was furious when Pickford married another one of his top stars, *Marilyn MILLER*, on July 30, 1922, at Pickfair, his sister's Beverly Hills estate. Miller received a Parisian divorce on November 2, 1927. Pickford wed actress *Mary Mulhern* at a country church near Del Monte, California, on August 12, 1930. Mulhern received a divorce, charging cruelty, in Los Angeles on February 26, 1932. Pickford died on January 3, 1933, at the same hospital where Olive Thomas had died thirteen years before.

PICKFORD, Mary
(1893-1979)

While working at the Biograph studios in New York City, Pickford met actor *Owen MOORE*. They were married on January 7, 1911, in a Jersey City, New Jersey, courtroom. In 1917, she met *Douglas FAIRBANKS*, with whom she fell in love, during a WWI liberty bond tour. In 1919, Fairbanks' wife, *Anna Beth Sully*, divorced him. At Fairbanks's urging, Pickford filed for divorce from Moore. On March 3, 1920, she received her decree in Minden, Nevada, on the grounds of desertion. Mary and Doug were married in Los Angeles on March 30, 1920. *Marjorie DAW* was maid-of-honor and *Robert Fairbanks*, brother of the groom, was best man. Doug's wedding present to Mary was Pickfair, their elegant Beverly Hills estate. They were soon being called "the most popular couple in the world." But in the thirties their careers faltered and the couple began to travel more. Doug preferred Europe, but Mary preferred Hollywood. On January 13, 1936, Pickford received a final decree of divorce in Los Angeles. She married actor *Charles "Buddy" ROGERS* on June 26, 1937, at the *Louis D. Lighton* estate in Bel-Air. In 1943, they adopted a six-year-old son, *Ronald Pickford Rogers*. In 1944, the couple adopted a six-month-old daughter, *Roxanne Pickford Rogers*. Their forty-one years of marriage ended in Pickford's death, at age eighty-six, on May 29, 1979, in Santa Monica, California. Her younger brother was actor-director *Jack PICKFORD* and her younger sister was actress *Lottie Pickford* (1895–1936).

PIDGEON, Walter
(1897-1984)

In 1922, the actor married *Edna Pickles*. Two years later, in 1924, she died giving birth to their daughter, *Edna Verne Pidgeon*. Pidgeon remarried in 1930, to *Ruth Walker*. Their fifty-four years of marriage ended in his death on September 25, 1984, in Santa Monica. He was eighty-seven.

PITTS, ZaSu
(1898-1963)

On July 23, 1920, the actress married *Thomas S. Gallery*, a sports manager, in Santa Ana, California. Their daughter, *Ann*, was born in 1923. That same year, the couple adopted *Marvin Carville La Marr*, the orphaned son of actress *Barbara LA MARR*, whom they renamed *Don Mike*. The couple separated in 1926, and, six years later, on April 26, 1932, the actress was granted a divorce in Los Angeles on the grounds of desertion. She married *John Edward Woodall*, a Pasadena real estate broker, in Minden, Nevada, on October 8, 1933. The union was kept a secret until February 12, 1934, when the couple left for a belated honeymoon in New York. Their twenty-nine years of marriage ended in her death from cancer on June 7, 1963, in Los Angeles.

PLESHETTE, Suzanne
(1937-)

Pleshette wed actor *Troy DONAHUE* on January 4, 1964. Nine months later, on September 8, 1964, she was granted a divorce in Santa Monica after testifying that their marital problems had begun seventeen days after the wedding. Since March 16, 1968, Pleshette has been married to Texas oilman *Thomas Joseph Gallagher III*.

PLUMMER, Christopher
(1927-)

On August 16, 1956, the Canadian-born actor married actress *Tammy Grimes*. Their daughter, actress *Amanda Plummer*, was born in 1957. Grimes received a divorce in April 1960. Plummer married British columnist *Patricia Audrey Lewis* on May 4, 1962. They were divorced in 1968. Since 1970, the actor has been married to *Elaine Taylor*.

POITIER, Sidney
(1924-)

On April 29, 1950, the actor-director married *Juanita Hardy*. The couple had four daughters: *Beverly*, born July 4, 1952; *Pamela*, born April 12, 1954; *Sherry*, born July 4, 1956; and *Gina*, born in 1961. In 1972, a daughter, *Anika*, was born to Poitier and actress *Joanna Shimkus*. Their second daughter, *Sydney*, was born in 1973. Divorced from Hardy in July of 1975, Poitier married Shimkus in Santa Monica on January 23, 1976.

PONS, Lily
(1898-1976)

In 1925, the opera singer and actress married *August Mesritz* of Holland. He encouraged her operatic career. After a lengthy separation, Mesritz received a divorce in Paris on December 29, 1933. Pons wed conductor *André Kostelanetz* at her home in

Silvermine, Connecticut, on June 2, 1938. *Geraldine FARRAR* attended her at her wedding. Twenty years later, on November 25, 1958, Pons received a divorce in Juarez, Mexico, on the grounds of incompatibility. She never remarried.

POWELL, Dick
(1904-1963)

In 1925, Powell wed *Maude Maund* who was from his childhood home of Little Rock, Arkansas. They were divorced two years later. On September 19, 1936, he married film star *Joan BLON-DELL* aboard the ocean liner *Santa Paula* before it sailed from Los Angeles to New York. His studio publicized the union as Powell's first marriage. On July 1, 1938, their daughter, *Ellen,* was born in Los Angeles. In February 1938, Powell had legally adopted Blondell's son, *Norman Barnes,* from her former marriage to a cameraman. His surname became Powell. Blondell's divorce hearing in Los Angeles on July 14, 1944, took four minutes. She charged Powell with numerous acts of cruelty. On August 19, 1945, Powell married film star *June ALLYSON* at the Los Angeles home of composer *Johnny Green. Louis B. Mayer* gave the bride away. The couple adopted a two-month-old daughter, *Pamela,* on August 10, 1948. A son, *Richard Keith,* was born on Christmas Eve, 1950. On March 31, 1961, Allyson won a 2.5 million-dollar divorce settlement and custody of their children on the grounds of cruelty. The decree, granted in Los Angeles, would have become final in one year, but the Powells were reunited. Their seventeen years of marriage ended in Powell's death from cancer on January 3, 1963, in Los Angeles at the age of fifty-eight.

POWELL, Eleanor
(1912-1982)

The dancer-actress married *Glenn FORD*, whom she had met during the first Hollywood war bond cavalcade, on October 24, 1943, at her Beverly Hills home. Their son, *Peter Newton Ford,* was born in 1945. Powell received an interlocutory decree of divorce in Santa Monica on November 23, 1959, after testifying that Ford was "very moody." She never remarried.

POWELL, Jane
(1929-   )

The singer-actress married professional ice skater *Geary Steffen* on November 5, 1949. The couple had two children: *Geary, Jr.*, born in 1951, and *Suzanne*, born in 1952. Powell received a divorce in Santa Monica on August 6, 1953, after testifying that "divergence of interests" had ruined their marriage. She was given custody of their children. She wed auto manufacturer *Patrick W. Nerney* (divorced from actress *Mona Freeman*) on November 9, 1954. Their daughter, *Lindsay*, was born in 1956. The marriage ended in divorce in 1963. On June 27, 1965, Powell married publicist *James Fitzgerald* in Sydney, Australia. Divorced from Fitzgerald in 1975, she married writer-producer *David Parlour* on October 21, 1978. They were divorced in 1981. On May 21, 1988, Powell married *Dick Moore*, a former child actor who is now a business executive and writer, in Connecticut.

POWELL, William
(1892-1984)

In April 1915, Powell wed actress *Eileen Wilson*. A son, *William David Powell*, was born in 1925. The marriage ended in divorce in 1931. Later that same year, on June 26, 1931, Powell married actress *Carole LOMBARD* at the Los Angeles home of her mother, *Elizabeth Peters*. Eighteen months later, on August 18, 1933, Lombard received a Reno divorce. She and Powell remained close friends. Powell was engaged to actress *Jean HARLOW* at the time of her death on June 7, 1937. On January 5, 1940, Powell wed actress *Diana "Mousie" Lewis* at a dude ranch near Warm Springs, Nevada. Their forty-four years of marriage ended in Powell's death on March 5, 1984, in Palm Springs, California. He was ninety-two.

POWER, Tyrone
(1913-1958)

He was the son of actor *Tyrone Power, Sr.*, and the grandson of Irish stage actor *Tyrone Power*. On April 23, 1939, Power married French-born actress *Annabella* at her Bel-Air home. She received an interlocutory divorce decree in Los Angeles in 1948, which became final on January 27, 1949. That same day, Power married actress *Linda Christian* at the Church of Santa Francesca Roma in Rome. A large crowd of spectators gathered outside the church, and an audience with *Pope Pius XII* followed. The couple had two daughters, both of whom became actresses. *Romina Francesca* (named for the church where they were married) was born in October 1951, followed by *Taryn Stephanie*, born on September 13, 1953. Christian received an interlocutory divorce decree in Los Angeles on May 3, 1955. She later married *Edmund PURDOM*. Power received a final divorce from her in London on August 8, 1956. On May 7, 1958, he married *Deborah Ann Minardos* in Tunica, Mississippi. Six months later, on November 15, 1958, Power died from a heart attack at the age of forty-four in Madrid, Spain. On January 22, 1959, Deborah Power gave birth to a son, *Tyrone Power IV*, now an actor, in Los Angeles.

PRENTISS, Paula
(1939-   )

In 1961, she married actor *Richard BENJAMIN*. The couple has a son, *Ross Alexander*, born on March 26, 1974.

PRESLEY, Elvis
(1935-1977)

Presley wed *Priscilla Beaulieu* on May 1, 1967, in Las Vegas. Their daughter, *Lisa Marie*, was born on February 1, 1968, in

Memphis, Tennessee. The Presleys were divorced on October 9, 1973. He never remarried.

PRESTON, Robert
(1918-1987)

Preston married actress *Catherine Craig* (née *Kay Feltus*), whom he had met when they were both students at the Pasadena Playhouse, on November 9, 1940. The couple was married forty-six years, until his death from cancer in Santa Barbara on March 21, 1987. He was sixty-eight.

PREVOST, Marie
(1898-1937)

The actress married *H.O. Gerke* on June 22, 1918, in Oceanside, California. The couple separated in May 1922, and Gerke received a divorce in Los Angeles in September 1923 on the grounds of desertion. She married film star *Kenneth Harlan* in Los Angeles on October 14, 1924. Three years later, on November 21, 1927, Prevost divorced Harlan in Los Angeles on charges of neglect and desertion. She never remarried.

PRICE, Vincent
(1911-)

On April 22, 1938, Price and actress *Edith Barrett* were married at St. Thomas Episcopal Church in New York City. Their son, *Vincent Barrett Price*, was born in 1941. Barrett was granted a divorce (and custody of their son) on May 10, 1948. The actor wed fashion designer *Mary Grant* in Tijuana, Mexico, on August 8, 1949. A daughter, *Mary Victoria*, was born in 1962. On August 17, 1973, Mary Grant Price filed for divorce in Santa Monica after twenty-four years of marriage. She was given custody of their daughter. Since November 3, 1974, Price has been married to actress *Coral Browne*.

PRINGLE, Aileen
(1895-   )

She was *Aileen Bisbee* when, in 1912, she married Jamaican planter *Sir Charles MacKenzie Pringle* in her native California. The couple separated after she began her acting career. On September 12, 1933, the actress filed for divorce in Kingston, Jamaica. When asked if she planned to remarry, her reply was: "Well, is it going to rain or snow?" She did not remarry until August 12, 1944, when she wed novelist *James Cain* in Santa Monica. The brief union ended in divorce in Los Angeles on September 12, 1947. She has not remarried.

PURDOM, Edmund
(1924-   )

in 1951, the actor married ballet dancer *Anita (Tita) Phillips* in his native England. The couple had two daughters: *Lillian*, born in 1952, and *Mariana*, born in 1954. Purdom filed for divorce in Santa Monica on January 3, 1955, charging his wife with extreme cruelty. But it was Phillips who received the divorce (and custody of their daughters) in Santa Monica on March 5, 1956. Purdom married actress and artist *Alicia Darr* in 1957. Darr received a divorce in Juarez, Mexico, in August of 1961. On March 25, 1962, Purdom married actress *Linda Christian* (divorced from *Tyrone POWER*) in Mexico City. Divorced in 1963, Purdom has not remarried.

QUAID, Dennis
(1954-   )

Quaid, the younger brother of *Randy QUAID*, married actress *Pamela J. Soles* on November 24, 1978. The marriage ended in divorce in 1983. On Valentine's Day, 1991, Quaid married actress *Meg RYAN* at the Bel-Air Hotel.

Q

QUAID, Randy
(1950-   )

The actor is the older brother of *Dennis QUAID*. He married model *Ella Marie Jolly* on May 11, 1980. Their daughter, *Amanda*, was born in 1983. The marriage ended in divorce in 1985. On October 5, 1989, Quaid married film production assistant *Evi Motolanez* in Montecito, California.

QUINN, Anthony
(1915-   )

Quinn wed actress *Katherine DEMILLE* on October 3, 1937, at All Saints Church in Los Angeles despite the objections of her father, *Cecil B. DeMille*. The Quinns had five children: *Christopher*, born in 1939; *Christina*, born in 1941; *Kathleen*, born in 1942; actor *Duncan Quinn*, born in 1945; and *Valentina*, born in 1952. Their son Christopher drowned in 1941. Quinn and DeMille were divorced on January 21, 1965, in Juarez, Mexico, on the grounds of incompatibility. Quinn said that he felt a sense of duty to his two sons in Italy. The sons, *Francesco Daniele*, born in March 1963, in Rome, and *Daniele Antonio*, born in April 1964, in Rome, were his children with Italian actress *Iolanda Addolori*. Quinn and Addolori were married at the Beverly Hills home of his agent, *Milton Grossman*, on January 2, 1966. A third son, *Lawrence Alexander*, was born in Italy in May 1966. Quinn also has a son, born in 1977, with *Ferdel Dunbar*.

RAFT, George
(1895-1980)

Early in 1932, the actor married secretary *Grayce Mulrooney* in Pennsylvania. The couple soon separated but were never divorced. The marriage ended in Mrs. Raft's death in 1969. Raft never remarried.

RAINER, Luise
(1910-)

The actress married playwright, screenwriter, and director *Clifford Odets* on January 8, 1937, at her Brentwood, California, home. Rainer received a divorce on May 14, 1940, in Santa Monica. She told the judge that quarrels about her husband's objections to her career were what had ruined their marriage. On July 12, 1945, she wed British publisher *Robert Knittel* at the Episcopal Church of the Ascension in New York City. The couple resides in London.

RAINES, Ella
(1921-1988)

On August 11, 1942, Raines eloped to Florida with *Capt. Kenneth S. Trout* of the U.S. Army. He left to fight in the war only eleven days later. Raines received a divorce in Los Angeles on December 18, 1945. On February 6, 1947, Raines married *Maj. Robin Olds* at Westwood Community Church in Los Angeles. The couple had two daughters: *Christina*, born in 1951, and *Susan*, born March 12, 1953. The couple settled in Colorado where Raines received a divorce in 1978 after thirty-one years of marriage.

RAINS, Claude
(1889-1967)

While on tour of the United States in 1913, the English-born actor married actress *Isabel Jeans*. The marriage ended in divorce after Rains returned to London. In 1920, he married and divorced actress *Marie Hemingway* in London. He married one of his students at the Royal Academy of Dramatic Arts, *Beatrix Lindsay Thomson*, in 1924. Eleven years later, on April 5, 1935, Rains divorced Thomson in Trenton, New Jersey, charging that she had deserted him in New York City in 1928. Three days later, on April 8, 1935, he wed Bronx-born actress *Frances Propper* at the Bronx County Building in New York City. Their daughter, *Jennifer*, was born in Los Angeles on January 24, 1938. After twenty-one years of marriage, the couple was divorced in 1956. Rains married for the fifth time on November 4, 1959, at his West Chester, Pennsylvania, home. His new wife was *Madame Agi Jambor*, a pianist and lecturer at Bryn Mawr College. Nine months later, on July 29, 1960, Jambor received a divorce in West Chester. Rains married writer *Rosemary Clark* at his West Chester home in August 1960. Rosemary Rains died from cancer at the age of forty-seven at their home in Sandwich, New Hampshire, on December 31, 1964.

RALSTON, Esther
(1902-)

Ralston married actor-agent *George Webb* at the Mission Inn in Riverside, California, on Christmas Day, 1925. Their daughter, *Mary Esther*, was born on August 10, 1931. The actress received a divorce in Santa Monica in March 1934 on the grounds of cruelty. She wed singer *Will Morgan* on June 9, 1935, at the Bel-Air home of friends. The Morgans were divorced in 1938. On August 6, 1939, she married newspaper man *Theodore (Ted) Lloyd* in Greenwich, Connecticut. The Lloyds had two children: *Judith*, born November 12, 1942, and *Theodore, Jr.*, born December 17, 1943. Divorced in 1954, Ralston has not remarried.

RALSTON, Vera Hruba
(1919-)

On March 15, 1952, the Czechoslovakian-born ice skating star married *Herbert Yates*, chief executive of Republic Studios. The couple was married in the Little Brown Church in the Valley in

North Hollywood. Their thirteen-year marriage ended in Yates' death, at age eighty-five, at their Sherman Oaks, California, home on February 3, 1966. Since June 16, 1973, Ralston has been married to businessman *Charles Alva*. The couple resides in Santa Barbara.

RATHBONE, Basil
(1892-1967)

Rathbone married actress *Ethel Marion Foreman* in his native England in October 1914. Their son, *Rodion*, was born in July 1915. Rathbone was divorced in America early in 1926. That same year, on April 18, 1926, he married screenwriter *Ouida Bergére* at the New York City home of architect *Joseph Thomas*. Many New York stage celebrities attended the reception that followed. In September 1939, the Rathbones, who were social leaders in Hollywood, adopted an eight-month-old daughter, *Cynthia*. Their forty-one years of marriage ended in his death on July 21, 1967, at their New York City home. He was seventy-five. Ouida Rathbone died in 1974.

RAY, Charles
(1891-1943)

On November 15, 1915, the film actor married *Clara Grant*. During the peak of his popularity, the Rays were considered to be one of Hollywood's most happily married couples, but they separated in 1932. Grant obtained a divorce in Los Angeles on May 3, 1935, charging cruelty, desertion, and non-support. She testified that Ray had been seen in the company of other women. Shortly after the decree became final in 1936, Ray married French-born *Yvonne Guerin*. He was widowed in 1942.

RAYE, Martha
(1916-)

The actress has been married and divorced six times. On May 30, 1937, she wed Hollywood make-up man *Hamilton (Buddy) Westmore* in Las Vegas. Four months later, on September 28,

1937, Raye received a divorce in Los Angeles, along with a court order restraining Westmore from molesting her. She married composer and arranger *David Rose* on October 8, 1938, in Ensenada, Mexico. She was granted a divorce in Los Angeles on May 17, 1940, testifying that Rose was "sullen and abusive." Rose later became the first husband of *Judy GARLAND*. Raye married hotel manager *Neal Lang* in a midnight ceremony at a Las Vegas hotel on May 25, 1941. That marriage ended in divorce in Juarez, Mexico, on February 3, 1944. A month later, on March 11, 1944, she announced that she had married dancer *Nick Condos* in California. Their daughter, *Melodye*, was born on February 22, 1943. Raye divorced Condos, charging extreme cruelty, on June 18, 1953, in Miami. Dancer *Thomas J. Begley* became her fifth husband in Arlington, Virginia, on April 22, 1954. Two years later, on October 6, 1956, she divorced Begley in Juarez, Mexico. She married *Robert O'Shea*, her former bodyguard, at the Teaneck, New Jersey, home of its mayor, *August Hannibal*, on November 7, 1958. Divorced from O'Shea in 1962, Raye has not remarried.

RAYMOND, Gene
(1908-)

On June 16, 1937, fifteen thousand people lined the streets to catch glimpses of the stars attending the wedding of Raymond to *Jeanette MACDONALD*. The wedding, held at Wilshire Boulevard Church in Los Angeles, is considered to be one of the most beautiful Hollywood has ever seen. The Raymonds were married twenty-seven years, until, on January 14, 1965, MacDonald died of a heart attack in Houston. Raymond was remarried on September 8, 1974, to *Nel Bentley Hees*.

REAGAN, Ronald
(1911-)

Reagan's marriage to actress *Jane WYMAN* took place in Glendale, California, on January 26, 1940. A daughter, singer-actress

Maureen Elizabeth Reagan, was born on January 4, 1941, and a son, *Michael*, was adopted in 1946. The marriage ended in divorce on June 28, 1948, in Los Angeles. The decree became final on July 9, 1949. Wyman charged extreme mental cruelty and was given custody of their children. Reagan married film actress *Nancy Davis* on March 4, 1952. *William HOLDEN* and his wife, actress *Brenda Marshall*, attended the couple. The Reagans have two children: *Patricia Ann*, born October 22, 1952, and *Ronald Prescott Reagan, Jr.*, born May 28, 1958.

REDFORD, Robert
(1937-)

The actor-director has been married to *Lola Jean Van Wagenen* since September 12, 1958. The couple has a daughter, *Shauna*, born in 1960, and a son, *Jamie*, born in 1962. The Redfords have been separated since 1985.

REDGRAVE, Lynn
(1943-)

The actress is the youngest child of *Sir Michael REDGRAVE* and *Rachel Kempson*. Her older sister is actress *Vanessa RED-GRAVE* and her brother is actor *Corin Redgrave*. On April 2, 1967, she wed actor-photographer *John Clark* at the New York City apartment of director *Sidney Lumet*. The Clarks have a son, *Benjamin*, born May 8, 1968, and two daughters, *Kelly*, born in 1970, and *Annabel*, born in 1981.

REDGRAVE, Sir Michael
(1908-1985)

While acting in the Liverpool Playhouse Company, Redgrave met actress *Rachel Kempson*. They were married on July 18, 1935. Their three children are all established actors: *Vanessa RED-*

GRAVE was born on January 30, 1937; *Corin William Redgrave* was born on July 16, 1939; and *Lynn Rachel REDGRAVE* was born on March 8, 1943. All three children were born in London. The couple was married nearly fifty years, until Sir Michael's death from Parkinson's Disease one day short of his seventy-seventh birthday, on March 21, 1985.

REDGRAVE, Vanessa
(1937-)

The oldest child of *Sir Michael REDGRAVE* and *Rachel Kempson*, she is the sister of actor *Corin Redgrave* and actress *Lynn REDGRAVE*. On April 29, 1962, she wed British film director *Tony Richardson* at Hammersmith registry office in London. The couple had two daughters: actress *Natasha Richardson*, born May 11, 1963, and *Joely Kim*, born January 9, 1965. Redgrave divorced Richardson in London on April 28, 1967, on the grounds of adultery. She has not remarried. On September 14, 1969, a son, *Carlos*, was born to Redgrave and actor *Franco Nero*.

REED, Donna
(1921-1986)

On January 30, 1943, Reed married make-up man *William C. Tuttle*. They were divorced in 1945. That same year, on June 15, 1945, she married her agent, *Tony Owen*, at Beverly Hills Community Church. The Owens adopted a daughter, *Penny*, and a son, *Tony, Jr.*, in the late forties. A second daughter, *Mary Ann*, was born in 1948, and a son, *Timothy*, was born in 1950. The Owens were divorced on June 10, 1971, after twenty-six years of marriage. Reed married *Col. Grover Asmus* on August 31, 1974. Their eleven years of marriage ended in Reed's death from cancer in Los Angeles on January 14, 1986. She was sixty-four.

REEVE, Christopher
(1952-)

Reeve has a son, *Matthew*, born in 1980, and a daughter, *Alexandra*, born in 1983, with British modeling agent *Gae Exton*.

REID, Wallace
(1891-1923)

On October 13, 1913, the actor, director, and screenwriter married *Dorothy DAVENPORT* at Christ Episcopal Church in Los Angeles. The Reids had two children: *Wallace, Jr.*, born in 1917, and an adopted daughter, *Betty Ann*. While being treated for head injuries received in a train crash, Reid became addicted to the drug morphine, used as a painkiller. He later became an alcoholic. Their marriage ended in his death at the age of thirty-two in a California sanitarium on January 18, 1923.

REMICK, Lee
(1935-)

Remick married *William Colleran*, a television director and producer, on August 3, 1957. A daughter, *Katherine Lee (Kate)*, was born on January 28, 1959, and a son, *Matthew*, was born on June 7, 1961. The Collerans were divorced on November 23, 1968, in Mexico. On December 18, 1970, she wed British director *William Rory "Kip" Gowens* at the Marylebone registry office in London.

REYNOLDS, Burt
(1936-)

Reynolds wed comedienne *Judy Carne* on June 28, 1963, in North Hollywood. Three years later, on October 25, 1966, the couple was divorced. On April 29, 1988, Reynolds wed actress *Loni Anderson* in Jupiter, Florida. In September 1988, the couple adopted an infant son, *Quinton Anderson*, named for the character Reynolds played on *Gunsmoke*.

REYNOLDS, Debbie
(1932-)

The celebrated marriage of *Debbie Reynolds* and singer *Eddie FISHER* took place at the Catskill Mountains resort Grossingers, in New York on September 26, 1955. Their daughter, actress *Carrie Frances FISHER*, was born on October 21, 1956, in Los Angeles. Their son, *Todd* (named for producer *Mike Todd*, a family friend), was born on February 24, 1958, in Burbank, California. Reynolds did not mention the widow of Mike Todd, actress *Elizabeth TAYLOR*, when she testified that "another woman" had ruined their marriage. On February 19, 1959, Reynolds was granted a divorce from Fisher in Los Angeles. On November 25, 1960, she married shoe manufacturer *Harry Karl* at the Los Angeles home of her sister. The marriage ended in divorce in 1975. Since 1984, Reynolds has been married to real estate developer *Richard Hamlett*.

RICHARDSON, Sir Ralph
(1902-1983)

Richardson wed actress *Muriel Hewitt* at Hampstead registry office in London on September 18, 1924. The couple had been married eighteen years when, on October 4, 1942, Hewitt died from suffocation while recovering from encephalitis in England. She was thirty-five. Richardson was remarried on January 26, 1944, to actress *Meriel Forbes-Robertson*, at Chelsea registry office in London. Their son, *Charles*, was born in London on January 1, 1945. The couple was married thirty-nine years, until the actor's death on October 10, 1983, in London at the age of eighty.

RIGG, Diana
(1938-)

After an eight-year romance with British writer-director *Philip Saville*, Rigg married Israeli artist *Manachem Gueffen* in London on July 6, 1973. The couple separated eleven months later and was divorced in 1976. On May 30, 1977, a daughter, *Rachel*, was born in London to Rigg and *Archibald (Archie) Hugh Stirling*, a former Scots Guards officer who became a film producer. Rigg and Stirling were married in New York City on March 25, 1982. They filed for divorce in 1990.

ROBARDS, Jason, Jr.
(1922-)

The son of actor *Jason Robards*, he married actress *Eleanor Pitman* on May 7, 1948. Three children were born: actor *Jason Nelson Robards III* in 1948, *Sarah Louise* in 1951, and *David* in 1956. The marriage ended in divorce in 1958. In 1959, Robards wed *Rachel Taylor*. They were divorced in Mexico in the spring of 1961. Later that year, on July 4, 1961, he married the widowed *Lauren BACALL* in Ensenada, Mexico. Their son, *Sam*, an actor, was born in New York City on December 16, 1961. The couple was divorced in Juarez, Mexico, on September 10, 1969, on the grounds of incompatibility. Since Valentine's Day, 1970, Robards has been married to actress *Lois O'Connor*. The couple has a daughter, *Shannon*, born in 1972, and a son, *Jake*, born August 25, 1974.

ROBERTSON, Cliff
(1925-)

In 1957, the actor married *Cynthia Stone*, the divorced wife of *Jack LEMMON*. Their daughter, *Stephanie*, was born in 1959. The marriage ended in divorce in the early sixties. On December 21, 1966, Robertson wed actress *Dina Merrill* at Hillwood, the Rock Creek estate of her mother, *Marjorie Merriweather Post*, near Washington, D.C. Their daughter, *Heather*, was born in September 1968. The couple separated in 1985 and was divorced in 1989, after twenty-three years of marriage.

ROBESON, Paul
(1898-1976)

The actor-singer married *Eslanda Cardozo Goode*, a student at Columbia University, on August 17, 1921. Their son, *Paul, Jr.*, was born on November 2, 1927. Eslanda Robeson became an author of two books, including a biography of her husband. Their forty-four years of marriage ended in her death at the age of sixty-eight on December 13, 1965, in New York City.

ROBINSON, Bill "Bojangles"
(1878-1949)

On November 14, 1907, the dancer-actor married *Lena Chase* in New York City. The couple separated in 1916 and was divorced in 1922. That same year, he wed *Fannie Clay*. Twenty-one years later, on June 19, 1943, Fannie Robinson received a Reno divorce. On January 27, 1944, he married dancer *Elaine Plaines* in Columbus, Ohio. The marriage ended in Robinson's death from a heart ailment in New York City on November 25, 1949. He was seventy-one.

ROBINSON, Edward, G.
(1893-1973)

Robinson married actress *Gladys Lloyd* on January 21, 1927. Lloyd had a daughter from a previous marriage. On March 19, 1933, their son, *Emanuel, Jr.*, (Robinson's real name was *Emanuel Goldenburg*) was born in New York City. After twenty years of marriage, Gladys Robinson received a divorce in Santa Monica on August 6, 1956. Robinson wed actress and costume designer *Jane Arden* on January 16, 1958, in Arlington, Virginia. The marriage ended in the actor's death on January 26, 1973, in Los Angeles. He was seventy-nine. His widow is now married to film director *George Sidney*.

ROGERS, Charles, "Buddy"
(1904-)

On June 26, 1937, Rogers wed film star *Mary PICKFORD* at the Bel-Air estate of *Louis D. Lighton*. In 1943, the couple adopted a six-year-old son, *Ronald*. In 1944, the couple adopted a six-month-old daughter, *Roxanne*. Their forty-one years of marriage ended in Pickford's death in Santa Monica on May 29, 1979. She was eighty-six. In 1981, Rogers married *Beverly Ricondo*.

ROGERS, Ginger
(1911-)

The actress has been married and divorced five times. She wed *Jack Edward Culpepper*, who performed in vaudeville using the name *Jack Pepper*, in New Orleans in 1928. They separated after ten months and were divorced in 1931. Rogers married film star *Lew AYRES* on November 14, 1934, at the Little Church of the Flowers in Glendale, California. *Janet GAYNOR* and *Mary BRIAN* were the bridesmaids. The couple separated in 1936 and was divorced in 1941. She married *John Calvin Briggs II*, a private in the marine corps, on January 16, 1943, at the First Methodist Church in Pasadena, California. They were divorced in Los Angeles on September 6, 1949. Rogers received an uncontested divorce decree after telling the judge that Briggs refused to come home at a decent hour. Six months to the day after first being introduced by mutual friend *Evelyn Keyes* in Paris, Rogers and French-born actor *Jacques Bergerac* were married. The ceremony took place on February 7, 1953, in Palm Springs, California. Their marriage ended in divorce in Santa Monica, on the grounds of mental cruelty, on July 9, 1957. Bergerac later married actress *Dorothy MALONE*. Rogers was wed for the fifth time on March 16, 1961, to actor-director *William Marshall*, who was divorced from *Michéle MORGAN*. Rogers and Marshall were married at the First Methodist Church in North Hollywood. They were divorced the following year.

ROGERS, Roy
(1912-)

Rogers married *Arlene Wilkins* at her family's home in Roswell, New Mexico, on June 14, 1936. The couple had three children: four-month-old *Cheryl Darlene* was adopted from Hope Cottage in Louisville, Kentucky, in 1941. A second daughter, *Linda Lou*, was born on April 18, 1943. *Roy Rogers, Jr.,* (nicknamed "Dusty") was born on October 28, 1946. Eight days later, on November 5, 1946, Arlene Rogers died suddenly from a bloodclot. His marriage to film actress *Dale EVANS* took place on December 31, 1947, at the Flying L Ranch in Davis, Oklahoma. A daughter, *Robin Elizabeth*, was born on August 26, 1950. The child was stricken with Downs Syndrome (mental retardation and physical malformation) as well as a heart condition. She died on August 24, 1952, two days before her second birthday, of complications from mumps. In October 1952, the couple adopted a three-fourths Choctaw Indian baby, *Mary Little Doe* (nicknamed "Dodie") from Hope Cottage in Dallas. Also that year, they adopted a six-year-old son, *Harry* from a foster home in Covington, Kentucky. He was renamed *John David Rogers* and nicknamed "Sandy." An eleven-year-old British daughter, *Marion*, was adopted in 1954. The next year, a Korean orphan, *Debbie*, was adopted. Debbie was killed in a bus crash near San Clemente, California, on August 17, 1964. While overseas in the service, Sandy choked to death in Germany on October 31, 1965. Dale Evans Rogers has written three books in memory of their children who have died: *Angel Unaware* (1953), *Dearest Debbie* (1965), and *Salute to Sandy* (1965). All the royalties from her books are donated to charity.

ROGERS, Will
(1879-1935)

The entertainer wed *Betty Blake* on November 25, 1908, at her mother's Arkansas home. The couple had four children: *William Vann Rogers* (actor *Will Rogers, Jr.*), born on October 20, 1911; *Mary Amelia*, born on May 18, 1913; *James Blake*, born on July 25, 1915; and *Fred Stone Rogers* (named for their comedian-friend *Fred Stone*), born in 1918. Fred died of diphtheria the following year. America was shocked into grief when, on August 15, 1935, Rogers and aviator *Wiley Post* were killed in a plane crash near Point Barrow, Alaska. Rogers was fifty-five.

ROLAND, Gilbert
(1905-)

On April 20, 1941, he eloped to Yuma, Arizona, with film star *Constance BENNETT*. The couple had two daughters: *Lorinda*, adopted soon after their marriage, and *Gyl Christina*, born in Los Angeles on December 11, 1941. In September of 1944, the couple separated. Bennett received a divorce on June 13, 1945, as well as custody of their daughters. Since December 12, 1954, Roland has been married to *Guillermina Cantu*.

ROLAND, Ruth
(1892-1937)

In 1917, the actress married *Lionel T. Kent*, a Los Angeles automobile dealer. The couple was divorced in 1919, but he continued to be her manager. In February 1929, she wed vaudeville star and theatre owner *Ben Bard*. They were married until her death after a long illness on September 22, 1937, in Los Angeles.

ROMAN, Ruth
(1924-)

In 1940, the actress married *Jack Flaxman*. The marriage ended in divorce the following year. Roman married *Mortimer Hall*, owner of a Los Angeles radio station, on December 17, 1950. A son, *Richard,* was born in 1952. Roman divorced Hall in Santa Monica on March 29, 1956, on the grounds of mental cruelty. She was given custody of their son. Hall later married actress *Diana LYNN.* On November 8, 1956, Roman wed agent *Budd Moss* in the El Panama Hotel in Panama City, Panama. Less than four years later, on August 10, 1960, the marriage was annulled in Santa Monica on the grounds that her divorce from Hall was not yet final when she married Moss. She has not remarried.

ROONEY, Mickey
(1920-)

The actor has been married eight times. His first wife was film star *Ava GARDNER,* whom he married in Ballard, California, on January 10, 1942. They separated less than a year later, and Gardner received an interlocutory divorce decree in Los Angeles on May 20, 1943. She testified that he had "told her repeatedly that he considered their marriage a mistake." On September 30, 1944, Rooney wed *Betty Jane Rase* (Miss Birmingham of 1944) in Birmingham, Alabama, while serving in the military. Two sons were born: *Joe Yule III* (Mickey Rooney was born *Joe Yule, Jr.*), on July 3, 1944, and *Timothy* in January of 1946. Rase was granted a divorce in Los Angeles on May 28, 1948. Actress *Martha Vickers* became Rooney's third wife on July 3, 1949, at Christ Memorial Unity Church in Los Angeles. Vickers obtained a divorce in Los Angeles on October 3, 1952. A few weeks later, on November 18, 1952, the actor wed model *Elaine Mahnken* at the Wee Kirk o'the Heather wedding chapel in Las Vegas. In May 1958, Rooney received a divorce from Mahnken in Mexico. He wed actress *Barbara Thomason* in Mexico that December. Mahnken received her divorce in Santa Monica on May 21, 1959. Rooney and Thomason had four children. Their first daughter, *Kelly Ann,* was born in Santa Monica on September 13, 1959. A second daughter, *Kerry,* was born on December 30, 1960. A son, *Kyle,* was born in Santa Monica on April 2, 1962. A third daughter, *Kimmy Sue,* was born in Santa Monica on September 13, 1963. The couple separated on January 21, 1966. Rooney filed for divorce three days later complaining that Yugoslavian actor *Milos Milocevic* was living at their Brentwood home and requested a court order to throw Milocevic out. On January 30, 1966, the Rooneys were reconciled. That night, Milocevic fatally shot Thomason and then himself at the Brentwood home. The widowed Rooney was remarried later that year, on September 6, 1966, to *Margie Lane*. The wedding took place at the Chapel of the West in Las Vegas. After three months of marriage, Lane filed for divorce in Los Angeles on December 23, 1966, charging mental cruelty. Rooney and secretary *Carolyn Hockett* were married in Mexico on April 12, 1969. They were remarried in Las Vegas on May 28, 1969. Hockett filed for divorce in Fort Lauderdale, Florida, in October 1974. Since July 28, 1978, Rooney has been married to singer *Jan Chamberlin*. The couple lives in Thousand Oaks, California.

ROTH, Lillian
(1910-1980)

The actress-singer was married and divorced five times. At eighteen, she became engaged to assistant director *David Lyons*, who died before they were married. On April 11, 1931, Roth married air force cadet *Willie Richards* in Atlanta. The marriage ended in divorce in May 1932. On January 29, 1933, she wed *Judge Benjamin Shalleck* in New York City. She received a divorce in Los Angeles on August 16, 1939, testifying that she was hindered in her career. In September 1940, she married *Mark Harris* in California. The union was annulled in Los Angeles on July 7, 1941, on the grounds that he had concealed his criminal activities from her. Later that year, she married *Victor Engel* in Nevada. Engel obtained a divorce in Los Angeles in 1945. In January 1947, Roth married socialite *T. Burt McGuire*, heir to the Funk and Wagnalls publishing fortune, in West New York, New Jersey. The couple separated in 1960. McGuire received a divorce in Phoenix on September 26, 1963, on the grounds of mental cruelty. Roth never remarried.

ROWLANDS, Gena
(1934-   )

On March 19, 1958, Rowlands married actor, director, and screenwriter *John CASSAVETES*. The couple had three children: *Nicholas*, born in 1959; *Alexander,* born in 1965; and *Zoe*, born in 1970. Their thirty years of marriage ended in Cassavetes's death after a long illness in Los Angeles on February 3, 1989, at the age of fifty-nine.

RUBENS, Alma
(1897-1931)

In August 1918, Rubens married actor *Franklyn Farnum*. She divorced him less than a month later on the grounds of cruelty, testifying that Farnum had abused her. She wed *Daniel Carson Goodman*, a physician, author, film director and producer, on August 12, 1923. The couple honeymooned in the Adirondacks. Rubens filed for divorce on January 10, 1925, in Los Angeles. The decree was granted on January 28, 1925. Both Rubens and her mother, *Theresa*, testified to "punches and slaps" the actress had received from Goodman. He did not contest the divorce. On January 30, 1926, Rubens married film star *Ricardo CORTEZ* in Riverside, California. The couple was separated when Rubens died from pneumonia on January 21, 1931, in her home in Los Angeles.

RUGGLES, Charles
(1886-1970)

The comic actor was the older brother of film director *Wesley Ruggles*, who married *Arline JUDGE*. On March 14, 1914, he married actress *Adele Rowland*. The union ended in divorce in the early twenties. He did not remarry until May 7, 1942, when he wed *Marion LaBarba* in Las Vegas. She was divorced from boxer *Fidel LaBarba*. The couple was married twenty-eight years, until the actor's death from cancer in Santa Monica on December 23, 1970. He was eighty-four.

RUSSELL, Gail
(1924-1961)

On July 31, 1949, the actress married *Guy MADISON*. Madison received a divorce in Los Angeles on October 6, 1954, testifying that Russell "cared nothing for their home or marriage." She never remarried.

RUSSELL, Jane
(1921-)

On April 24, 1943, Russell eloped to Las Vegas with football player *Bob Waterfield*. On February 15, 1952, they adopted a newborn daughter, *Tracy*. Later that year, in December, they adopted fifteen-month-old *Tommy Kavanaugh*, son of an English carpenter. In 1956, a third child, nine-month-old *Robert John* was adopted. Russell divorced Waterfield in Los Angeles in July 1968, charging physical abuse. She was given custody of the two older children. On August 25, 1968, she wed actor Roger Barrett at the Community Presbyterian Church in Beverly Hills. Less than three months later, on November 17, 1968, Barrett died of a heart attack. Russell married real estate broker *John Calvin Peoples* in a "kaftan ceremony" in Santa Barbara on January 31, 1974. All six members of the wedding party wore kaftans. The couple now lives in Sedona, Arizona.

RUSSELL, Rosalind
(1908-1976)

Russell married producer *Frederick Brisson* on October 25, 1941, at Mission Santa Ynez in Solvang, California. A son, *Lance,* was born in Hollywood on May 7, 1943. Their thirty-five years of marriage ended in Russell's death from cancer on November 28, 1976, in Los Angeles. She was sixty-three.

RUTHERFORD, Ann
(1917-)

On December 26, 1942, the actress married *David May II*, of the May Co. department store family, at the Los Angeles home of his parents. The couple adopted a daughter, *Gloria*. David May was granted a divorce in Juarez, Mexico, on June 6, 1953, on the grounds of incompatibility. Rutherford was given custody of Gloria. May later married *Lana TURNER*. Since 1953, Rutherford has been married to producer *William Dozier* (divorced from *Joan FONTAINE*). The couple resides in Beverly Hills.

RUTHERFORD, Dame Margaret
(1892-1972)

On March 26, 1945, Rutherford married actor-director (*James Buckley*) *Stringer Davis* in Beaconsfield Parish Church, Buckinghamshire, England. The couple adopted four adults to be their children: actress *Damaris Hayman*, writer *Gordon Langley Hall*, teacher *John Hibberd*, and a third son, the child of a close friend, also named *John*. In 1968, Gordon Hall had a surgical sex change and became *Dawn Langley Hall*. She published a biography of her mother in 1983. The Davises were married twenty-seven years, until Dame Margaret's death on May 22, 1972, at their home in Chalfont St. Peter, Buckinghamshire, England. She was eighty.

RYAN, Meg
(1963-   )

The actress married *Dennis QUAID* on Valentine's Day, 1991, at the Bel-Air Hotel.

RYAN, Robert
(1909-1973)

Ryan wed actress *Jessica Cadwalader* at St. Thomas Episcopal Church in Los Angeles on March 11, 1939. The Ryans had two sons: *Timothy*, born in 1946, and *Cheyney*, born in 1948, and a daughter, *Lisa*, born in 1952. The actor was widowed on May 22, 1972, when Cadwalader died of cancer in New York City at the age of fifty-two.

SAINT, Eva Marie
(1924-   )

On October 27, 1951, the actress married television producer *Jeffrey Hayden*. The couple has a son, *Darrell*, born April 2, 1955, and a daughter, *Laurette*, born July 19, 1958. Both children were born in New York City.

ST. JOHN, Jill
(1940-   )

The actress married laundry heir *Neil Durbin* in 1957. The marriage ended in divorce in 1959. On March 24, 1960, she wed *Lance Reventlow*, the only son of heiress *Barbara Hutton*. Reventlow's father was Danish *Count Court von Haugwitz-Reventlow*. The wedding took place at the Mark Hopkins Hotel in San Francisco. Three years later, on October 30, 1963, the couple was divorced in Los Angeles. She married singer *Jack Jones* (the son of *Allan JONES* and *Irene Hervey*) on October 15, 1967, at the Beverly Hills home of producer *William Dozier*. They were divorced in 1969. In June 1990, St. John married *Robert WAGNER* at his West Los Angeles ranch.

SANDERS, George
(1906-1972)

In the fall of 1942, *Elsie M. Poole* (an actress known professionally as *Susan Larson*) announced that she and Sanders had been married on October 27, 1940. They were divorced in 1948. The actor married *Zsa Zsa GABOR* on April 2, 1949, in a Las Vegas wedding chapel. Gabor received an interlocutory divorce decree in Los Angeles on April 1, 1954. The decree became final the following year. In February 1959, Sanders and actress *Benita HUME*, the widow of *Ronald COLMAN*, were married in Madrid, Spain, The couple was married until her death in England on November 1, 1967. Sanders married *Magda Gabor*, the older sister of his former wife Zsa Zsa Gabor, on December 5, 1970, at the courthouse in Indio, California. It was Magda Gabor's fifth marriage. "He just wanted to get back in the family. He missed me. I always liked George, but when a son-in-law comes back, I really like it," said *Jolie Gabor*, Magda's mother. Six weeks later, the marriage ended in divorce.

SARANDON, Susan
(1946-)

She was *Susan Tomalin* when, on September 16, 1967, she married actor *Chris Sarandon*. The couple remained friends after their divorce in 1979. The actress has a daughter, *Eva Maria Livia*, born in 1985, with Italian director and screenwriter *Franco Amurri*. In May 1989, a son, *Jack Henry*, was born to Sarandon and actor *Tim Robbins* in New York City.

SCHELL, Maria
(1926-)

The actress married German film director *Horst Häechler* on April 27, 1957. Their son, *Oliver*, was born in 1962. Häechler received a divorce in Germany in January 1966. Since September 28, 1966, Schell has been married to director *Veit Relins*. The couple was married in Munich, Germany. Her brother, actor *Maximilian Schell*, has never married.

SCHILDKRAUT, Joseph
(1895-1964)

In 1923, Schildkraut wed actress *Elise Bartlett*. She received a divorce in 1931. The actor married British-born *Mary McKay* in Vienna on May 25, 1932. He was widowed in 1961, after thirty-one years of marriage. In 1963, Schildkraut married *Leonora Rogers*. The marriage ended in his death from a heart attack on January 21, 1964, at their home in New York City. He was sixty-eight.

SCHWARZENEGGER, Arnold
(1947-)

The Austrian-born actor married television journalist *Maria Shriver*, a niece of John F. Kennedy, on April 26, 1986. The couple was married at St. Francis Xavier's Roman Catholic Church in Hyannis, Massachusetts. Their daughter, *Katherine Eunice* (Eunice is the name of Shriver's mother), was born in Santa Monica on December 13, 1989.

SCOTT, George C.
(1927-)

The actor has been married five times. On August 31, 1951, Scott wed Irish-born actress *Carolyn Hughes*. A daughter, *Victoria*, was born in 1952. Separated in 1953, the couple was divorced in 1954. That same year, Scott married actress *Patricia (Pat) Reed*. A son, *Matthew*, was born in 1957, and a daughter, *Devon*, who became an actress, was born in 1959. The marriage ended in divorce. In 1960, Scott married actress *Colleen DEWHURST*. Two sons were born: *Alexander* in 1961 and *Campbell*, an actor, in 1962. The couple was divorced in Juarez, Mexico, in July 1965. On July 4, 1967, Scott and Dewhurst were remarried at his South Salem, New York, farm. They were divorced for the second time in Santo Domingo on February 3, 1972. Since September 13, 1972, Scott has been married to actress *Trish Van Devere*. The couple was married in Santa Monica, California.

SCOTT, Randolph
(1903-1987)

On March 23, 1936, Scott wed *Mariana du Pont Somerville*, a member of the socially prominent du Pont family, in Charlotte, North Carolina. Separated in 1938, Somerville received a divorce in 1939. The actor married socialite *Marie Patricia Stillman* at the courthouse in Riverside, California, on March 3, 1944. The couple adopted a son, *Christopher*, and a daughter, *Sandra*. The Scotts had been married one day short of forty-three years when the actor died on March 2, 1987, in Los Angeles. He was eighty-four.

SEBERG, Jean
(1939-1979)

On September 5, 1958, the actress wed French attorney *François Moreuil* at Trinity Lutheran Church in her hometown of Marshalltown, Iowa. Two years later, on September 20, 1960, Seberg was granted a divorce in Marshalltown on the grounds of cruel and inhumane treatment. Seberg married French diplomat, novelist, and film director *Romain Gary* on October 16, 1962, in Sarrola-Carcopino, Corsica. At the time of their marriage, the couple had a son, *Alexandre Diego*, born on July 17, 1962, in Barcelona, Spain. The Garys were divorced in Paris on July 1, 1970. A daughter, *Nina Hart Gary*, was born on August 23, 1970, in Geneva, Switzerland, but died two days later. On March 12, 1972, the actress married film director *Dennis Berry* in the Chapel of the Bells in Las Vegas. They separated in 1978. Seberg married Algerian-born *Ahmed Hasni* at the American Church in Paris on May 31, 1979. Since she had never been divorced from Berry, the marriage was not legal. The union ended in Seberg's death, a possible suicide, in Paris on August 30, 1979. The actress was forty.

SELLECK, Tom
(1945-)

Selleck married model *Jacquelyn Ray* in 1970. Ray had a son, *Kevin*, from a former marriage. The couple separated in 1979 and was divorced in 1982. On August 7, 1987, Selleck wed British actress *Jillie Mack*, who had appeared in the London production of *Cats*. The couple was married in Incline Village, Nevada. Their daughter, *Hannah Margaret Mack Selleck*, was born on December 16, 1988.

SELLERS, Peter
(1925-1980)

Sellers married actress *Anne Hayes* in London on September 15, 1951. The couple had two children: *Michael,* born in April 1954, and *Sarah,* born in 1958. Sellers received a divorce in London on March 7, 1963, charging Hayes with adultery. He wed Swedish-born actress *Britt Ekland* at the registry office in Guildford, England, on February 19, 1964, four weeks after they first met. Their daughter, *Victoria,* was born in January 1965. Ekland obtained a divorce on December 18, 1968, in London, on the grounds of cruelty. Sellers and *Miranda Quarry* were married in London on August 24, 1970. After a long separation, Quarry divorced him in London in September 1974 on the grounds of irretrievable breakdown. On February 18, 1977, Sellers and actress *Lynne Frederick* were married in Paris. The actor died three years later, on July 24, 1980, from a heart attack in London at the age of fifty-four.

SHARIF, Omar
(1932-   )

Sharif married Egyptian film star *Faten Hamama* on February 5, 1955. The couple had one son, *Tarek,* born in 1957. The couple separated in 1966. They were divorced in 1974. Since January 7, 1977, Sharif has been married to actress *Sohair Ramzi.*

SHEARER, Moira
(1926-   )

On February 25, 1950, the dancer-actress married librarian, writer, and lecturer *Ludovic Kennedy* in the chapel of Hampton Court Palace, near London.

SHEARER, Norma
(1900-1983)

Shearer married production executive *Irving Grant Thalberg* on September 29, 1927, in the garden of his Beverly Hills home. Their son, *Irving, Jr.*, was born in Los Angeles on August 24, 1930. Their daughter, *Katherine*, was born on June 14, 1935, also in Los Angeles. The Thalbergs had been married eight years when, on September 14, 1936, Irving Thalberg died of pneumonia at the age of thirty-seven at their Santa Monica home. Shearer married ski instructor *Martin Arrouge* on August 23, 1942, at the Church of the Good Shepherd in Beverly Hills. Their forty years of marriage ended in Shearer's death from bronchial pneumonia on June 12, 1983, in Woodland Hills, California. Her brother, *Douglas Shearer*, was a cameraman, and her sister, *Athole*, married and divorced film director *Howard Hawks*.

SHEEN, Martin
(1940-)

The actor, who was born *Ramon Estevez*, married his wife, *Janet*, in 1961. The couple has three sons: actor *Emilio Estevez*, born in 1962 in New York City; actor *Ramon Estevez*, born in 1963; *Carlos,* actor *Charlie Sheen*, born September 3, 1965 in Los Angeles; and a daughter, *Renée*, born in 1967.

SHEPHERD, Cybill
(1950-)

After a romance with film director *Peter Bogdanovich*, Shepherd married automotive parts manufacturer *David Ford* in 1978. Their daughter, *Clementine*, was born in 1979. The marriage ended in divorce in 1982. She wed Los Angeles chiropractor *Bruce Oppenheim* at her Los Angeles home on March 1, 1987. Twins, a daughter, *Ariel*, and a son, *Zachariah*, were born in Los

Angeles on October 6, 1987. The couple separated in February 1989. They were divorced in Los Angeles in November 1989.

SHERIDAN, Ann
(1915-1967)

Her first marriage, to actor *Edward Norris* in August 1936, ended in divorce in October of 1937. On January 5, 1942, she married actor *George BRENT* at the Palm Beach, Florida, home of his sister, *Mrs. Sam H. Harris*. Exactly one year later, on January 5, 1943, Sheridan received a divorce in Mexico City, Mexico. In June 1966, the actress wed her stage co-star, *Scott McKay*. The marriage ended in her death, at the age of fifty-one, on January 21, 1967, in Los Angeles.

SHIRLEY, Anne
(1918-)

On August 22, 1937, the actress married *John PAYNE* in Santa Barbara. Their daughter, *Julie Anne*, was born on August 10, 1940. The union ended in divorce on February 19, 1942, in Los Angeles. Shirley charged Payne with cruelty and told the judge that she was "desperately unhappy." She married producer *Adrian Scott* in Las Vegas on February 9, 1945. They were divorced in 1948. On October 19, 1949, Shirley wed producer, director, and writer *Charles Lederer* (son of *Reine Davies*, the sister of *Marion DAVIES*). The wedding took place at the Manhattan home of *Bennett Cerf*. A son, *Daniel Davies Lederer*, was born in August 1950. The couple resided in Bel-Air until Lederer's death, at the age of sixty-five, after a long illness on March 5, 1976.

SHORE, Dinah
(1921-)

On December 5, 1943, the singer-actress married *George MONTGOMERY* in Las Vegas. Their daughter, *Melissa Ann*, was born in 1948. Their son, *John David*, was adopted in 1954. The eighteen-year marriage, considered to be one of Hollywood's most ideal, ended in divorce on May 9, 1962. The decree, granted in Santa Monica, became final on May 9, 1963. Later that month, on May 26, 1963, Shore wed *Maurice Fabian Smith*, a contractor and professional tennis player, at the Palm Springs, California, home of *Judge Joseph Ciano*. The couple separated a year later, and on August 21, 1964, Shore was granted a divorce in Indio, California. She testified that her husband was overly critical. She has not remarried.

SIDNEY, Sylvia
(1910-   )

On October 1, 1935, Sidney married writer and publisher *Bennett Cerf* at the courthouse in Phoenix, Arizona. Eight months later, on April 9, 1936, Sidney was granted a divorce decree in Los Angeles. The actress, who charged Cerf with cruelty, testified that he objected to her career. She married actor *Luther Adler* in London on August 13, 1938. Their son, *Jacob* (nicknamed Jody), was born in New York City on October 22, 1939. Sidney filed for divorce on the grounds of mental suffering in Los Angeles on January 11, 1946. The decree was granted later that year. In 1947, Sidney wed agent and publicist *Carleton W. Alsop*. She filed for divorce in Los Angeles on March 22, 1951, charging him with extreme cruelty. The divorce was granted later that year. Sidney has not remarried.

SIGNORET, Simone
(1921-1985)

In 1948, the actress married French film director *Yves Allegret*. At the time of their marriage, the couple had a daughter, *Catherine*, born in 1946. The marriage ended in divorce in 1949. On December 22, 1951, Signoret wed French singer and actor *Yves Montand* in Saint-Paul, France. The Montands were married forty-three years, until her death from cancer on September 30, 1985, at their country home in Normandy, France.

SILLS, Milton
(1882-1930)

Sills married actress *Gladys Edith Wynne* in England in 1910. Their daughter, *Dorothy*, was born two years later. Gladys Sills received a divorce in Los Angeles on October 11, 1926. The next day, the actor married *Doris KENYON* on the shores of Lake Silver in Ausable Forks, New York. The couple had one son, *Kenyon Clarence Sills*, born in 1927. Less than four years later, on September 15, 1930, Sills died suddenly of a heart attack while playing tennis at their Santa Monica home. He was forty-eight. His son, Kenyon, a geologist, died in 1971.

SILVERS, Phil
(1912-1985)

Silvers married former Miss America (of 1942) *Jo-Carroll Dennison* on March 12, 1945, in Los Angeles. The couple was divorced in 1950. The comedian married actress *Evelyn Patrick* on October 21, 1956. The couple had five daughters: *Tracey*, born June 27, 1957; *Nancey*, born January 19, 1959; twins, *Candy* and *Cathy*, born May 27, 1961; and *Laury*, born January 19, 1964. Divorced from Patrick in 1965, Silvers never remarried.

SIMMONS, Jean
(1929-   )

On December 21, 1950, she wed actor *Stewart GRANGER* in Tucson, Arizona. Their daughter, *Tracy* (named for co-star *Spencer Tracy*), was born in June 1956. Her marriage to Granger ended in divorce in Nogales, Arizona, on August 12, 1960. Simmons charged mental cruelty and was given custody of Tracy. That same year, on November 1, 1960, she married film director *Richard Brooks* in Salinas, California. A daughter, *Kate* (named for *Katharine HEPBURN*), was born in July 1961. Simmons and Brooks were divorced in 1977.

SINATRA, Frank
(1915-)

The singer-actor married *Nancy Barbato* in his native New Jersey on February 4, 1939. Singer *Nancy Sinatra* was born in June 1940, and a son, *Frank Wayne*, followed in January 1944. A second daughter, *Christina*, was born in 1948. Barbato was granted an interlocutory divorce decree (to be final in one year) on the grounds of mental cruelty in Santa Monica on October 30, 1951. In her testimony she stated that Sinatra ignored her, stayed out late many nights, and sometimes had not come home at all. Sinatra sought a Nevada decree, which would become final immediately, in order to marry film star *Ava GARDNER*. Sinatra and Gardner were married, after a well-publicized courtship, on November 7, 1951. The ceremony was held at the Philadelphia home of friends, *Mr. and Mrs. Lester Sacks*. Separated in 1954, Gardner received a divorce decree in Mexico City on July 5, 1957, charging desertion. On July 19, 1966, Sinatra wed actress *Mia FARROW* at the Las Vegas home of *Jack Entratter*, owner of the Sands Hotel. Farrow divorced Sinatra in Juarez, Mexico, on August 16, 1968. Since July 11, 1976, Sinatra has been married to *Barbara Marx*, the widow of *Zeppo Marx*. The wedding took place at the Rancho Mirage (near Palm Springs), home of former ambassador and publisher *Walter H. Annenberg*.

SKELTON, Red
(1913-)

In June 1931, the comedian married *Edna Marie Stillwell* of Kansas City, Missouri. She became his manager and one of the first women gag writers in radio. She divorced Skelton in Los Angeles on February 11, 1943, testifying that "he stayed out late and came in early." She continued to be his manager and later married film director *Frank Borzage*. In March 1945, Skelton married model *Georgia Maureen Davis*. The couple had a daughter, *Valentina Maris*, born May 5, 1947, and a son, *Richard Freeman*, born in 1948. Richard died of leukemia at the age of nine on May 10, 1958. Skelton and Davis were divorced in San Francisco on October 4, 1973, after twenty-eight years of marriage. Five days later, on October 9, 1973, Skelton wed Palm Springs photographer and sportswoman *Lothian Toland* at San Francisco's First Unitarian Church.

SMITH, Alexis
(1921-)

Smith wed actor *Craig STEVENS* at the Church of the Recessional, Forest Lawn, Glendale, California, on June 18, 1944. The couple has no children.

SMITH, Dame Maggie
(1934-)

Smith married actor *Robert Stephens* secretly in May 1967. The couple had two sons; *Christopher*, born June 19, 1967, and *Toby*, born April 21, 1969. Smith filed for divorce from Stephens on July 18, 1974. Later that same year, she married screenwriter *Beverley Cross*.

SOMMER, Elke
(1941-)

The German-born actress married writer *Joe Hyams* on November 19, 1964.

SOTHERN, Ann
(1909-)

One minute after midnight, on September 27, 1936, she wed bandleader and actor *Roger Pryor* at Hollywood Congregational Church. After testifying that Pryor's insistence on flying constituted cruelty, Sothern divorced Pryor in Los Angeles on May 7, 1942. ''We separated twice before our final separation. And all three breakups were due to the same thing, airplanes,'' Sothern stated. On May 23, 1943, Sothern wed actor *Robert Sterling* at the Community Church in Ventura, California. A daughter, *Patricia Ann* (actress *Tisha Sterling*), was born on December 10, 1944. The Sterlings were divorced in Los Angeles on March 8, 1949. Sothern received custody of their daughter. She has not remarried.

SPACEK, Sissy
(1949-)

The actress wed art director *Jack Fisk* on April 12, 1974, in a small chapel in Santa Monica, California. Their daughter, *Schuyler Elizabeth,* was born in July 1982.

STACK, Robert
(1919-)

On January 23, 1956, Stack married model *Rosemarie Bowe* in Beverly Hills. The Stacks have two children, *Elizabeth Langford*, born in 1957, and *Charles Robert*, born May 22, 1958. The actor's brother, *James L. Stack*, was married to *Wanda HENDRIX*.

STALLONE, Sylvester
(1946-)

On December 28, 1974, he wed *Sasha Czack*, whom he had met when they were both ushers at the Baronet movie theater in New York City. The couple had two sons: *Sage*, born in May 1976, and *Seargeoh*, born in 1979. Divorced in the fall of 1985, Stallone wed Danish-born actress and model *Brigitte Nielsen* that winter, on December 15, 1985. The wedding was held at the

Beverly Hills home of producer *Irwin Winkler*. In July 1987, the Stallones filed for divorce in Los Angeles on the grounds of irreconcilable differences and are now divorced.

STANWYCK, Barbara
(1907 – 1990)

On August 26, 1928, she married vaudeville comedian *Frank Fay* at the Missouri Theatre in St. Louis, Missouri. They adopted a ten-month-old son, *Dion Anthony Fay*, on December 5, 1932. The marriage ended in divorce in Los Angeles on December 30, 1935. On May 14, 1939, Stanwyck and film star *Robert TAYLOR* were married at the San Diego home of friends, *Mr. and Mrs. Thomas Whelan*. Twelve years later, on February 21, 1951, Stanwyck was granted a divorce in Los Angeles after testifying that Taylor had requested the divorce. The couple had separated in 1950. Stanwyck never remarried.

STAPLETON, Jean
(1923 –)

The actress married theatrical director and producer *William H. Putch* on October 26, 1957. Their daughter, *Pamela*, was born in 1959, and their son, *John*, was born in 1961. Both of their children became professional actors. The couple founded the Totem Pole Playhouse in Fayetteville, Pennsylvania, together. They had been married twenty-five years when Putch died of a heart attack, at the age of sixty, in Syracuse, New York, on November 23, 1983.

STAPLETON, Maureen
(1925 –)

In July 1949, the actress married business manager *Max Allentuck*. The couple has a son, *Daniel*, born in 1950, and a daughter, *Catherine*, born in 1954. They were divorced in February 1959. In July 1963, Stapleton married playwright *David Rayfiel*, from whom she is now divorced.

STARR, Ringo
(1940-   )

Starr married Liverpool hairdresser *Maureen Mary Cox* on February 11, 1965, at Caxton Hall registry office in London. They had two sons, *Zak*, born September 13, 1965, and *Jason*, born August 19, 1967; and a daughter, *Lee*, born November 17, 1970. Cox divorced Starr in London on the grounds of adultery on July 17, 1975. On April 27, 1981, Starr wed American actress *Barbara Bach* in London.

STEENBURGERN, Mary
(1953-   )

On September 29, 1980, the actress wed *Malcolm MCDOWELL* in New York City. Their daughter, *Lilly*, was born in January 1981, and their son, *Charlie*, was born in 1983. Steenburgern filed for divorce on September 11, 1989, and the decree was granted in 1990.

STEIGER, Rod
(1925-   )

In 1952, Steiger wed actress *Sally Grace*. The couple separated a few months later and was divorced in 1958. The actor married *Claire BLOOM* in Los Angeles on September 19, 1959. Their daughter, *Anna Justine*, now an opera singer, was born on February 13, 1960. The Steigers were divorced in 1969. On April 23, 1973, he married *Sherry Nelson*, a former ballet dancer and secretary, in Los Angeles. Nelson received a divorce in Los Angeles in the fall of 1979. Steiger has not remarried.

STEVENS, Craig
(1918-   )

Stevens wed actress *Alexis SMITH* on June 18, 1944, at the Church of the Recessional, Forest Lawn, Glendale, California. The couple has no children.

STEWART, Anita
(1895-1961)

Stewart married actor *Rudolph Cameron* in May 1918, while working at a film studio in New York City. The marriage ended in divorce on July 2, 1928, in Los Angeles. Stewart testified that Cameron had said "he was sick of married life." She wed New York banker *George Peabody Converse* on the patio of Château Elysée, an apartment house in Los Angeles, on July 24, 1929. The couple spent their honeymoon in Europe. The marriage ended in divorce in 1946. She never remarried. Her sister, actress *Lucille Lee Stewart*, married and divorced actor-director *Ralph Ince*, the brother of *Thomas H. Ince*.

STEWART, James
(1908-   )

Long known as "Hollywood's most eligible bachelor," Stewart was once quoted as saying: "Most successful marriages are those in which the people concerned are young enough to adapt their actions and thoughts to each other. When a fellow's been a bachelor quite awhile he sort of gets in the habit of it." Nevertheless, he married *Gloria Hatrick McLean* on August 9, 1949, at the Brentwood Presbyterian Church. At the time of their marriage, McLean had two sons, *Ronald* and *Michael*, from a former marriage. Twin daughters, *Judy* and *Kelly*, were born to the Stewarts on May 7, 1951. The couple resides in Beverly Hills. Ronald was killed in Vietnam.

STREEP, Meryl
(1951-)

On September 30, 1978, the actress married sculptor *Donald J. Gummer* at her parents' Mystic, Connecticut, home. The couple has three children: *Henry*, born November 14, 1979; *Mary Willa*, born August 4, 1983; and *Grace*, born in May 1986. All of their children were born in New York City.

STREISAND, Barbra
(1942-)

Streisand and actor *Elliott GOULD* were married in Baltimore, Maryland, on March 21, 1963. Their son, *Jason Emanuel Gould*, was born on December 29, 1966, in New York City. On July 1, 1971, Streisand and Gould filed for divorce in Santo Domingo and were divorced within seven days. Streisand has not remarried.

STUART, Gloria
(1910-)

In June 1930, Stuart married sculptor *Blair Gordon Newell*. The couple was divorced early in 1934. That same year, on July 29, 1934, she wed screenwriter *Arthur Sheekman* in Agua Caliente, Mexico. A daughter, *Sylvia*, was born on June 10, 1935. Their forty-three years of marriage ended in Sheekman's death from arteriosclerosis at the age of seventy-six on January 12, 1978, in Santa Monica. Stuart has not remarried.

SULLAVAN, Margaret
(1911-1960)

On Christmas Day, 1931, the actress married *Henry FONDA* at the Kernan Hotel in Baltimore, Maryland. The couple separated four months later and was divorced in 1933. She eloped to Yuma, Arizona, on November 25, 1934, with film director *William Wyler*. She filed for divorce in Mexico on March 13, 1936. Later that year, on November 15, 1936, she wed agent-producer *Leland Hayward* in Newport, Rhode Island. Three children were born: actress *Brooke Hayward* in 1937, *Bridget* in 1939, and *William Leland* in 1941. The Haywards were divorced in April 1948, after eleven years of marriage. In 1950, she married her fourth husband, British industrialist *Kenneth Arthur Wagg*. On January 1, 1960, the actress died, a suicide, in New Haven, Connecticut. She was forty-eight.

SWANSON, Gloria
(1899-1983)

On her seventeenth birthday, March 27, 1916, she eloped to Pasadena, California, with actor *Wallace BEERY*. The first of her six marriages, it ended in divorce two years later when, on December 13, 1918, Beery obtained a divorce on the grounds of desertion. In December 1919, she wed *Herbert K. Somborn*, president of Equity Pictures, at the Hotel Alexandria in Los Angeles. A daughter, *Gloria Swanson Somborn*, was born in Los Angeles on October 7, 1920. The couple separated in May 1921, and Somborn received an uncontested divorce in Los Angeles on September 19, 1923. He testified that his wife had put her career above everything else. That same year, Swanson adopted an infant son, *Joseph*, named after her father. Her third marriage, in Paris, on January 28, 1925, was front page news. Swanson wed *Henri, Marquis de la Falaise de la Courdraye*, whom she had met while filming *Madame Sans Gene* (1925) in France. When the couple arrived in America, they were greeted in New York City by a parade and a brass band. Five years later, on November 6, 1930, the couple was divorced in Los Angeles. They had often been separated while pursuing separate careers. Henri later married *Constance BENNETT*. Swanson wed her fourth husband, Irish-born sportsman and actor *Michael Farmer*, in Elmsford, New York, on August 16, 1931, in a ceremony performed by the mayor, *John Murray*. Soon after, they began to have doubts about the legality of their marriage because at the time of the ceremony, Swanson's divorce from Henri was not yet final. They were remarried in Yuma, Arizona, on November 9, 1931. A daughter, *Michele Bridget Farmer*, was born in London on April 5, 1932. The couple was divorced in Los Angeles on November 7, 1934. Swanson testified that Farmer was excessively quarrelsome and delighted in humiliating her in front of friends. *Lois Wilson* testified on her behalf, and Swanson was given custody of Michele. She did not remarry until January 29, 1945, when she wed retired businessman *George W. Davey* in Union City, New Jersey. They separated forty-four days later and were divorced in 1946. She was married for the sixth time in New York City on February 2, 1976, to *William Dufty*, the author of a book on sugar addiction. "We have all these mutual interests and have been traveling around promoting his book. It just seems silly not to get married," Swanson said. The marriage ended in her death from a heart ailment on April 4, 1983, in New York City. She was eighty-four. Her son, Joseph, died in 1975.

SWEET, Blanche
(1896-1986)

Sweet married director-actor *Marshall "Mickey" Neilan* on June 8, 1922, at the county clerk's office in Chicago. After a long separation, Sweet divorced Neilan in Los Angeles on October 21, 1929. She told the judge that she had been unhappy since she had married him. On October 9, 1935, she wed actor *Raymond Hackett* in Greenwich, Connecticut. Their twenty-two years of marriage ended in Hackett's death, at age fifty-three, on July 7, 1958, in Los Angeles. Sweet never remarried.

TALMADGE, Constance
(1900-1973)

The film star was the younger sister of *Norma TALMADGE* and *Natalie Talmadge*, who married *Buster KEATON*. On December 26, 1920, she eloped to Greenwich, Connecticut, with tobacco manufacturer *John Pialoglu*. The couple was married in a double wedding with *Dorothy GISH* and *James Rennie*. Eighteen months later, on June 1, 1922, the actress received a divorce in Los Angeles, charging mental cruelty. Talmadge married *Capt. Alistair MacIntosh* in California in February 1926. She was granted a divorce in Edinburgh, Scotland, on October 15, 1927, on the grounds of misconduct. She married Chicago department store heir *Townsend Netcher* on May 8, 1929. The wedding took place at the Beverly Hills home of Buster and Natalie Keaton. Divorced, she wed New York Stockbroker *Walter Michael Giblin* in 1939. The couple was married twenty-five years, until Giblin's death on May 1, 1964, in New York City.

TALMADGE, Norma
(1897-1957)

In October 1917, the actress married producer *Joseph M. Schenck* in Connecticut. Schenck guided her career, and Talmadge became one of the biggest stars of the silent era. The couple separated in 1928. Talmadge received a divorce in Juarez, Mexico, on April 14, 1934, on the grounds of incompatibility. Schenck took the blame for the divorce, saying that he had neglected her after becoming president of United Artists. Nine days later, on April 23, 1934, Talmadge wed comedian *George Jessel* in a ceremony held at Atlantic City's Ambassador Hotel and performed by the mayor of that city, *Harry Bacharach*. "I've never been happier in my life. Is there anything more a man can say?" asked Jessel. The union ended in divorce on August 11, 1939, in Juarez, Mexico, on the grounds of incompatibility. On December 4, 1946, Talmadge married Beverly Hills physician *Dr. Carvel James* in Las Vegas. Their eleven years of marriage ended in her death, at age sixty, on December 24, 1957, in Las Vegas. Her younger sisters were *Natalie Talmadge*, who married *Buster KEATON*, and actress *Constance TALMADGE*.

TANDY, Jessica
(1909-)

In 1932, the British-born actress wed actor *Jack HAWKINS*. Their daughter, *Susan*, was born in 1934. The marriage ended in divorce in 1940. On September 27, 1942, she married actor *Hume CRONYN*. The Cronyns have a son, *Christopher*, born in 1946, and a daughter, *Tandy*, born in 1947.

TATE, Sharon
(1943-1969)

In January 1968, the actress wed Polish filmmaker *Roman Polanski* in London. Polanski was in London writing a film script when, on the night of August 8, 1969, Tate and four others were slain in the couple's rented Beverly Hills home.

TAYLOR, Elizabeth
(1932-)

The actress has been married seven times and divorced six times. On May 6, 1950, Taylor was escorted up the aisle in a $3,500 wedding gown by her father, *Francis Taylor*, to wed hotel heir *Conrad Nicholas Hilton, Jr.*, at the Church of the Good Shepherd in Beverly Hills. Seven hundred film stars attended the ceremony while a countless number of fans waited outside. Six months and twenty-five days later, on January 29, 1951, a sobbing Taylor was granted a divorce in Los Angeles on the grounds of extreme mental cruelty. She testified that Hilton cursed her and ignored her at Hollywood parties. On February 21, 1952, she wed British actor *Michael WILDING* at Caxton Hall registry office in London. *Michael Wilding, Jr.*, who became an actor, was born in 1953, and *Christopher Wilding* was born in 1955. Taylor received a divorce in Acapulco, Mexico, on January 31, 1957. Two days later, on February 2, 1957, the mayor of Acapulco married her to producer *Mike Todd*, who was divorced from *Joan BLONDELL*. Their daughter, *Elizabeth Frances Todd*, was born in New York City on August 6, 1957. The Todds had been married thirteen months when, on March 22, 1958, the producer's plane crashed in the Zuni Mountains, ninety miles west of Albuquerque, New Mexico. Everybody on board was killed. Among those comforting the widow was singer *Eddie FISHER*, the husband of *Debbie REYNOLDS*, and a close friend of Todd's. A romance blossomed as Fisher's marriage to Reynolds failed. In her divorce suit, Reynolds never mentioned Taylor by name, but testified that "another woman" had wrecked their marriage. The well-publicized love triangle ended when Fisher and Taylor were married at Temple Beth Sholom in Las Vegas on May 12, 1959. While filming *Cleopatra* (1963) in Italy, Taylor fell in love with her leading man, *Richard BURTON*. On March 5, 1964, Taylor divorced Fisher in Puerto Vallarta, Mexico. She was given custody of Liza Todd, whom Fisher had legally adopted. Burton was divorced from his wife, *Sybil Williams Burton*, and on March 15, 1964, Burton and Taylor were married in Montreal, Canada. Meanwhile, in 1961, Taylor had adopted a handicapped German girl, *Maria Burton Carson*. The separations and reconciliations of the Burtons received much notice in the press, until, on June 26, 1974, Taylor divorced Burton on the grounds of incompatibility in Gstaad, Switzerland. The Burtons remarried on October 10, 1975, in a mudhut village on a Botswana game preserve. The union lasted less than a year; on July 30, 1976, Richard Burton received a Haitian divorce. Husband number seven was former Navy Secretary, later to become Senator, *John W. Warner*, whom she married on his farm outside Middleburg, Virginia, on December 4, 1976. On November 5, 1982, Taylor received a no-fault divorce in Virginia.

TAYLOR, Estelle
(1899-1958)

In 1913, at the age of fourteen, she wed *Kenneth Malcolm Peacock*, a banker in her hometown of Wilmington, Delaware. The couple separated in 1918, when she went to New York to study acting. She divorced Peacock in Philadelphia on January 9, 1925, charging cruel and barbarious treatment. A month later, on February 7, 1925, she wed World Heavyweight Boxing Champion *Jack Dempsey*, who had been her co-star on Broadway and in film. The couple was married at the First Presbyterian Church in San Diego. Dempsey received a divorce in Reno on September 21, 1931. He testified that her acting career had ruined their marriage. In May 1943, Taylor wed producer and agent *Paul Small*. They were divorced in 1946.

TAYLOR, Robert
(1911 - 1969)

On May 14, 1939, Taylor and film star *Barbara STANWYCK* were married at the San Diego home of friends, *Mr. and Mrs. Thomas Whelan*. Eleven years later, on February 21, 1951, Stanwyck received a divorce in Los Angeles after testifying that Taylor had requested the divorce. Taylor married actress *Ursula Theiss*, the ex-wife of German director *George Theiss*, on May 24, 1959. The wedding took place aboard a boat on Jackson Lake, Jackson, Wyoming, at the foot of Grand Teton Mountain. The Taylors had a son, *Terrence*, born in 1955, and a daughter, *Theresa*, born August 16, 1959. Their fifteen years of marriage ended in Taylor's death from cancer on June 8, 1969, in Santa Monica. He was fifty-seven.

TEASDALE, Verree
(1906-   )

On August 25, 1934, the actress married *Adolphe MENJOU* in the Los Angeles chambers of *Judge James H. Pope*. They adopted a son, *Peter Adolphe Menjou*, in 1937. Their twenty-nine years of marriage ended in Menjou's death, at the age of seventy-three, from hepatitis on October 29, 1963, in Beverly Hills. The actress has not remarried.

TELLEGEN, Lou
(1881 - 1934)

In 1905, the actor married artist *Jeanne de Broukére* in Paris. The couple had one daughter, *Diane*. The marriage ended in divorce after two years. He married opera singer and actress *Geraldine FARRAR* at her New York City home on February 8, 1916. Farrar divorced Tellegen in New York City on January 23, 1923. She charged misconduct and alleged that Tellegen had committed adultery on several occasions. Later that year, on December 17, 1923, the actor married *Isabel Craven Dilworth,* the daughter of a wealthy Philadelphia glass manufacturer, in Rutherford, New Jersey. The marriage was not announced until February 17, 1925, in Hollywood. The couple had one son, *Rexford*, born in June 1924, in Jacksonville, Florida. Isabel Tellegen was granted a divorce in Los Angeles on November 22, 1928. On March 9, 1930, Tellegen married actress-dancer *Eva Casanova* in Asbury Park, New Jersey. The marriage ended in his suicide in Los Angeles on October 29, 1934. He was fifty-two.

TEMPLE, Shirley
(1928-   )

On September 19, 1945, at the age of seventeen, she married actor *John Agar*, whom she had met at a house party given by *ZaSu PITTS*, in a "quiet, old-fashioned" ceremony at Wilshire Methodist Church in Los Angeles. Their daughter, *Linda Susan*, was born on January 30, 1948, in Santa Monica. Temple testified that Agar "drank to excess, romanced with other women, and even drove her to thinking of suicide" when she won a divorce (and custody of their daughter) in Los Angeles on December 5, 1949. She married television executive Charles Black on December 16, 1950, in Del Monte, California. The Blacks have a son, *Charles, Jr.*, born April 28, 1952, in Washington, D.C., and a daughter, *Lori*, born April 9, 1954, in Santa Monica.

TERRY, Alice
(1899-)

The actress married film director *Rex Ingram* in Pasadena, California, in November 1921. Ingram had been her director before their marriage and continued to guide her career with success. The Ingrams were married for thirty-eight years, until his death at the age of fifty-eight on July 22, 1950, in Los Angeles. Terry has not remarried.

THAXTER, Phyllis
(1921-)

In 1944, Thaxter married film executive *James Aubrey*. The couple had a daughter, *Schuyler*, born in 1945, who became an actress, and a son, *James, Jr.*, born in 1953. Divorced in 1962, she wed publisher *Gilbert Lea* that same year.

THOMAS, Danny
(1914-1991)

The actor married singer *Rose Marie Cassaniti* in Michigan on January 15, 1936. The couple has three children: *Margaret Julia*, better known as actress-writer *Marlo Thomas*, born November 21, 1937; *Theresa Cecelia*, born in 1943; and *Anthony Charles*, born in 1948. Marlo Thomas wed talk show host *Phil Donohue* in 1981. Thomas died from a heart attack at his Beverly Hills home on February 6, 1991. He was seventy-seven years old.

THOMAS, Olive
(1897-1920)

She was *Olive Elaine Duffy* when, in about 1913, she married *Bernard Krug Thomas* in Pennsylvania. The marriage ended in divorce in 1915 soon after she arrived in New York City to begin her career. In May 1917, she wed actor-director *Jack PICK-FORD*. On September 20, 1920, Thomas died at the American Hospital in Neuilly, France, from an overdose of bichloride of mercury tablets. The circumstances surrounding her death remain a mystery.

TIERNEY, Gene
(1920-   )

On June 1, 1941, the actress eloped with designer *Oleg Cassini* to Las Vegas. The couple had two daughters: *Daria*, born October 14, 1943, and *Christina*, born in 1949. Tierney divorced her husband in Santa Monica on February 28, 1952, testifying that Cassini was more interested in his tennis game than in their marriage. She married Houston oilman *Howard Lee* (divorced from *Hedy LAMARR*) on July 11, 1960, at the Community Church in Aspen, Colorado. She was widowed in 1980.

TOBIN, Genevieve
(1901-   )

The actress wed film director *William Keighley* on September 19, 1938. Their forty-five years of marriage ended in Keighley's death at the age of ninety-four on June 24, 1984, in Beverly Hills.

TODD, Thelma
(1905-1935)

On July 10, 1932, she eloped to Prescott, Arizona, with her agent, *Pasquale De Cicco*. Less than two years later, on March 2, 1934, Todd won a divorce in Los Angeles charging extreme cruelty.

TONE, Franchot
(1905 - 1968)

Tone's four wives were all actresses. On October 11, 1935, he married *Joan CRAWFORD* in Englewood Cliffs, New Jersey. Crawford received a divorce in Los Angeles on April 11, 1939, on the grounds of mental cruelty. She testified that Tone had told her: "I am sorry we married. Marriage was a mistake for me. I'm not the marrying kind and I want my freedom." They remained friends. On October 8, 1941, he wed *Jean WALLACE* in Yuma, Arizona. The couple had two sons, *Pascal Franchot*, born July 29, 1943, and *Thomas Jefferson*, born September 16, 1945. Wallace was granted a divorce in Los Angeles on August 23, 1948. The decree became final on September 30, 1949. In 1951, Tone landed in the hospital after a fight with actor *Tom Neal* over the affections of actress *Barbara Payton*. Tone and Payton were married in her hometown of Cloquet, Minnesota, on September 28, 1951. Tone filed for divorce in Los Angeles, charging extreme mental cruelty, on November 20, 1951, after fifty-three days of marriage. The decree was granted in 1952, and Payton later married (and divorced) Tom Neal. In 1956, Tone married *Dolores Dorn-Heft* in Canada. The marriage was kept a secret until March 1958. Divorced in 1959, the actor never remarried.

TORN, Rip
(1931 -   )

On January 15, 1955, the actor married actress *Ann Wedgeworth*. A daughter, *Danae*, was born in 1956. The marriage ended in divorce the following year. On September 11, 1963, Torn announced that he had been married to actress *Geraldine PAGE* for the past nine months. But in later years both Torn and Page confessed that they couldn't remember exactly when they had been married. Their daughter, *Angelica*, was born on February 17, 1964. Twin sons, *Anthony* and *Jonathan* were born on June 9, 1965. The marriage ended in Page's death at the age of sixty-two on June 13, 1987, in New York City.

TRACY, Lee
(1898-1968)

The actor eloped to Yuma, Arizona, on July 19, 1938, with socialite divorcée *Helen Thomas Wyse*. The couple was married for
thirty years, until Tracy's death from cancer on October 18,
1968, in Santa Monica. He was seventy.

TRACY, Spencer
(1900-1967)

On September 12, 1923, Tracy married actress *Louise Treadwell*
in Cincinnati, Ohio. Their son, *John*, was born in June 1924.
Their daughter, *Louise* (nicknamed "Susie"), was born in 1932.
The couple remained married, although estranged, until Tracy's
death. The actor died on June 10, 1967, from a heart attack at his
home in Beverly Hills. He was sixty-seven.

TREVOR, Claire
(1909-   )

The actress married radio producer *Clark Andrews* on July 27,
1938. Less than four years later, on July 13, 1942, Trevor divorced Andrews in Los Angeles. She charged Andrews with in-
difference and living beyond his means. The decree was not to
become final until July 1943, but Trevor married *Lieut. Cyclos
Dunsmoore* of the navy in Tijuana, Mexico, in April 1943. She did
not announce her marriage until she received her final divorce
decree from Andrews on July 24, 1943. A son, *Charles Cyclos
Dunsmoore*, was born in 1944. The union ended in divorce in
1947. Trevor married producer *Milton Bren* on November 14,
1948. She was widowed in 1979.

TUFTS, Sonny
(1911-1970)

The actor wed dancer *Barbara Dare* on December 5, 1938, in
Fort Lee, New Jersey. The union ended in divorce after fifteen

years of marriage (including a three-year separation) in Los Angeles on November 9, 1953. Tufts never remarried.

TURNER, Kathleen
(1954-)

Turner married real estate executive *Jay Weiss* in 1984. The couple has one daughter, *Rachel*, born in the fall of 1987.

TURNER, Lana
(1920-)

The actress has been married eight times. She eloped to Las Vegas on February 13, 1940, with musician *Artie Shaw*. The couple was married by *Judge Marshall* at four o'clock in the morning. Turner received a divorce from Shaw in September 1941. Shaw later wed actresses *Ava GARDNER* and *Evelyn KEYES*. Turner wed restaurateur *Stephan Crane* in Las Vegas on July 17, 1942. She was again married by Judge Marshall who greeted her with "Welcome back, Lana!" In December 1942, the couple discovered that they had been married before Crane's divorce from his first wife was final. Turner obtained an annulment on these grounds (and custody of their unborn child) in Los Angeles on February 4, 1943. Crane and Turner were remarried in Tijuana, Mexico, on March 14, 1943. Their daughter, *Cheryl Christine*, was born on July 25, 1943, in Los Angeles. On April 8, 1944, Turner filed for divorce from Crane in Los Angeles. The decree was granted later that year. She was married for the fourth time on April 26, 1948, to *Henry J. (Bob) Topping* (divorced from *Arline JUDGE*), the heir to a tin-plate fortune. The ceremony took place at the Hollywood home of a friend, *William R. Wilkerson*. The actress received a divorce from Topping on December 15, 1952, in Carson City, Nevada. Actor *Lex BARKER* became her fifth husband on September 7, 1953, in Turin, Italy. Four years later, on June 28, 1957, she filed for divorce in Santa Monica charging Barker with "cruel and inhumane conduct." On November 27, 1960, she wed *Fred May*, of the May Co. department store family. May was divorced from actress *Ann RUTHERFORD*. Two years later, in October 1962, Turner received a divorce in Juarez, Mexico. In June 1965, she was married for the seventh time, to writer *Robert Eaton*. The couple was married at the Arlington, Virginia, home of Eaton's father. The union ended in divorce four years later, on April 1, 1969. Turner, who received the decree in Santa Monica, called Eaton an "absentee spouse." She wed nightclub hypnotist *Ronald Dante* in Las Vegas on May 8, 1969. Divorced from Dante that December, the actress has not remarried.

TURPIN, Ben
(1874-1940)

In 1907, the comedian married *Carrie LeMieux*. They were married eighteen years, until, on October 1, 1925, LeMieux died in Quebec, Canada, after a long illness at the age of forty-three. Turpin was remarried on July 7, 1926, to *Babette Elizabeth Dietz*. They were married at the Church of the Good Shepherd in Beverly Hills. Their fourteen years of marriage ended in Turpin's death from a heart attack on July 1, 1940, in Santa Monica. He was sixty-five.

TWELVETREES, Helen
(1907-1958)

In 1927, *Helen Jurgens* eloped to Greenwich, Connecticut, with actor and artist *Clark Twelvetrees*. The marriage ended in divorce in Los Angeles on March 26, 1930, on the grounds of cruelty. The interlocutory decree became final on April 1, 1931. Later that month, on April 21, 1931, she wed *Frank Woody*, a Los Angeles real estate man, in Santa Cruz, California. The couple had one son, *Jack Bryan Woody*, born on October 26, 1932. She received a divorce from Woody in Los Angeles on April 15, 1936, after testifying that Woody had abused her with unseemly language. She was given custody of their son. In 1946, she wed an air force captain, Conrad Payne, and settled in Har-

risburg, Pennsylvania. On February 13, 1958, she committed suicide in Harrisburg. She was forty-nine.

TYSON, Cicely
(1932?-   )

The actress married jazz musician *Miles Davis* in November
1981, at Bill Cosby's farm near Amherst, Massachusetts. The
couple filed for divorce in December 1988, and the decree was
granted in 1989.

ULLMAN, Liv
(1939-)

In 1960, the actress married psychiatrist *Dr. Gappe Stang* in Oslo, Norway. They were divorced in 1965. Ullman has a daughter, *Linn*, born in 1965, with Swedish film director *Ingmar Bergman*. She married real estate agent Richard Saunders in Rome in September 1985.

ULRIC, Lenore
(1892-1970)

On May 23, 1927, Ulric married actor *Sidney Blackmer* in Croton-On-Hudson, New York. They were divorced on August 6, 1933, in Mexico, on the grounds of incompatibility. Ulric, who never remarried, was once quoted as saying: ''I don't think I'm comfortable to live with. I have a temper. I'm difficult. I'm too quick and too impulsive. And men have a right to be comfortable.''

USTINOV, Sir Peter
(1921-)

The actor, director, and screenwriter married *Isolde Denham*, the daughter of playwright *Reginald Denham*, in London in 1940. Their daughter, *Tamara*, was born in London on July 25, 1945. The Ustinovs were divorced in London in the late forties. On February 15, 1954, Ustinov wed French-Canadian actress *Suzanne Cloutier* at the Chelsea registry office in London. The couple had three children: *Pavla*, born June 2, 1954, in Los Angeles; *Igor*, born April 30, 1956, in London; and *Andrea*, born March 30, 1959, in Los Angeles. Their seventeen years of marriage ended in divorce in 1971. On June 21, 1972, Ustinov married French press agent *Helene deu Lau d'Allemans* in Corsica.

VALENTINO, Rudolph
(1895-1926)

In November 1919, Valentino married actress *Jean Acker* in Mexico. The couple separated only a few days later, and Acker received a divorce in Los Angeles in January 1922. The interlocutory decree became final on March 12, 1923. Three days later, on March 15, 1923, he married actress, set designer, and scenarist *Natacha Rambova* in Crown Point, Indiana. Rambova tried to guide her husband's career, but under her guidance his popularity began to wane. On January 19, 1926, she received a divorce in Paris on the grounds of desertion. Valentino was engaged to *Pola NEGRI* when, on August 23, 1926, he died following surgery in New York City at the age of thirty-one.

VALLEE, Rudy
(1901-1986)

In 1928, the musician and actor married *Leonie Cauchois*. The couple received an annulment later that same year. On July 6, 1931, Vallee married *Fay Webb*, daughter of a Santa Monica policeman, in West Orange, New Jersey. Webb was granted a divorce in Los Angeles on May 20, 1936, after testifying that Vallee "knew how to torment me and did." Actress *Jane GREER* became Vallee's third wife on December 2, 1943, in the Westwood Village Community Chapel in Los Angeles. Eight months later, on July 27, 1944, Greer received a divorce in Los Angeles. She told the judge that her husband had called her "beautiful but dumb." Vallee married *Eleanor Kathleen Norris* on September 4, 1949, at the Corpus Christi Roman Catholic Church in Oakland, California. At the wedding reception at a nearby country club, the bride's veil brushed against a candle and caught fire. Vallee immediately grabbed the veil and crushed the flames with his bare hands. Neither the bride nor Vallee was hurt. Their thirty-six years of marriage ended in his death, at age eighty-four, on July 3, 1986, at their home in the Hollywood hills.

VALLI, Alida
(1921-)

Valli married Italian pianist and composer *Oscar de Mejo* in 1944. The couple had two sons: *Carlos*, born in 1945, and *Lorenzo*, born in 1950. Divorced in 1952, Valli has not remarried.

VAN DYKE, Dick
(1925-)

On February 12, 1948, Van Dyke married his childhood sweetheart, *Marjorie Willetts,* on the "Bride and Groom" radio show. The couple has four children: *Christian*, born in 1950; *Barry*, born in 1951; *Stacey,* born in 1955; and *Carrie Beth*, born in 1961.

VELEZ, Lupe
(1908-1944)

After a well-publicized romance with *Gary Cooper*, Velez married swimmer and actor *Johnny WEISSMULLER* on October 8, 1933, in Las Vegas. They separated in 1934, again in 1935, and for the last time on July 5, 1938. Velez received a divorce in Los Angeles on August 15, 1938.

VERA-ELLEN
(1926-1982)

In 1945, the dancer and actress married dancer *Robert Hightower*. The marriage ended in divorce only a year later, in 1946. On November 19, 1954, she married oilman *Victor Rothschild* at St. Paul's Lutheran Church in the San Fernando Valley, near Los Angeles. The Rothschilds had one daughter born on March 3, 1963. She died three months later on June 22, 1963. Divorced in 1966, Vera-Ellen never remarried.

VERDON, Gwen
(1925-)

The actress, dancer, and singer married Hollywood writer *James Henaghan* in 1942. Their son, actor *James O'Farrell*, was born in 1943. The marriage ended in divorce in June 1947. In April 1960, Verdon wed dancer and choreographer *Bob Fosse*. Their daughter, *Nicole*, was born on March 24, 1963. The Fosses were divorced in 1979.

VIDOR, Florence
(1895-1977)

She was *Florence Arto* when she married *King Vidor*, who became a film director, in her native Texas in 1915. The couple headed for Hollywood, where their daughter, *Suzanne*, was born on December 26, 1918. The Vidors were divorced in Los Angeles in 1925. King Vidor later married *Eleanor BOARDMAN*. Florence Vidor married violinist *Jascha Heifetz* at Mayfair House in New York City on August 20, 1928. A son, *Robert*, was born in 1930, and a daughter, *Josepha*, was born in 1932. Seventeen years after their wedding, on January 3, 1946, Heifetz was granted an interlocutory divorce decree in Santa Ana, California, after testifying that Vidor belittled his musical ability. She was given custody of their children. She never remarried.

WAGNER, Robert
(1930-)

The actor first married *Natalie WOOD* on December 28, 1956, at the Scottsdale Methodist Church in Scottsdale, Arizona. Four years later, on April 17, 1962, Wood filed for divorce in Santa Monica, charging mental cruelty. The decree was granted later that year. Wagner married actress *Marian Marshall* at the Bronx County courthouse in New York City on July 21, 1963. A daughter, *Katharine (Kate)*, was born on May 12, 1964. The marriage ended in divorce in October 1971. On July 16, 1972, Wagner and Wood were remarried aboard the yacht *Rambling Rose* off the coast of Southern California. Wood had a daughter, *Natasha*, from an in-between marriage to producer *Richard Gregson*. Wagner's and Wood's daughter, *Courtney Brooke*, was born on March 11, 1974. On the night of November 29, 1981, Wood lost her footing aboard a yacht off Catalina Island, California, and drowned at the age of forty-three. Eight years later, in June 1990, Wagner married actress *Jill ST. JOHN* at his ranch in the Santa Monica Mountains, near Los Angeles.

WALKER, Robert
(1918-1951)

In New York City, early in his career, he met actress and model *Phyllis Isley*. They were married exactly thirteen weeks later, on January 2, 1939. They had two sons, both of whom became actors: *Robert Walker, Jr.*, was born on April 15, 1940, and *Michael Walker* was born on March 13, 1941. In 1942, the couple moved to Hollywood, where producer *David O. Selznick* changed Isley's name to *Jennifer JONES* and put her under a long-term contract. Selznick and Jones became romantically linked, while Walker's success at this time was only moderate. Jones divorced Walker in Los Angeles on June 20, 1945, on the grounds of mental cruelty. She married Selznick in 1949. On July 9, 1948, Walker married *Barbara Ford*, the daughter of director *John Ford*, at the Beverly Hills Club in Beverly Hills. The couple separated six weeks later. Ford was granted a divorce in Los Angeles on December 16, 1948, on the grounds of extreme cruelty.

WALLACE, Jean
(1923-1990)

On October 8, 1941, the actress eloped to Yuma, Arizona, with *Franchot TONE*. The couple had two sons: *Pascal Franchot*, born July 29, 1943, and *Thomas Jefferson*, born September 16, 1945. Wallace was granted a divorce in Los Angeles on August 23, 1948. The decree became final on September 30, 1949. She married *Capt. Jim Randall* in San Diego on January 30, 1950. Six months later, in June 1950, Wallace asked for an annulment in Los Angeles. The annulment was granted in November 1950. On September 4, 1951, Wallace married *Cornel WILDE* in the Los Angeles chambers of *Judge Arthur Crum*. Their son, *Cornel Wallace Wilde*, was born in the late sixties. The Wildes were divorced in 1981 after thirty years of marriage. Wallace never remarried.

WALLACH, Eli
(1915-   )

On March 5, 1948, Wallach married actress *Anne JACKSON*. The couple has three children: Peter, born February 20, 1951; *Roberta*, born in 1955; and *Katherine*, born July 13, 1958.

WALSH, Raoul
(1887-1980)

The actor-director married film star *Miriam COOPER* in February 1916 at a Hopi Indian reservation near Albuquerque, New Mexico. The couple adopted two sons from the New York Foundling Hospital: *Jackie*, in 1918, and *Bobby*, in 1922. Cooper received a divorce in Los Angeles on the grounds of incompatibility in 1926. The decree became final in 1927. Later that year, Walsh married socialite *Lorraine Walker*. They were divorced in 1937. Early in 1941, he wed *Edna Mary Simpson*, the daughter of a horse breeder, in Lexintgon, Kentucky. Their thirty-nine years of marriage ended in Walsh's death on December 31, 1980, at his ranch in the Simi Valley of California. He was ninety-three.

WAYNE, David
(1914-   )

Wayne married actress *Jane Gordon* on December 21, 1941, at the Little Church Around the Corner in New York City. Twin daughters, *Melinda* and *Susan*, were born in 1946. A son, *Timothy* was born in 1948.

WAYNE, John
(1907-1979)

Wayne married *Josephine Saenz*, the daughter of a Dominican Republic businessman, on June 24, 1933. The wedding was held at the Bel-Air estate of *Loretta YOUNG*. The couple had four children: *Michael*, born in 1934; *Antonia Maria,* born in 1936; *Patrick,* born in 1937; and *Melinda Ann,* born in 1939. Saenz received a divorce in November 1944, which became final in 1945. Three weeks later, on January 17, 1946, he wed Mexican singer-dancer *Esperanza "Chata" Baur*, at the United Presbyterian Church in Long Beach, California. The marriage was a stormy one, ending with both Wayne and Baur simultaneously receiving divorce decrees in Los Angeles on October 28, 1953. On November 1, 1954, he married Peruvian actress *Pilar Pallette* in a ninety-second ceremony in Kona, Hawaii. Three children were born: *Aissa* on March 31, 1956, in Burbank, California; *John Ethan* on February 22, 1962, in Encino, California; and *Marissa* on February 22, 1966, in San Fernando, California. Wayne and Pallette separated in 1973, but remained married until his death from cancer in Los Angeles on June 11, 1979. The actor was seventy-two.

WEAVER, Sigourney
(1949-   )

In 1984, Weaver married actor *Jim Simpson*, whom she had met when they both studied drama at Yale. Their daughter, *Charlotte*, was born in April 1990.

WEISSMULLER, Johnny
(1904-1984)

The swimmer-actor married musical comedy actress *Bobbe Arnst* on February 28, 1931, in Fort Lauderdale, Florida, after a two-week courtship. Less than two years later, on October 4, 1932, Arnst received a divorce in Los Angeles. She told the judge that Weissmuller rarely came home for meals. Weissmuller married film star *Lupe VELEZ* on October 8, 1933, in Las Vegas. The marriage was marked by many separations and reconciliations. Finally, on August 15, 1938, Velez obtained a divorce in Los Angeles. A year later, on August 20, 1939, Weissmuller and San Francisco socialite *Beryel Scott* were married in Garfield, New Jersey, by *Mayor John Gabriel*. Three children were born: *John Scott* on September 23, 1940; *Wendy Ann* on June 1, 1942; and *Heidi Elizabeth* on July 20, 1943. All three of the children were born in Los Angeles. Weismuller was divorced from Scott in Reno on January 29, 1948. Five hours later, he wed professional golfer *Allene Gates* in Reno. Gates received a divorce late in 1962. On April 23, 1963, Weissmuller wed Bavarian-born *Maria Bauman Brock*, a widow with one daughter, *Lisa*. The couple was married at the Dunes Hotel in Las Vegas. The twenty-year marriage ended in Weissmuller's death at the age of seventy-nine on January 20, 1984, at his home in Acapulco, Mexico. His daughter, Heidi, was killed in a car accident in 1962.

WELCH, Raquel
(1940-   )

On May 8, 1959, *Raquel Tejada* wed her high school sweetheart, *James Westley Welch*. The couple had two children: *Damon*, born in 1959, and actress-model *Tahnee Welch*, born in 1961. The marriage ended in divorce in 1964. She married press agent *Patrick Curtis*, who had helped build her into a star, on Valentine's Day, 1967, in Paris. Curtis adopted her two children, but the couple separated in March 1971. She filed for divorce in September 1971, and the decree became final in 1972. Welch married French film writer and producer *André Weinfeld* on July 5, 1980. The ceremony was held at a resort hotel in Carlo San Lucas, Mexico. The couple was divorced in September 1990.

WELD, Tuesday
(1943-   )

In October 1965, the actress married writer *Claude Harz*. A daughter, *Natasha*, was born in 1966. The couple was divorced in 1971. In 1975, Weld married *Dudley MOORE*. A son, *Patrick*, was born in March 1976. The marriage ended in divorce in 1980.

WELLES, Orson
(1915-1985)

Welles married actress *Virginia Nicholson* in December 1934. The couple had one daughter, *Christopher*, born in New York City on March 27, 1938. The marriage ended in divorce in 1940. Welles and film star *Rita HAYWORTH* were married in Santa Monica on September 7, 1943. *Rebecca Welles* was born on December 17, 1944. Hayworth received a divorce in November 1948. On May 8, 1955, Welles married Italian actress *Paola Mori, Countess Di Girfalco*, in London. Their daughter, *Beatrice*, was born in New York City in November 1955. Their thirty years of marriage ended in his death from a heart attack, at the age of seventy, on October 10, 1985, at their Los Angeles home. Paola Mori Welles died in 1986.

WEST, Mae
(1892-1980)

West had long been known as Hollywood's bachelor girl when, in 1935, it was discovered that she had married a vaudeville performer, *Hal Wallace*, in Milwaukee in April 1911. West at first denied it, but eight years later, after a long and bitter suit, she received a divorce from Wallace in Los Angeles on August 4, 1943.

WHITE, Pearl
(1889-1938)

White married actor *Victor Sutherland* on October 12, 1907, in Oklahoma City, Oklahoma. The couple was divorced in 1914, after a long separation. The actress wed film director and actor *Wallace McCutcheon* in 1919. Two years later, on July 20, 1921, White divorced McCutcheon in Providence, Rhode Island, on the grounds of neglect to provide. She never remarried.

WHITTY, Dame May
(1865-1948)

In August 1892, Whitty married actor *Ben Webster*, who was descended from an old English theatrical family. Their daughter, actress and director *Margaret Webster*, was born on March 15, 1905. Their fifty-five years of marriage ended in Webster's death at the age of eighty-two on February 26, 1947, in Los Angeles.

WIDMARK, Richard
(1914-   )

The actor married drama student *Ora Jean Hazelwood* on April 5, 1942. They have one daughter, *Anne*, born in 1945, who married baseball player *Sandy Koufax*.

WILDE, Cornel
(1915-1989)

On September 21, 1937, Wilde eloped to Elkton, Maryland, with actress *Patricia Knight*. Their daughter, *Wendy Wilde*, was born in Los Angeles on February 22, 1943. Patricia Wilde received a Reno divorce on August 30, 1951, on the grounds of mental cruelty, after fourteen years of marriage. Five days later, on September 4, 1951, the actor, producer, and director married actress *Jean WALLACE* in the Los Angeles chambers of *Judge Arthur Crum*. Their son, *Cornel Wallace Wilde*, was born in the late sixties. The Wildes were divorced in 1981, after thirty years of marriage.

WILDER, Gene
(1935-   )

Wilder married playwright-actress *Mary Mercier* on July 22, 1960. Divorced, he wed *Mary Joan Schutz* on October 27, 1967. He adopted her daughter from a former marriage, *Katharine Anastasia* They were divorced in 1974. In 1984, Wilder married comedienne *Gilda Radner*. Five years later, on May 20, 1989, Radner died of cancer in Los Angeles at the age of forty-two.

WILDING, Michael
(1912-1979)

The actor married *Kay Young*, an actress, in his native England in 1938. They were divorced in 1941. Wilding married film star *Elizabeth TAYLOR* on February 21, 1952, at Caxton Hall registry office in London. *Michael Wilding, Jr.*, who became an actor, was born in 1953, followed by *Christopher Wilding*, born in 1955. Taylor received a divorce in Acapulco, Mexico, on January 31, 1957. She married producer *Mike Todd* two days later. On February 12, 1958, Wilding married socialite *Susan Nell* in Nevada. She was granted a divorce in London on July 23, 1962, on the grounds of adultery. On July 15, 1964, he married actress *Margaret LEIGHTON* in Los Angeles. Their twelve years of marriage ended in Leighton's death, at the age of fifty-three, after a long illness, on January 13, 1976, in Chichester, England.

WILLIAMS, Esther
(1923-   )

In 1940, the swimmer-actress married medical intern *Dr. Leonard Kovner*, in San Francisco. They were divorced in September 1944. On November 25, 1945, Williams wed radio announcer and singer *Ben Gage*. The Gages had three children: *Benjamin Stanton Gage, Jr.*, born in 1949; *Kimball Austin*, born in 1950; and *Susan Tenney*, born in 1953. Their marriage ended in divorce in Santa Monica on April 8, 1958, on the grounds of mental cruelty. Williams was given custody of their children as well as most of their community property. In 1967, she wed actor *Fernando LAMAS* in Europe. They were remarried on December 31, 1969, at the Founder's Church of Religious Science near Hollywood. On October 8, 1982, Lamas died from cancer in Los Angeles at the age of sixty-seven.

WILLIAMS, Robin
(1952-)

Williams wed dancer *Valerie Velardi* in San Francisco on June 4, 1978. Their son, *Zachary*, was born in 1983. The couple separated in 1987 and was divorced in 1988. On April 30, 1989, Williams married *Marsha Garces*, Zachary's former nanny, at Lake Tahoe. Their daughter, *Zelda*, was born in New York City on July 31, 1989.

WILLIS, Bruce
(1955-)

Willis married actress *Demi MOORE* in Las Vegas on November 21, 1987. Their daughter, *Rumer Glenn*, was born on August 16, 1988, in Paducah, Kentucky.

WINDSOR, Claire
(1897-1972)

In 1917, the actress, then known as *Clara Viola Cronk*, married William T. Bowes. A son, *William, Jr.*, was born in 1918. The marriage ended in divorce in 1920, shortly after she arrived in Hollywood. On May 14, 1925, she wed film star *Bert LYTELL* in the Presidenca Room of the Juarez, Mexico, city hall. Two years later, on August 9, 1927, Windsor received a divorce in Los Angeles on the grounds of cruelty. She never remarried.

WINGER, Debra
(1955-)

In March 1986, the actress surprised her friends and fans when she wed actor *Timothy Hutton* in Big Sur, California. Their son, *Emmanuel Noah*, was born in Los Angeles on April 29, 1987. Hutton filed for divorce in December 1989.

WINNINGER, Charles
(1884-1969)

The actor married *Blanche Ring*, his Broadway co-star, at the Boston home of his mother on November 5, 1912. Blanche Ring's sister, *Frances*, also an actress, married film star *Thomas MEIGHAN*. After a twenty-two year separation, the Winningers were divorced in Los Angeles on June 12, 1951. Later that summer, on August 10, 1951, Winninger married his secretary, a former actress named *Gertrude Walker*, in Juarez, Mexico. They were married until the actor's death on January 19, 1969, at their home in Palm Springs, California. He was eighty-four.

WINTERS, Shelley
(1922-)

On January 1, 1942, the actress wed *Paul Mack Mayer*, a Chicago textile salesman, in New York City. The marriage ended in divorce in Los Angeles in 1948. Winters married Italian-born actor *Vittorio Gassman* in Juarez, Mexico, on April 28, 1952. Their daughter, *Vittoria*, was born on February 14, 1953, in Los Angeles. She divorced Gassman in Los Angeles in 1954. On May 4, 1957, she wed actor *Anthony Franciosa*. Three years later, on

November 18, 1960, Winters was granted a divorce in Santa Monica, charging cruel and inhuman treatment. She has not remarried.

WITHERS, Jane
(1926-   )

On September 20, 1947, Withers married Texas oilman turned film producer *William Moss* at the First Congregational Church in Hollywood. Three children were born: Wendy Leigh on September 26, 1948; *William Paul III* on July 9, 1950; and *Walter Randall*, nicknamed "Randy," in December 1951. All of their children were born in Santa Monica. Withers was granted a divorce in Santa Monica on July 12, 1954, after testifying that Moss drank and gambled to excess. Moss later married *Ann MILLER*. On October 23, 1955, Withers wed singer *Kenneth Edward Errair*, a former member of the Four Freshmen singing group, aboard the yacht *Flamba* in Newport Beach, California. Their son, *Kenneth, Jr.*, was born on May 19, 1957, followed by a daughter, *Kendall*, born on March 4, 1960. The Errairs had been married twelve years when, on June 14, 1968, Kenneth Errair was killed in a plane crash at Bass Lake Airport near Madera, California. On Valentine's Day, 1985, Withers married her business manager, *Thomas Pierson*. Her son Randy died of cancer on January 15, 1986.

WOOD, Natalie
(1938-1981)

Wood first married actor *Robert WAGNER* on December 28, 1957, at the Scottsdale Methodist Church in Scottsdale, Arizona. She filed for divorce on April 17, 1962, in Santa Monica, charging cruelty. The decree was granted later that same year. On May 30, 1969, Wood married British agent and producer *Richard Gregson* in a Russian Orthodox ceremony in Hollywood. A daughter, *Natasha*, was born on September 29, 1970. Wood filed for divorce in Santa Monica on August 4, 1971. On July 16,

1972, Wood and Wagner were remarried aboard the yacht *Rambling Rose* off the coast of Southern California. Wagner had a daughter, *Katharine*, from an in-between marriage to actress *Marian Marshall*. A daughter, *Courtney Brooke*, was born to Wood and Wagner on March 11, 1974. On the night of November 29, 1981, Wood lost her footing aboard a yacht off Catalina Island, California, and was drowned. She was forty-three.

WOODS, James
(1947-   )

The actor wed model *Kathryn Greko* in 1980. Divorced in 1983, the couple continued to date until 1985, when Woods met *Sarah Owen*, a rider for a horse trainer. Woods and Owen were married in Beverly Hills on July 2, 1989.

WOODWARD, Joanne
(1930-   )

On January 29, 1958, Woodward married actor, director, and producer *Paul NEWMAN* in Las Vegas. The couple has co-starred together and Woodward has been directed by Newman in one film. The couple has three daughters: *Elinor* (the name of Woodward's mother), born in 1959; *Melissa*, born in 1961; and *Claire*, born in 1965.

WRAY, Fay
(1907-   )

On June 15, 1928, Wray married writer and Rhodes Scholar *John Monk Saunders* at Calvary Methodist Church in Easton, Maryland. A daughter, *Susan Cary Saunders*, who became an actress, was born on September 24, 1936. The couple separated in February 1938, and Wray received a divorce in California in December 1939, which became final in December 1940. The actress wed screenwriter *Robert Riskin* on August 23, 1942, at the St. Regis Hotel in New York City. Their son, *Robert, Jr.*, was born on July 23, 1943, in New York City. Their daughter, *Victoria*, was born in Los Angeles in 1945. Their thirteen years of marriage ended in Riskin's death, at the age of fifty-eight, after a long illness, in Woodland Hills, California on September 20, 1955. Since 1971, Wray has been married to neurosurgeon *Sanford (Sandy) Rothenberg*. The couple lives in Studio City, California.

WRIGHT, Teresa
(1918-   )

The actress married novelist and screenwriter *Niven Busch* at the Van Nuys, California, home of friends, *Mr. and Mrs. Winston Miller*, on May 23, 1942. The couple had a son, *Niven Terrence*, born December 2, 1944, and a daughter, *Mary Kelly*, born September 12, 1947. Both of their children were born in Los Angeles. They separated in 1951, and Wright received a divorce in Santa Monica on November 25, 1952. She married widowed playwright *Robert Woodruff Anderson* in Los Angeles on December 11, 1959. The couple was divorced in 1978.

WYATT, Jane
(1911-   )

On November 9, 1935, the actress married *Edgar Bethune Ward*, a Harvard student who became an investment broker, in Santa Fe, New Mexico. The Wards have two sons: *Christopher*, born June 16, 1937, and *Michael*, born September 10, 1943. The couple resides in Beverly Hills.

WYMAN, Jane
(1914-   )

Early in 1937, Wyman eloped to New Orleans with clothing manufacturer *Myron Futterman* The couple separated a few months later and was divorced in December 1938. Her marriage to actor *Ronald REAGAN* took place in Glendale, California, on January

26, 1940. A daughter, singer-actress *Maureen Elizabeth Reagan*, was born on January 4, 1941. A son, *Michael*, was adopted in 1946. Charging her husband with extreme mental cruelty, Wyman received a divorce (and custody of their children) on June 28, 1948, in Los Angeles. The decree became final on July 18, 1949. On November 1, 1952, Wyman wed orchestra leader *Fred Karger* at the El Montecito Presbyterian Church in Santa Barbara, California. Wyman divorced Karger in Los Angeles on December 7, 1954. The decree became final on December 30, 1955. In March 1961, Wyman and Karger were remarried. Karger received a divorce on March 9, 1965, in Los Angeles, after testifying that Wyman had ''walked out on him.'' Wyman has not remarried.

WYMORE, Patrice
(1926-)

Four thousand spectators gathered outside the Lutheran chapel in Nice, France, when the actress wed *Errol FLYNN* on October 23, 1950. A daughter, *Arnella Roma*, was born in Rome on Christmas Day, 1953. Although separated, the couple was married until Flynn's death from a heart attack on October 14, 1959, in Vancouver, Canada. He was fifty. Wymore, who now lives in Jamaica, has not remarried.

WYNN, Ed
(1886-1966)

On September 5, 1914, the actor wed *Hilda Keenan*, the daughter of silent film star *Frank Keenan*, in New York City. Their son, actor *Keenan WYNN*, was born on July 27, 1916, in New York City. The couple had been married twenty-six years when, on May 13, 1937, Hilda Wynn received a Reno divorce. A month later, on June 15, 1937, Wynn wed dancer *Frieda Mierse* in New York City. Mierse obtained a divorce in Reno two years later, on December 12, 1939. On July 31, 1946, Wynn married *Dorothy Elizabeth Nesbitt* in the Little Church of the West in Las Vegas.

Eight years later, on March 1, 1955, Nesbitt received a divorce in Santa Monica. Wynn never remarried.

WYNN, Keenan
(1916-1986)

On September 30, 1938, the actor, who was the son of *Ed WYNN*, married *Eve Abbott*. The couple had two sons: *Edmund*, born April 27, 1941, and screen writer *Tracy Keenan Wynn*, born in 1945. Abbott received a divorce in Juarez, Mexico, on January 25, 1947. Four hours later, she married Wynn's best friend, actor *Van JOHNSON*. Wynn married model *Betty Jane Butler* in a proxy ceremony in Tijuana, Mexico, on January 11, 1949. Separated in 1952, Butler received a divorce in Los Angeles on June 29, 1953, after testifying that Wynn was too friendly with his ex-wife. Wynn married *Sharley Jean Hudson* in Puerto Rico on January 8, 1954. They were remarried six months later at the Little Brown Church in the Valley in California. A daughter, *Hilda* (named for Wynn's mother, *Hilda Keenan*), was born later that same year. A second daughter, *Edwynna*, was born on February 2, 1960. Their thirty-two years of marriage ended in Wynn's death from cancer on October 14, 1986, at their Brentwood, California, home. He was seventy.

WYNTER, Dana
(1930-)

In 1956, the actress married lawyer *Gregson Bautzer*. Their son, *Mark Ragan Bautzer*, was born on January 29, 1960. The couple separated in 1964, but did not divorce until 1981.

YORK, Michael
(1942-)

York met photographer *Patricia McCallum* when *Glamour* magazine sent her to photograph him in his London apartment. They were married on March 27, 1968, the actor's twenty-sixth birthday. The couple resides in London.

YORK, Susannah
(1942-)

York married actor-writer *Michael Wells* in 1960. They have a daughter, *Sasha*, born May 9, 1972, and a son, *Orlando*, born June 9, 1973. The couple lives on a farm in Sussex, England.

YOUNG, Clara Kimball
(1890-1960)

She was *Clara Kimball* when, in 1912, she wed actor-director *James Young*. He guided her career successfully, and she became one of the brightest stars of the WW I era. The couple was divorced in 1916. That same year, she wed her agent, *Harry Garson*. Garson tried to direct her career with the same success, but failed. Her stardom waned in the early twenties. The Garsons were divorced after ten years of marriage. In 1928, she wed *Dr. Arthur S. Fauman*. Widowed in 1937, she never remarried.

YOUNG, Gig
(1913-1978)

The actor was married five times. In 1939, he wed actress *Sheila Stapler*. They were divorced in 1947. Early in 1950, he married *Sophia Rosenstein*, a drama coach at Warner Brothers studios. Rosenstein died of cancer late in 1952. On December 28, 1956, Young married actress *Elizabeth MONTGOMERY*. The union ended in divorce in January 1963. That same year, on September 18, 1963, Young married real estate agent *Elaine Whitman*. A daughter, *Jennifer*, was born in 1964. Elaine Young received a divorce in Santa Monica on November 23, 1966. The actor did not marry again until September 27, 1978, when he wed German actress *Kim Schmidt*. Three weeks later, on October 19, 1978, Young shot Schmidt, who was thirty-one, and then himself in their New York City apartment.

YOUNG, Loretta
(1913-)

She eloped to Yuma, Arizona, on January 26, 1930, with actor *Grant Withers*. The marriage was annulled in 1931. On July 3, 1940, Young wed producer and writer *Thomas H. Lewis* at the Church of St. Paul in the Westwood area of Los Angeles. Her brother, *Jack*, gave the bride away, and her sister, *Georgianna*, was maid-of-honor. A son, *Christopher Paul*, was born on August 1, 1944, in Los Angeles. The couple then adopted a daughter, *Judy*. A second son, *Peter*, was born on July 15, 1945, in Los Angeles. Young divorced Lewis in Los Angeles on October 21, 1969, on the grounds of desertion, after twenty-nine years of marriage. She has not remarried. Her sisters are actresses *Polly Ann Young*, *Georgianna Young* (who is married to *Ricardo Montalban*), and *Sally Blane*.

YOUNG, Robert
(1907-)

Since 1933, the actor has been married to *Elizabeth Louise Henderson*, whom he had met in high school. The Youngs have four daughters: *Carol Anne*, born in 1933; *Barbara Queen*, born in 1937; *Elizabeth Louise*, born in 1943, and *Kathleen Joy*, born in 1945.

YURKA, Blanche
(1887-1974)

Yurka married actor *Ian Keith* in Chicago in September 1922. The couple separated seven weeks later. The actress received a divorce from Keith in Chicago on January 27, 1928, charging her husband with cruelty. She never remarried.

ZORINA, Vera
(1917-)

On Christmas Eve, 1938, the dancer-actress married choreographer *George Balanchine* on Staten Island. Seven years later, on January 17, 1946, Zorina received a Reno divorce on the grounds of cruelty. On April 2, 1946, she married *Goddard Lieberson*, president of Columbia Records. The couple had two sons: *Peter*, born October 25, 1946, and *Jonathan*, born in 1948. Their thirty-one years of marriage ended in Lieberson's death in 1977.

Stars Who Never Married

"My work is my wife"
—Mack Sennett

BEATTY, Warren (1937–)
BEY, Turhan (1920–)
BISSET, Jacqueline (1944–)
BOGARDE, Dirk (1920–)
BONDI, Beulah (1892–1981)
CHAMBERLAIN, Richard (1935–)
CHAPLIN, Geraldine (1944–)*
CHRISTIE, Julie (1941–)
CLIFT, Montgomery (1920–1966)
DALTON, Timothy (1946–)
DEAN, James (1931–1955)
FITZGERALD, Barry (1888–1961)
GARBO, Greta (1905–1990)
GERE, Richard (1949–)
GIELGUD, Sir John (1904–)
GISH, Lillian (1896–)
GRANGER, Farley (1925–)
HAINES, William (1900–1973)
HERSHEY, Barbara (1948–)*
HUNTER, Tab (1931–)
KAHN, Madeline (1942–)
KEATON, Diane (1946–)
MCCALLISTER, Lon (1923–)
MCDOWELL, Roddy (1928–)
MINEO, Sal (1939–1976)
NOVARRO, Ramon (1899–1968)
PACINO, Al (1940–)
PHILBIN, Mary (1903–)
REEVE, Christopher (1952–)*
ROBSON, Dame Flora (1902–1984)
ROMERO, Cesar (1907–)
SCHELL, Maximilian (1930–)
SCOTT, Lizabeth (1922–)
SENNETT, Mack (1880–1960)
SIMON, Simone (1911–)
TOMLIN, Lily (1939–)

TRAVOLTA, John (1954–)
WEBB, Clifton (1891–1966)
WILSON, Lois (1896–1988)
WONG, Anna May (1907–1961)
*See individual entries for information on the children of these
stars.

Index

Bold indicates person with main entry.

Abbott, Bud	1	Allman, Gregg	57
Abbott, Diahnne	83	Almond, Paul	41
Abraham, F. Murray	1	**Allyson, June**	4–5, 247
Acker, Jean	305	**Ameche, Don**	5
Adams, Edie	1, 155	**Ames, Adrienne**	5–6
Adams, Neile	199	**Ames, Leon**	6
Addolori, Iolanda	253	Amurri, Franco	274
Addy, Wesley	149	**Anderson, Dame Judith**	6
Adler, Buddy	189	Anderson, Loni	262
Adler, Luther	280	Anderson, Robert Woodruff	320
Adrain, Gilbert	122	**Andress, Ursula**	6
Adoree, Renee	1–2, 220	Andrews, Clark	299
Agar, John	295	**Andrews, Dana**	7
Aherne, Brian	2, 113	**Andrews, Julie**	7
Aimee, Anouk	109	Angel, Heather	114
Alberghetti, Anna Maria	2	**Angeli, Pier**	7–8, 72
Albert, Eddie	2–3, 202	Annabella	249
Albert, Eddie, Jr.	2, 202	**Ann-Margret**	8
Albright, Lola	51	**Arbuckle, Roscoe "Fatty"**	8, 92
Alda, Alan	3, 3	**Arden, Eve**	8–9
Alda, Robert	3, 3	Arden, Jane	265
Alderman, Harry Myrl	98	**Arkin, Alan**	9
Alessandrini, Goffredo	200	**Arlen, Richard**	9
Alexander, Jane	3	**Arliss, George**	9
Allegret, Yves	280	Arliss, Leslie	9
Allen, Adrienne	208	**Arnaz, Desi**	10, 15
Allen, Fred	4, 206	Arnaz, Desi, Jr.	10, 16, 215
Allen, Gracie	4, 42	Arnaz, Lucy	10, 15
Allen, Peter	214	Arnold, Elliott	159
Allen, Woody	4, 104	Arnst, Bobbe	312

Arquette, Rosanna 10
Arthur, Jean 10, 52
Ashcroft, Dame Peggy 11
Asher, Irving 179
Asher, William 217
Asherson, Renee 86
Ashley, Elizabeth 11, 243
Astaire, Fred 11–12
Astin, John 90
Astor, Mary 12, 189
Attenborough, Michael 12–13
Attenborough, Sir
  Richard 12–13
Aubrey, James 296
Autry, Gene 13
Avalon, Frankie 13
Aykroyd, Dan 13
Ayres, Agnes 14
Ayres, Lew 14, 265

Bacall, Lauren 15, 263
Bach, Barbara 286
Bacharach, Burt 85
Bailey, David 83
Baker, Carroll 15
Baker, Virginia 240
Bakish, Shakira 46
Balanchine, George 327
Ball, Lucille 10, 15–16
Ballard, Lucien K. 233
Bancroft, Anne 16, 40
Bankhead, Tallulah 16
Banks, Marty 108
Banky, Vilma 16–17, 180
Bannister, Harry 135
Bara, Theda 17
Bardot, Brigitte 17, 112
Bari, Lynn 17–18, 120
Barker, Jess 143
Barker, Lex 18, 71, 300
Barkin, Ellen 18
Baron, Lita 46
Barreto, Bruno 157
Barrett, Edith 250

Barrie, Wendy
Barrymore, Diana 19,
Barrymore, Ethel 19–20,
Barrymore, John 19, 20, 2
  64
Barrymore, John, Jr. 20,
Barrymore, Lionel 19,
Barrymore, Maurice 19,
Barthelmess, Richard
Bartlett, Dusty
Bartlett, Elise
Bartlett, Sydney S.
Baryshnikov, Mikhail
Basinger, Kim
Bauer, Steve
Baum, Florence
Baur, Esperanza "Chata"
Baxter, Anne 2
Baxter, Warner
Bayne, Beverly 22–2
Beatty, Warren 49, 198
Beaulieu, Priscilla
Beery, Noah 2
Beery, Noah, Jr.
Beery, Wallace 23, 2
Begley, Ed
Begley, Ed, Jr.
Begley, Thomas J.
Belafonte, Harry
Belafonte, Shari
Bel Geddes, Barbara
Bell, Rex 2
Bellamy, Ralph
Belushi, Jim 2
Belushi, John 2
Benjamin, Richard 2
Bennett, Barbara
Bennett, Constance 26, 27,
  289
Bennett, Enid 2
Bennett, Hazel Hastings
Bennett, Joan 26, 27, 17
Bennett, Richard
Benny, Jack

Bergen, Candice 28, 28
Bergen, Edgar 28, 28
Bergen, Polly 28–29
Bergerac, Jacques 201, 265
Bergere, Ouida 257
Bergman, Ingmar 303
Bergman, Ingrid 29
Berle, Milton 29–30
Bern, Paul 136
Berry, Dennis 276
Bertolini, Countess Lydia 37
Best, Edna 203
Bey, Turhan 329
Bisset, Jacqueline 329
Black, Charles 295
Black, Karen 30
Blackmer, Sidney 303
Blaine, Vivian 30
Blair, Betsy 167
Blair, Janet 30–31
Blane, Sally 324
Blondell, Joan 31, 247, 293
Bloom, Claire 31, 286
Blyth, Ann 32
Boardman, Eleanor 32, 307
Boetticher, Bud 239
Bogarde, Dirk 329
Bogart, Humphrey 15, 32–33, 193
Bogdanovich, Peter 278
Bolger, Ray 33
Bond, Ward 33
Bondi, Beulah 329
Bono, Sonny 57
Boone, Debby 33, 105
Boone, Pat 33–34, 106
Booth, Shirley 34
Borgnine, Ernest 34, 212
Borzage, Frank 282
Boulting, Ray 214
Bow, Clara 24, 35
Bowe, Rosemarie 284
Boyd, William 35
Boyer, Charles 35

Brabin, Charles J. 17
Bracken, Eddie 36
Bradley, Grace 35
Brady, Alice 36
Branagh, Kenneth 36
Brando, Marlon 36
Bransfield, Marjorie 25
Brazzi, Rosanno 37
Bren, Milton 299
Brent, George 37–38, 56, 279
Brett, Jeremy 208
Brian, Mary 14, 38, 104, 265
Brice, Lew 58
Bridges, Beau 38
Bridges, Jeff 38, 38
Bridges, Lloyd 38, 38
Brisson, Frederick 271
Britt, May 77
Broderick, Helen 67
Bromfield, John 47
Bronson, Betty 39
Bronson, Charles 39
Brooks, Geraldine 39
Brooks, Louise 39–40, 78
Brooks, Mel 16, 40
Brooks, Rand 108
Brown, Clarence 163
Brown, George Hanley 235
Brown, Harry Joe 96
Browne, Carol 251
Bruce, Virginia 40–41, 124
Bryant, Charles 227
Brynner, Yul 41
Bryson, Winifred 22
Bujold, Genevieve 41
Burke, Billie 41–42
Burns, George 4, 42
Burstyn, Ellen 42
Burstyn, Neil 42
Burton, Richard 42–43, 109, 293
Burton, Robert "Skip" 30
Busch, Mae 43
Bushman, Francis X. 22, 43–44

Butler, Betty Jane	322	**Caulfield, Joan**	10, **52**
Buttons, Red	**44**	Cauchois, Leonie	305
Butts, Robert Dale	98	**Chadwick, Helene**	**52**
Byrne, Gabriel	18	Chamberlain, Jan	269
		Chamberlain, Richard	**329**
Caan, James	**45**	**Champion, Gower**	**52–53**, 53
Cabot, Bruce	6	**Champion, Marge**	52, **53**
Cadwalader, Jessica	272	**Chandler, Helen**	19, **53**
Caesar, Sid	**45**	**Chandler, Jeff**	**53–54**
Cagney, James	**45**	**Chaney, Lon**	**54**
Cagney, James, Jr.	45	Chaney, Lon, Jr.	54
Caine, Michael	**45–46**	**Chaplin, Charlie**	40, **54–55**, 55,
Calhern, Louis	**46**, 56	78, 125, 137, 228	
Calhoun, Alice	**46**	**Chaplin, Geraldine**	55, 55, **329**
Calhoun, Roy	**46–47**	Chaplin, Michael John	55
Calvet, Corinne	**47**	**Charisse, Cyd**	**55**, 205
Cameron, Rudolph	287	Charisse, Nico	55
Campbell, Webster	130	Charriers, Jacques	17
Candoli, Pete	1	**Chase, Chevy**	**56**
Cannon, Dyan	**47**, 128–129	**Chase, Ilka**	46, **56**
Cantor, Eddie	**48**	**Chatterton, Ruth**	37, **56–57**, 114
Carabella, Flora	208	**Cher**	**57**
Carlin, Jacqueline	56	Cherrill, Virginia	128
Carlisle, Kitty	**48**	**Chevalier, Maurice**	**57**
Carne, Judy	261	Childs, Doris Sellers	33
Carol, Sue	**48–49**, 173	Christian, Linda	249
Caron, Leslie	**49**	**Christie, Julie**	**329**
Carradine, John	**49–50**, 146	Churchill, Marguerite	234
Carradine, David	49, 146	Cilento, Diane	61
Carradine, Keith	49, 50	Cimber, Matt	202
Carradine, Robert	49	Claessen, David	126
Carroll, Diahann	73	**Claire, Ina**	**57–58**, 124
Carroll, John	235	Clark, John	259
Carroll, Madeleine	**50**, 141	**Clark, Marguerite**	**58**
Carroll, Nancy	**50–51**	**Clark, Petula**	**58**
Carson, Jack	**51**	**Clarke, Mae**	**58**
Carver, Kathryn	210	**Clayburgh, Jill**	**59**
Casanova, Eva	295	**Clift, Montgomery**	**329**
Cassaniti, Rose Marie	296	**Close, Glenn**	**59**
Cassavetes, John	**51**, 269	Cloutier, Susan	303
Cassidy, David	161, 185	**Cody, Lew**	**59**, 72, 231
Cassidy, Jack	161	Cohn, Harry	139
Cassidy, Shaun	161	**Colbert, Claudette**	**59–60**
Cates, Phoebe	**51**, 171	Colleran, William	261

Collins, Joan 60
Collins, John Hancock 73
Collyer, June 60, 97
Colman, Ronald 60–61, 151, 184, 273
Compson, Betty 61, 192
Compton, Betty 179
Connery, Jason 61
Connery, Sean 61
Conte, John 209
Conti, Tom 62
Conway, Jack 43
Conwell, Mary Bessie 102
Coogan, Jackie 62, 127
Coombs, Guy 230
Cooper, Gary 62–63, 306
Cooper, Dame Gladys 63
Cooper, Jackie 63
Cooper, Miriam 64, 310
Cooper, Rosemary 166
Cornell, Katherine 242
Cortez, Ricardo 64, 270
Cosby, Bill 302
Costello, Dolores 20, 64–65, 65
Costello, Helene 65
Costello, Lou 65
Costello, Maurice 20, 64, 65–66
Costner, Kevin 66
Cotten, Joseph 66
Courtenay, Tom 66
Courtland, Jerome 28
Coyne, Jeanne 167
Craig, Catherine 250
Crain, Jeanne 66–67
Crane, James L. 36
Crane, Ward 165
Crawford, Broderick 67
Crawford, Christina 68
Crawford, Joan 67–68, 102, 298
Crawford, Lester 67
Creighton, Cleva 54
Crisp, Donald 68
Cromwell, Richard 179
Cronyn, Hume 68–69, 292

Crosby, Bing 48, 69
Cross, Beverley 283
Cruise, Tom 69
Cruze, James 61
Crystal, Billy 69
Curtis, Alan 207
Curtis, Jamie Lee 70, 70, 184
Curtis, Patrick 313
Curtis, Tony 70, 70, 184
Cusak, Cyril 157
Cusak, Sinead 157

Dafoe, Willem 71
Dahl, Arlene 18, 71, 176
Dahl, Roald 227
Dahl, Tessa Sophia 228
Dailey, Dan 71–72, 235
Dalton, Dorothy 59, 72, 134
Dalton, Timothy 329
Damita, Lila 72, 111
Damone, Vic 7, 72–73
Dana, Barbara 9
Dana, Viola 73
Danderidge, Dorothy 73–74
Daniels, Bebe 74, 189, 192
Daniels, Jeff 74
Dare, Barbara 299
Darin, Bobby 74–75, 80
Darnell, Linda 75
Dassin, Jules 211
Davenport, Dorothy 75, 261
David, Charles Henri 92
Davies, Helen Bradford 243
Davies, Marion 75–76, 279
Davis, Bette 76
Davis, Geena 76–77, 126
Davis, Georgia Maureen 282
Davis, Jerome 210
Davis, Mildred 77, 187
Davis, Miles 302
Davis, Nancy 259
Davis, Ossie 77, 80
Davis, Sammy, Jr. 77–78
Davis, Stringer 272

Daw, Marjorie	40, **78**, 101	Dors, Diana	87
Dawber, Pam	136	Douglas, Kirk	**88**, 88
Dawson, Dickie	87	Douglas, Melvyn	88
Day, Dennis	32	Douglas, Michael	**88**, 88
Day, Doris	78–79	Dove, Billie	88–89
Day, Laraine	79	Dozier, William	271, 273
Dean, James	329	Drake, Betsy	128
Deane, Doris	8	Dressler, Marie	89
DeCamp, Rosemary	79	Drew, Ellen	89
De Carlo, Yvonne	80	Drew, Georgianna	19, 20–21
Dee, Francis	80, 195	Dreyfuss, Richard	90
Dee, Ruby	77, 80	Dru, Joanne	142
Dee, Sandra	74, 80–81	Dubrinsky, Morris	95
Dega, Igor	93	Duff, Howard	191
De Haven, Gloria	5, **81**, 242	Duke, Patty	90
De Havilland, Olivia	81–82	Dunaway, Faye	90
De Laurentiis, Dino	201	Dunne, Irene	91
Delmar, Ethel	160	Dunstan, Dorothy	123
Del Rio, Dolores	82	Durante, Jimmy	91
De Mille, Cecil B.	180	Durbin, Deanna	91–92
De Mille, Katherine	82–83, 253	Durfee, Minta	8, **92**
Dempster, Carol	83	Duryea, Dan	92
Deneuve, Catherine	83, 208	Dura, Steffi	235
Denham, Reginald	303	Duvall, Robert	92
De Niro, Robert	83	Dvorak, Ann	93
Dennis, Sandy	84		
Derek, John	6	Eagels, Jeanne	95
DeToth, Andre	174	Eastwood, Clint	95
Devine, Andy	84	Edelstein, Rick	167
DeVithas, Mary	205	Eddy, Nelson	27, **95**
De Vito, Danny	84	Edwards, Blake	7
Dewhurst, Colleen	84–85, 275	Eggar, Samantha	95
Dexter, Elliott	85, 87	Eilers, Sally	96, 123
Dickinson, Angie	85	Ekberg, Anita	96
Dietrich, Marlene	85	Ekland, Britt	277
DiMaggio, Joe	216	Eldridge, Florence	96, 202
Dix, Richard	86	Elliott, Denholm	97
Dixon, Donna	13	Emerson, Faye	97
Donahue, Phil	296	Emery, John	16
Donahue, Troy	86, 246	Erickson, Leif	102
Donat, Robert	86	Ernst, Hugh "Bud"	116
Donen, Stanley	214	Errair, Kenneth Edward	318
Donlevy, Brian	87, 190	Erway, Ben	123
Doro, Marie	85, **87**	Erwin, Stuart	60, **97**

Esmond, Jill 236
Estevez, Emilio 278
Estevez, Ramon 278
Etting, Ruth **98**
Evans, Dale **98–99**, 266
Evans, Dame Edith **99**
Evans, Madge **99**
Evans, Robert 197

Fabray, Nanette **101**
Fair, Elinor 35
Fairbanks, Douglas 68, 78, **101,** 102, 103, 117, 219–220, 244
Fairbanks, Douglas, Jr. 67, 101, **102**
Fairbanks, Robert 101, 244
Farentino, James 11
Farmer, Frances **102**
Farmer, Michael 289
Farnum, Dustin **102–103,** 103
Farnum, Franklyn 270
Farnum, William 102, **103**
Farrar, Geraldine 103, 247, 295
Farrell, Charles **103–104**
Farrell, Glenda **104**
Farrow, John 104, 237
Farrow, Mia 4, **104–105,** 237, 282
Farrow, Stephanie 105, 237
Farrow, Tisa 105, 237
Fawcett, Farrah **105,** 237
Fay, Frank 285
Faye, Alice **105,** 137, 205
Falk, Harry G. 90
Fazenda, Louise **105–106,** 155
Fenton, Leslie 93
Fenwick, Irene 21
Ferrer, Jose **106**
Ferrer, Mel **106–107,** 146
Field, Betty **107,** 191
Field, Sally **107**
Fields, Dame Gracie **107–108**
Fields, W.C. **108**
Finch, Peter **108**

Finney, Albert **109**
Fisher, Carrie **109,** 109, 262
Fisher, Eddie 109, **109–110,** 262, 293
Fisk, Jack 284
Fitzgerald, Barry **329**
Fitzgerald, Geraldine **110**
Fitzmaurice, George 26
Fleming, Rhonda **110**
Fleming, Susan 206
Fletcher, Bramwell 19, 53
Flynn, Errol 72, **111,** 142, 321
Flynn, Maurice 73
Foch, Nina **111**
Foley, Red 33
Foley, Shirley 33
Fonda, Bridget 113
Fonda, Henry **111–112,** 112, 113, 288
Fonda, Jane 17, 112, **112–113,** 113
Fonda, Peter 112, **113**
Fontaine, Joan 2, 81, **113–114,** 191, 271
Forbes, Ralph 56, **114**
Forbes-Robertson, Meriel 262
Ford, Glenn **114–115,** 247
Ford, Harrison **115**
Ford, John 309
Forde, Victoria 216
Foreman, Ethel Marion 257
Forwood, Anthony 159
Fosse, Bob 307
Foster, Norman 59
Fox, Michael J. **115**
Franciosa, Anthony 317
Francis, Kay **115**
Francis, Noel M. 105
Franklin, Sidney 27
Frederick Lynne 277
Frederick, Pauline **116**
Freeman, Mona 248
Friedlob, Bert 240
Friml, Rudolf 2
Furness, Betty **116**

Gable, Clark 101, **117**, 188
Gabor, Eva **117–118**, 119
Gabor, Zsa Zsa 118, **118–119**, 273
Gage, Ben 315
Gahagan, Helen 88
Gallagher, Richard "Skeets" 119
Gannoway, Al 47
Garbo, Greta **329**
Gardiner, Edward 34
Gardner, Ava **119**, 170, 268, 282, 300
Garfein, Jack 15
Garfield, David Pattom 120
Garfield, John **119–120**
Garland, Judy 17–18, **120–121**, 214, 258
Garner, James **121**
Garner, Peggy Ann **121**
Garrett, Betty **121**, 241
Garson, Greer **122**, 229
Gassman, Vittorio 317
Gaul, Patricia 126
Gaynor, Janet 14, **122**, 265
Gaynor, Mitzi **123**
George, Gladys **123**
Gere, Richard **329**
Gero, Mark 215
Geston, Susan 38
Gibbons, Cedric 82
Gibson, Helen 123
Gibson, Hoot 96, **123**
Gibson, Mel **124**
Gielgud, Sir John **329**
Gilbert, John 40, 57, **124**, 162
Gelbert, Ray 239
Gilmore, Virginia 41
Gish, Dorothy **124–125**, 291
Gish, Lilian 125, **329**
Gist, Robert 221
Glass, Gaston 2
Gleason, Jackie **125**
Goddard, Paulette 54, **125–126**, 211
Goldberg, Whoopi 126

Goldblum, Jeff 76, **126**
Goldwyn, Samuel 16, 180, 203
Goodman, Daniel Carson 270
Gorcey, Leo 206
Gordon, Jane 311
Gordon, Ruth **126–127**
Goudal, Jetta **127**
Gould, Elliott **127**, 288
Gowens, Kip 261
Grable, Betty 62, **127–128**
Grace, Sally 286
Graham, Mona 200
Granger, Farley **329**
Granger, Stewart **128**, 281
Grant, Cary 47, **128–129**, 257
Granville, Bonita **129**
Grayson, Kathryn **129**
Green, Johnny 4, 116
Greene, Luther 6
Greer, Jane **130**, 305
Gregory, Paul 122
Gregson, Richard 309, 318
Greko, Kathryn 319
Grey, Yvonne 87
Griesman, Alan 107
Grieve, Harold 127
Griffith, Corinne **130**
Griffith, Melanie **130**, 144
Griffith, Peter 144
Grimes, Tammy 246
Guest, Christopher 70
Guiness, Sir Alec **131**
Gurie, Sigrid **131**
Guzman, Claudio 2

Hackett, Raymond 290
Hackman, Gene **133**
Haechler, Horst 274
Hagan, Uta 106
Hagman, Heidi 133
Hagman, Larry **133**, 204
Haines, Patricia 45
Haines, William **329**
Hale, Barbara **133**

Hale, Sonnie	209
Hale, William	133
Haley, Jack	**133**, 215
Haley, Jack, Jr.	133, 215
Halford, Genevieve	125
Hall, Mortimer	267
Hall, Peter	49
Hallam, Julie	157
Hamilton, George	**134**
Hamilton, Neil	**134**
Hamlin, Harry	6
Hammerstein, Arthur	72, 134
Hammerstein, Elaine	72, **134**
Hanks, Tom	**134**
Hanley, William B.	169
Harding, Ann	**135**
Hardwicke, Sir Cedric	**135**
Hardwicke, Edward	135
Hardy, Oliver	**135–136**
Harlan, Kenneth	250
Harlow, Jean	**136**
Harmon, Mark	**136**
Harris, Julie	**136–137**
Harris, Mildred	54, **137**
Harris, Phil	105, **137**
Harris, Richard	138
Harrison, Carey	138
Harrison, George	**137–138**
Harrison, Noel	138
Harrison, Sir Rex	**138**, 168, 240
Hart, Moss	48
Hart, William S.	**138–139**
Hart-Davis, Rupert Charles	11
Harvey, Laurence	**139**, 185
Haver, June	**139**, 198
Haver, Phyllis	**139–140**
Havoc, June	**140**, 182
Hawkins, Jack	69, **140**, 292
Hawks, Howard	278
Hawks, Kenneth	12, 189
Hawn, Goldie	**140–141**
Hayden, Jeffrey	273
Hayden, Sterling	50, **141**
Haydon, Julie	**141–142**
Hayes, Anne	277
Hayes, Helen	**142**
Hayman, Damaris	272
Haymes, Dick	111, **142–143**, 144
Hays, Kathryn	114
Hayward, Brook	288
Hayward, Leland	288
Hayward, Lews	191
Hayward, Susan	**143**
Hayworth, Rita	5, 142, **143–144**, 313
Headley, Glenne	200
Hedren, Tippi	130, **144**
Heerman, Victor	213
Heflin, Van	**144**
Hemingway, Mariel	**144**
Henaghan, James	307
Henderson, Lyle "Skitch"	97
Hendricks, Ray	79
Hendrix, Wanda	**145**, 223, 284
Henie, Sonja	**145**
Henreid, Paul	**146**
Hepburn, Audrey	107, **146**
Hepburn, Katharine	**146**, 236, 281
Herbert, Richard	121
Herron, Mark	120
Hershey, Barbara	50, **146**, **329**
Hersholt, Allan	147
Hersholt, Jean	**147**
Hervey, Irene	160
Heston, Charleton	**147**
Hewitt, Muriel	262
Hightower, Robert	306
Hill, Phyllis	106
Hiller, Dame Wendy	**147**
Hitower, Rosalind	88
Hodiak, John	22, **147**
Hoffa, Portland	4
Hoffman, Dustin	**148**
Holden, William	**148**, 259
Holliday, Judy	**148**
Holm, Celeste	**148–49**
Holm, Peter	60

Holt, Jack   149
Holt, Jennifer   149
Holt, Tim   149
Hope, Bob   149
Hopkins, Miriam   149–150
Hopper, Hedda   150
Hopper, Jerry   152
Hornblow, Arthur, Jr.   190
Horne, Lena   150
Horne, James W.   63
Horne, June   63
Horne, Victoria   233
Horton, Peter   243
Hoshelle, Marjorie   53
Hough, Stanley   243
House, Dorothy Irene   84
Houseman, John   151
Howard, Leslie   151
Howard, Ronald   151
Hoyt, Julia   46
Hudson, Bill   141
Hudson, Rock   151
Hughes, Carolyn   275
Hughes, Harriet   108
Hughes, Howard   220, 243
Hume, Benita   60, 151–152, 184,
    273
Hunt, Marsha   152
Hunter, Jeffrey   152
Hunter, Tab   329
Hurt, John   152–153
Hurt, Mary Beth   153
Hurt, William   153
Hussey, Olivia   204
Huston, Anjelica   153
Huston, John   153–154, 154, 170
Huston, Walter   153, 154
Hutchinson, Nicholas   11
Hutton, Betty   1, 154–155
Hutton, Timothy   317
Hyams, Leila   155
Hyer, Martha   106, 155

Ingels, Marty   162

Ingram, Rex   296
Ipar, Alim   40
Ireland, Jill   39
Ireland, John   142
Irons Jeremy   157
Isley, Phyllis   309
Irving, Amy   157

Jackson, Anne   159, 310
Jackson, Glenda   159
Jacobs, Elaine   20
James, Edgar   125
James, Harry   127
Jeans, Isabel   255
Jeffries, Fran   143
Jeffries, Lang   110
Jessel, George   291
Johann, Zita   151
Johns, Glynis   159
Johnson, Don   130
Johnson, Maggie   95
Johnson, Richard   232
Johnson, Van   159–160, 322
Johnston, Jimmy   129
Jolson, Al   160, 166
Jones, Allan   160–161, 273
Jones, Jack   160, 161, 273
Jones, Jennifer   161, 309
Jones, Shirley   161–162, 185
Jordan, Al   78
Jourdan, Louis   162
Joy, Leatrice   124, 162
Joyce, Alice   162–163, 220
Judge, Arline   145, 163, 270, 300
Jurado, Katy   34

Kahn, Madeline   329
Kanin, Garson   126
Karger, Fred   321
Karloff, Boris   165
Kashfi, Anna   36
Kass, Ronald   60
Kaufmann, Christine   70
Kaye, Danny   165

Keaton, Buster   165–166, 291–292
Keaton, Diane   329
Keaton, Michael   166
Keel, Howard   166
Keeler, Ruby   160, 166–167
Keenan, Frank   321
Keighley, William   297
Keith, Ian   324
Kellerman, Annette   167
Kellerman, Sally   167
Kelly, Gene   167
Kelly, Grace   168
Kelly, Gregory   126
Kelly, Nancy   168, 233
Kendall, Kay   138, 168–169, 240
Kendall, Suzy   218
Kennedy, Cheryl   66
Kennedy, Madge   169
Kennedy, Patricia   181
Kenyon, Doris   169, 281
Kerr, Deborah   170
Keyes, Evelyn   119, 153, 170, 300
Kidman, Nicole   69
Kingsley, Ben   170–171
Kinglsey, Sidney   99
Kingston, Winifred   103
Kinski, Klaus   171
Kinski, Nastassja   171
Kirkland, Alexander   183
Kirkland, Jack   50
Kirkwood, James   183
Kitt, Eartha   171
Kline, Kevin   51, 171
Knight, Patricia   314
Knight, Sandra   230
Korda, Alexander   233
Kostelanetz, Andre   246
Koufax, Sandy   314
Kovacs, Ernie   1

Ladd, Alan   49, 173
Ladd, Alana   49, 173
Ladd, David   49, 173

Lahr, Bert   173
Lake, Veronica   173–174
La Marr, Barbara   174, 245
Lamarr, Hedy   27, 175, 190, 297
Lamas, Fernando   176, 316
Lamour, Dorothy   176
Lamphere, Dorothy   62
Lancaster, Burt   176–177
Lanchester, Elsa   177, 180
Landi, Elissa   177
Landis, Carole   177–178
Lane, Lola   14
Lane, Marjorie   87
Langdon, Dorothy   104
Langdon, Harry   178
Lange, Jessica   178
Lansbury, Angela   179
Lanza, Mario   179
Laplante, Laura   179
Larocque, Rod   16–17, 180
Larson, Susan   273
Lasser, Louis   4
Lattanzi, Matt   229
Laughlin, Michael   49
Laughton, Charles   177, 180
Laurel, Stan   180–181
Laurie, Piper   181
Lavorel, Henri   50
Lawford, Peter   181–182
Lawrence, Doreen   140
Lawrence, Florence   182
Lawson, Leigh   214
LeCompte, Elizabeth   71
Lederer, Charles   279
Lederer, Francis   182, 202
Lee, Dixie   48, 69
Lee, Gypsy Rose   140, 182–183
Lee, John Griffith   221
Lee, Kathy   41, 48
Lee, Lila   74, 183, 192
Leigh, Janet   70, 183–184
Leigh, Vivien   184, 236
Leighton, Margaret   139, 184–185
Lemmon, Jack   185, 263

Lennon, John 185
Lennon, Julian 185
Lenz, Kay 185
Leonard, Robert Z. 224
Leslie, Joan 32, 186
Lewes, Samantha 134
Lewis, Diana "Mousie" 248
Lewis, Jerry 186
Lewis, Thomas H. 324
Lieberson, Goddard 327
Lindfors, Viveca 186
Lithgow, John 186
Litvak, Anatole 150
Livingstone, Mary 28
Lloyd, Gladys 264
Lloyd, Harold 77, 187
Lloyd, Harold Clayton, Jr 77, 187
Loder, John 175
Logan, Jacqueline 187
Lollobrigidia, Gina 187
Lombard, Carole 117, 188, 248
Long, Shelley 188
Loren, Sophia 188
Lorre, Peter 188–189
Louise, Anita 189
Love, Bessie 12, 189
Loveridge, Marguerite 203
Loy, Myrna 27, 175, 190
Luft, Lorna 120
Luft, Sid 120
Lugosi, Bela 87, 190–191
Lugosi, Lilian Arch 87
Lukas, Paul 107, 191
Lumet, Sidney 150, 259
Lupino, Ida 113, 191
Lvovsky, Celia 188
Lynn, Betty 32
Lynn, Diana 191–192, 268
Lyon, Ben 74, 192
Lyons, David 269
Lytell, Burt 192–193, 316
Lyton, Henry 209

MacArthur, Charles 142

MacArthur, Mary 142
McAvoy, May 195
McCallister, Lon 329
McCallum, David 39
McCambridge, Mercedes 195
McCartney, Paul 195
McCrea, Joel 80, 195–196
McCutheon, Wallace 314
MacDonald, Jeanette 196, 258
MacDougall, Ranald 101
McDowell, Malcolm 196, 286
McDowell, Roddy 329
McGillis, Kelly 196
MacGraw, Ali 197, 199
McGuire, Dorothy 197
Mack, Jillie 276
Mack, Willard 116
McKay, Scott 279
MacKenna, Kenneth 115
MacKenna, Virginia 97
McLaglen, Andrew V. 197
McLaglen, Victor 197–198
MacLaine, Shirley 198
McLaughlin, Emily 152
McLean, Gloria 287
MacMahon, Aline 198
MacMurray, Fred 139, 198
McQueen, Steve 197, 199
MacRae, Gordon 199
MacWilliams, Caroline 166
Madison, Guy 199–200, 270
Madonna 242
Magnani, Anna 200
Mahnken, Elaine 268
Main, Marjorie 200
Maitland, Mollie 203
Major, Isabelle Lunds 103
Majors, Lee 105
Malden, Karl 200
Malkovich, John 200
Malle, Louis 28
Mallory, Boots 203
Malone, Dorothy 201, 266
Mangano, Silvana 201

Mansfield, Jayne	**201–202**	Menken, Grace	32, 193
March, Elspeth	128	Menken, Helen	32, 193
March, Fredric	96, **202**	Mercier, Mary	315
Margo	2, 3, 182, **202**	**Mercouri, Melina**	**211**
Markey, Enid	**202–203**	**Meredith, Burgess**	125, **211**
Markey, Gene	27, 175, 190	Merivale, Philip	63
Markle, Fletcher	195	**Merkel, Una**	**211**
Marquand, Tina	217	**Merman, Ethel**	34, **212**
Marsh, Mae	**203**	Merrick, Lynn	227
Marshall, Brenda	148, 259	Merril, Gary	76
Marshall, Hervert	**203**	Merrill, Dina	263
Marshall, Marian	309	Merry, Eleanor	221
Marshall, William	222, 266	Methot, Mayo	32
Martin, Dean	**204**	Michaels, Janet	37
Martin, Dean Jr.	204	Midgley, Leslie	116
Martin, Mary	133, **204**	**Midler, Bette**	**212**
Martin, Steve	**204**	Mierse, Frieda	321
Martin, Tony	55, 105, **205**	**Milland, Ray**	**212–213**
Marvin, Lee	**205**	**Miller, Ann**	**213**, 318
Marx, Chico	**205**	Miller, Arthur	216
Marx, Groucho	**206**	**Miller, Marilyn**	**213**, 244
Marx, Harpo	**206**	Miller, Ruth	35
Marx, Zeppo	282	**Mills, Hayley**	**214**, 214
Mason, James	**206–207**	**Mills, John**	**214**, 214
Mason, Marsha	**207**	Mills, Juliet	214
Mason, Pauline	119	Mills, Martin	1
Massey, Ilona	**207**	Milocevic, Milos	268
Massey, Raymond	**207–208**	**Mimieux, Yvette**	**214**
Mastroianni, Marcello	83, **208**	**Mineo, Sal**	**329**
Mathison, Melissa	115	**Minnelli, Liza**	120, 133, **214–215**
Matthau, Walter	**208**	Minnelli, Vincente	120, 214
Matthews, Jessie	**209**	**Minter, Mary Miles**	**215**
Matthews, Joyce	29	Minty, Barbara	199
Mattis, Dee Jay	45	**Miranda, Carmen**	**215**
Mature, Victor	**209**	Mitchum, Chris	215
Maxwell, Marilyn	**209–210**	Mitchum, Jim	215
May, Mary Louise	33	**Mitchum, Robert**	**215**
Mayer, Louis B.	5	**Mix, Tom**	**216**
Mayo, Virginia	**210**	**Monroe, Marilyn**	**216**
Medina, Patricia	66	Montand, Yves	280
Meehan, John	115	**Montez, Maria**	**216–217**
Meighan, Thomas	210, 317	**Montgomery, Elizabeth**	**217**,
Melcher, Martin	79	217–218, 323	
Menjou, Adolphe	**210–211**, 294	Montgomery, Florence	9

Montgomery, George   **217**, 279
Montgomery, Robert   217, **217–218**
Moore, Colleen   **218**
Moore, Demi   **218**, 316
Moore, Dick   248
Moore, Dudley   **218–219**, 313
Moore, Gracie   **219**
Moore, Joanna   236
Moore, Mary Tyler   **219**
Moore, Owen   101, **219–220**, 220, 244
Moore, Terry   **220**, 243
Moore, Tom   1, 162, 219, **220–221**
Moorehead, Agnes   **221**
Morant, Angela   170
Moreno, Antonio   **221**
Moreno, Rita   **221**
Morgan, Dennis   **222**
Morgan, Helen   **222**
Morgan, Michele   **222**, 266
Morgan, Robert   80
Morgan, Will   256
Mori, Paola   313
Morosco, Walter   130
Morse, John Hollingsworth   96
Morton, Gary   16
Moss, William   213, 318
Mostel, Zero   **223**
Moussa, Ibrahim   171
Movita   37
Mulhern, Mary   244
Mulligan, Gerry   84
Muni, Paul   **223**
Murfin, Jane   68
Murphy, Audie   145, **223–224**
Murphy, George   **224**
Murray, Bill   **224**
Murray, Mae   **224–225**
Myers, Carmel   189, **225**

Nagel, Conrad   **227**
Nathan, George Jean   141
Nazimova, Alla   **227**

Neagle, Dame Anna   **227**
Neal, Frances   144
Neal, Patricia   **228**
Neal, Tom   298
Neff, Hildegarde   **228**
Negri, Pola   225, **228–229**, 305
Neilan, Marshall "Mickey"   290
Nelson, Oscar Harmon, Jr.   76
Nelson, Ralph   148
Nero, Frank   260
Newly, Anthony   60
Newman, Paul   **229**, 319
Newton-John, Olivia   **229**
Ney, Richard   122, **229**
Niblo, Fred   27
Nicholas, Harold   73
Nicholson, Jack   **230**
Nicholson, Virginia   313
Nickerson, Connie   36
Nielsen, Brigitte   284
Nielson, Lois   180
Nilsson, Anna Q.   **230**
Nimoy, Leonard   **230**
Niven, David   **230–231**
Nixon, Marian   192
Normand, Mabel   1, 59, 220, **231**
Norris, Edward   279
North, Sheree   **231**
Novak, Kim   **232**
Novarro, Ramon   329

Oakie, Jack   **233**
Oberon, Merle   **233**
O'Brien, Edmond   168, **233**
O'Brien, George   **234**
O'Brien, Margaret   5, **234**
O'Brien, Pat   **234**
O'Connor, Donald   **235**
O'Connor, Lois   263
O'Curran, Charles   154
Odets, Clifford   255
O'Farrell, James   307
O'Hara, Maureen   **235**
O'Keefe, Dennis   **235–236**

Olivier, Sir Laurence   184, **236**
Olmstead, Gertrude   225
Olson, Jeanne   91
Olson, Nancy   155
O'Neal, Ryan   105, **236–237**, 237
O'Neal, Tatum   236, **237**
O'Neil, Eugene   55
O'Neil, Oona   55
O'Neill, Terrence   90
Ono, Yoko   185
Orleneff, Paul   227
O'Shea, Michael   210
O'Sullivan, Maureen   104, **237**
O'Toole, Peter   **238**
Owen, Tony   260

Pacino, Al   **329**
Page, Geraldine   **239**
Paget, Debra   **239**
Paige, Janis   **239–240**
Palance, Holly   240
Palance, Jack   **240**
Palastranga, David Anthony   228
Pallette, Pilar   311
Palmer, Lilli   138, **240**
Parker, Eleanor   **240–241**
Parker, Steve   198
Parks, Hildy   63
Parks, Larry   121, **241**
Parry, Flower   62
Paterson, Pat   35
Patrick, Evelyn   281
Patrick, Gail   **241**
Paul, Vaughn   91
Payne, John   81, **241–242**, 279
Payton, Barbara   298
Peacock, Diana   153
Peck, Gregory   **242**
Penn, Leonard   123
Penn, Sean   **242**
Peppard, George   11, **243**
Pepper, Jack   265
Perkins, Anthony   **243**
Perlberg, William   17

Perlman, Rhea   84
Perry, Antoinette   211
Perry, Kathyrn   220
Peters, Brandon   149
Peters, Jean   220, **243**
Pfeiffer, Michelle   **243**
Philbin, Mary   **329**
Phillips, Mary   32
Pickard, Helena   135
Pickford, Jack   1, 213, 220, **244, 245,** 297
Pickford, Lottie   245
Pickford, Mary   68, 78, 101, 102, 213, 219, 244, **244–245,** 265
Pickles, Edna   245
Pidgeon, Walter   **245**
Pitt, Archie   107
Pittman, Eleanor   263
Pitts, ZaSu   174, **245,** 295
Plaines, Elaine   264
Pleshette, Suzanne   86, **246**
Plimpton, Martha   50
Plowright, Joan   236
Plummer, Amanda   246
Plummer, Christopher   **246**
Poitier, Sidney   **246**
Polanski, Roman   292
Pollan, Tracy   115
Pons, Lily   **246–247**
Ponti, Carlo   188
Powell, Dick   4, 5, 31, **247**
Powell, Eleanor   114, **247–248**
Powell, Jane   **248**
Powell, William   136, 188, **248**
Power, Tyrone   249, **249,** 251
Power, Tyrone, Sr   249
Power, Tyrone, IV   249
Preminger, Otto   183
Prentiss, Paula   26, **249**
Presley, Elvis   **249–250**
Presnell, Robert, Jr.   152
Preston, Robert   **250**
Previn, Andre   104
Prevost, Marie   **250**

Price, Vincent   **250–251**
Price, Will   235
Pringle, Aileen   **252**
Propper, Frances   256
Pryor, Roger   283
Purdom, Edmund   249, **252**

Quaid, Dennis   **253**, 253
Quaid, Randy   253, **253**
Quinn, Anthony   82, **253**

Rabe, David   59
Rackmil, Milton R.   30
Radner, Gilda   315
Raft, George   **255**
Rain, Jeramie   90
Rainer, Luise   **255**
Raines, Ella   **255**
Rains, Claude   **255–256**
Ralston, Esther   144, **256**
Ralston, Jobyna   9
Ralston, Vera Hruba   **256–257**
Rambova, Natacha   305
Ramiz, Sohair   277
Rankin, Doris   21
Raphael, Ida   181
Rathbone, Basil   19, **257**
Rawlins, Judy   73
Ray, Charles   **257**
Ray, Jacquelyn   276
Raye, Martha   120, **257–258**
Raye, Thelma Victoria   60
Raymond, Aileen   214
Raymond, Gene   196, **258**
Reagan, Maureen
    Elizabeth   259, 321
Reagan, Ronald   **258–259**, 320
Redford, Robert   **259**
Redgrave, Corin   259, 260
Redgrave, Lynn   **259**, 260
Redgrave, Sir Michael   259,
    259–260, 260
Redgrave, Vanessa   259, **260**
Reed, Donna   **260**

Reed, Maxwell   60
Reed, Patricia   275
Reeve, Christopher   **261**, 329
Reeves, Ruth   66
Reid, Wallace   75, **261**
Reiner, Rob   70
Relins, Veit   274
Remick, Lee   **261**
Rennie, James   124
Reynolds, Burt   **261–262**
Reynolds, Debbie   109, **262**, 293
Rice, Elmer   107
Richardson, Natasha   260
Richardson, Sir Ralph   **262**
Richardson, Tony   260
Rickard, Gwendolyn   33
Rigg, Diana   **263**
Riley, Lewis   82
Ring, Blanche   317
Riskin, Robert   320
Riva, Maria   85
Robards, Jason, Jr.   15, **263**
Robbins, Tim   274
Roberts, Rachel   138
Robertson, Annatte   152
Robertson, Cliff   185, **263–264**
Robeson, Paul   **264**
Robinson, Bill "Bojangles"   264
Robinson, Edward G.   **264–265**
Robson, Dame Flora   329
Rogers, Charles "Buddy"   245,
    265
Rogers, Ginger   14, 201, 222,
    265–266
Rogers, Mimi   69
Rogers, Roy   98, **266**
Rogers, Will   **267**
Rogers, Will, Jr.   267
Roland, Gilbert   26, **267**
Roland, Ruth   **267**
Roman, Ruth   192, **267–268**
Romero, Cesar   329
Rooney, Mickey   119, **268–269**
Rose, David   120, 258

Rosenstein, Sophia 323
Ross, Frank 52
Rossellini, Isabella 29
Rossellini, Roberto 29
Roth, Lillian **269**
Roth, Philip 31
Rowan, Dan 181
Rowland, Adele 270
Rowlands, Gena 51, **269–270**
Roxanne 44
Rubens, Alma 64, **270**
Rubenstein, Arthur 169
Rubin, Walter 40
Ruggles, Charles 163, **270**
Ruggles, Wesley 163, 270
Rush, Barbara 152
Russell, Gail 199, 270
Russell, Jane **271**
Russell, Kurt 141
Russell, Lee 203
Russell, Rosalind **271**
Rutherford, Ann 113, **271**, 301
Rutherford, Dame Margaret **272**
Ryan, Meg 253, **272**
Ryan, Robert **272**
Ryan, Sheila 45

Sagal, Bovis 53
Saint, Eva Marie **273**
St. John, Jill 161, **273**, 309
Salaman, Merula 131
Salmi, Albert 121
Salter, Harry 182
Sanders, George 118, 152,
273–274
San Juan, Olga 233
Sarandon, Chris 274
Sarandon, Susan **274**
Sargent, Herbert 39
Saura, Carlos 55
Saville, Philip 263
Sayers, Dora L. 114
Schaefer, Natalie 46
Schell, Maria **274**

Schell, Maximilian 274
Schenck, Joseph M. 291
Schildkraut, Joseph **274**
Schmidt, Kim 324
Schmidt, Lars 29
Schulberg, Budd 39
Schwarzenegger, Arnold **275**
Scott, Adrian 279
Scott, George C. 84, **275**
Scott, Lizabeth 329
Scott, Randolph **275–276**
Sebastian, David 215
Sebastian, Dorothy 35
Seberg, Jean **276**
Seiter, William 179
Selleck, Tom **276**
Sellers, Peter **277**
Selznik, David O. 161, 165, 211, 309
Sennett, Mack 231, 329
Serato, Massimo 200
Seymour, Jane 13
Sharif, Omar **277**
Shaw, Artie 170, 300
Shearer, Moira **277**
Shearer, Norma 189, **278**
Sheen, Charlie 278
Sheen, Martin **278**
Shelton, John 129
Shepherd, Cybill **278–279**
Shepherd, Sam 178
Sheridan, Ann 37, **279**
Shirley, Anne 241, **279**
Shore, Dinah 217, **279–280**
Shriver, Maria 275
Sidney, George 265
Sidney, Sylvia **280**
Siebe, Rudolf 85
Siegel, Donald 186
Signoret, Simone **280**
Sills, Milton 169, **281**
Silvers, Phil **281**
Sim, Sheila 12
Simmons, Jean 128, **281**
Simon, Neal 207

Simon, Paul	109
Simon, Simone	329
Simpson, Dorothy	38
Simpson, Jim	312
Sinatra, Frank 77, 104, 119, **282**	
Sinatra, Nancy	282
Skeekman, Arthur	288
Skelton, Red	**282–83**
Small, Paul	294
Smith, Alexis	**283**, 287
Smith, Betty	1
Smith, Dame Maggie	**283**
Soles, Pamela J.	253
Sommer, Elke	**283**
Sorel, Sonia	49
Sothern, Ann	**283–284**
Spacek, Sissy	**284**
Spielberg, Steven	157
Springs, Helena	83
Stack, Robert	145, **284**
Stahl, Ray	155
Stallone, Sylvester	**284–285**
Stanley, Louise	235
Stanwyck, Barbara	**285**, 294
Stapler, Sheila	323
Stapleton, Jean	**285**
Stapleton, Maureen	**285–286**
Starke, John	59
Starr, Ringo	**286**
Steele, Anthony	96
Steenburgern, Mary	196, **286**
Steiger, Rod	31, **286**
Sterling, Robert	284
Sterling, Tisha	284
Stern, Tom	95
Stevens, Craig	283, **287**
Stewart, Anita	**287**
Stewart, James	**287**
Stewart, Lucille Lee	286
Stewart, Marianne	46
Stone, Fred	267
Stone, Jeff	47
Strange, Michael	19, 20
Strasberg, Lee	15

Strasberg, Paula	15
Streep, Meryl	**288**
Street, David	239
Streisand, Barbra	127, **288**
Stuart, Gloria	**288**
Stuart, Nick	48
Sullavan, Margaret 111, **288–289**	
Sunderland, Ninetta "Nan"	154
Sutherland, Edward	39
Sutherland, Victor	314
Swanson, Gloria 23, 26, **289–290**	
Sweet, Blanche	**290**
Swope, Topo	197
Talmadge, Constance 73, 125, 192, **291**, 291, 292	
Talmadge, Natalie	291
Talmadge, Norma 165, 291, **291**	
Tandy, Jessica	140, **292**
Tariipaia, Tarita	37
Tate, Sharon	**292**
Taylor, Elizabeth 31, 42, 43, 109, 262, **292–293**, 315	
Taylor, Eloise	234
Taylor, Estelle	**293–294**
Taylor, Robert	285, **294**
Taylor, William Desmond	231
Taylor-Young, Leigh	236
Tchinarova, Tamara	108
Teasdale, Verree	211, **294**
Tell, Michael	90
Tellegen, Lou	103, **295**
Temple, Shirley	**295**
Tendler, Harriet	39
Tennant, Victoria	204
Terry, Alice	**296**
Thalberg, Irving Grant	278
Thaxter, Phyllis	**296**
Theiss, George	294
Thomas, Danny	**296**
Thomas, Marjorie	138
Thomas, Marlo	269
Thomas, Olive	244, **296–297**
Thomason, Barbara	268

Thompson, Carlos 240
Thompson, Emma 36
Thomson, Barry 56
Tierney, Gene 175, **297**
Tinker, Grant 219
Tobin, Genevieve **297**
Todd, Michael 293, 315
Todd, Thelma **297**
Tomasini, George 38
Tomlin, Lily 329
Tone, Franchot 68, **298**, 310
Torn, Rip 239, **298**
Tracy, Lee **299**
Tracy, Spencer **299**
Travolta, John **329**
Treadwell, Louise 299
Trevor, Claire **299**
Trinkonis, Gus 140
Tubb, Barry 196
Tufts, Sonny **299–300**
Turner, Kathleen **300**
Turner, Lana 18, 119, 163, 170, 271, **300–301**
Turner, Yolanda 108
Turpin, Ben 301
Tuttle, William C. 260
Twelvetrees, Clark 301
Twelvetrees, Helen 301–302
Tyson, Cicely **302**

Ullman, Liv **303**
Ulric, Lenore **303**
Urwick, Joy 209
Ustinov, Sir Peter **303**

Vadim, Roger 17, 83, 112
Valentino, Rudolph 225, 228, **305**
Vallee, Rudy 130, **305**
Vallee, Yvonne 57
Valli, Alida **306**
Valli, Virginia 103
Van Devere, Trish 275
Van Dyke, Dick **306**
Van Nutter, Rick 96

Velardi, Valerie 316
Velez, Lupe **306**, 312
Vera-Ellen **306**
Verdon, Gwen **307**
Verne, Kaaren 189
Vernon, Frances Willard "Bill" 45
Vickers, Martha 268
Vickery, James 84
Vidal, Henri 222
Vidor, Charles 170
Vidor, Florence 32, **307**
Voysey, Ella Annesley 86

Wagner, Robert 273, **309**, 318, 319
Walker, Gertrude 317
Walker, Michael 161, 309
Walker, Robert 161, **309**
Walker, Robert, Jr. 161, 309
Wallace, Fred 89
Wallace, Hal 313
Wallace, Jean 298, **310**, 315
Wallach, Eli 159, **310**
Wallis, Hal B. 105, 155
Walsh, Raoul 64, **310–311**
Walton, Helen 178
Wanger, Walter 27
Warren, Fran 87
Wayne, David **311**
Wayne, John **311**
Weaver, Sigourney **312**
Webb, Clifton 330
Webb, George 256
Webster, Ben 314
Webster, Margret 314
Wedgeworth, Ann 298
Weidler, George 78
Weidler, Virginia 78
Weinfeld, Andre 313
Weissmuller, Johnny 306, **312**
Welch, Raquel **312–313**
Weld, Tuesday 218–219, **313**
Welles, Orson 143, **313**
Wellman, William A. 52
Wells, Michael 323

Wenham, Jane 109
West, Mae 313–314
Westcott, Frances 28
Westover, Winifred 138
Whitcomb, Jon 38
White, Loray 77
White, Olive Ann 103
White, Pearl **314**
Whittaker, James 57
Whitty, Dame May **314**
Widmark, Richard **314**
Wilcox, Herbert 227
Wilcox, Robert 19
Wilde, Cornel 310, **314–315**
Wilder, Gene **315**
Wilding, Michael 185, 292, **315**
Wilding, Michael, Jr. 293, 315
Willard, Catherine 25
Willat, Irvan 88
Williams, Bill 133
Williams, Cara 21
Williams, Esther 176, **315–316**
Williams, Robin **316**
Willis, Bruce 218, **316**
Wilson, Eileen 248
Wilson, Kara 62
Wilson, Lois 330
Wilson, Rita 134
Wilton, Penelope 208
Windsor, Claire 192, **316–317**
Winger, Debra **317**
Winkler, Irwin 285
Winniger, Charles 210, **317**
Winters, Shelley **317–318**
Wirt, Robert 47
Withers, Grant 324
Withers, Jane 32, 213, **318**

Witte, Jackie 229
Wolders, Robert 233
Wolf, Peter 90
Wong, Anna May 330
Wood, Evelyn 161
Wood, Natalie 309, **318–319**
Woods, James **319**
Woodward, Joanne 229, **319**
Worth, Constance 37
Wray, Fay **319–320**
Wright, Robin 242
Wright, Teresa **320**
Wyatt, Jane **320**
Wyman, Jane 258, **320–321**
Wymore, Patrice 111, **321**
Wynn, Ed **321–322**, 322
Wynn, Keenan 159, 321, **322**
Wynne, Gladys Edith 281
Wynter, Dana **322**

York, Michael **323**
York, Susannah **323**
Young, Clara Kimball **323**
Young, Collier 113, 191
Young, Georgianna 324
Young, Gig 217, **323–324**
Young, James 323
Young, Kay 315
Young, Loretta 311, **324**
Young, Polly Ann 324
Young, Robert **324**
Youngs, Gail 92
Yurka, Blanche **325**

Ziegfeld, Florenz 4, 244
Zober, Sandi 230